D1389194

THE CELTS

Also by Simon Jenkins

THE CELTS

A SCEPTICAL HISTORY

SIMON JENKINS

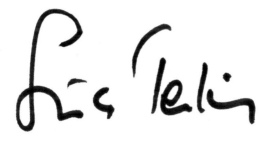

P

PROFILE BOOKS

First published in Great Britain in 2022 by
Profile Books Ltd
29 Cloth Fair
London
EC1A 7JQ

www.profilebooks.com

1 3 5 7 9 10 8 6 4 2

Typeset in Sabon by MacGuru Ltd
Printed and bound in Great Britain by Clays Ltd, Elcograf S.p.A.

A CIP catalogue record for this book is available from the British Library.

ISBN 978 1 78816 880 9
eISBN 978 1 78283 886 9

FSC
www.fsc.org
MIX
Paper from
responsible sources
FSC® C018072

For Dashiell and Nia

Contents

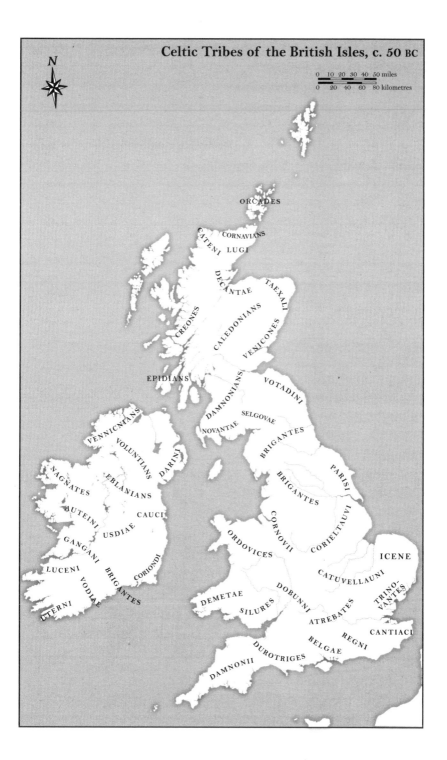

Celtic Tribes of the British Isles, c. 50 BC

N

0 10 20 30 40 50 miles
0   20   40   60   80 kilometres

ORCADES

CATENI CORNAVIANS
LUGI

DECANTAE TAEXALI

CREONES CALEDONIANS VENICONES

EPIDIANS

DAMNONIANS VOTADINI
SELGOVAE
NOVANTAE
BRIGANTES

VENNICNIANS
VOLUNTIANS DARINI BRIGANTES PARISI

NAGNATES EBLANIANS BRIGANTES CORIELTAUVI
AUTEINI CAUCI
USDIAE ORDOVICES CORNOVII ICENE
GANGANI CATUVELLAUNI
LUCENI BRIGANTES CORIONDI
VODIAE DEMETAE DOBUNNI TRINO-VANTES
UTERNI SILURES ATREBATES CANTIACI
REGNI
BELGAE
DUROTRIGES
DAMNONII

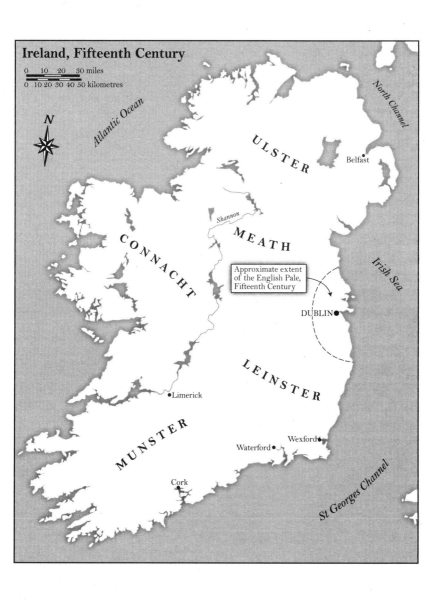

Ireland, Fifteenth Century

0   10   20   30 miles
0 10 20 30 40 50 kilometres

Atlantic Ocean

North Channel

ULSTER

Belfast

Shannon

MEATH

Irish Sea

Approximate extent
of the English Pale,
Fifteenth Century

CONNACHT

DUBLIN

LEINSTER

Limerick

MUNSTER

Wexford

Waterford

Cork

St Georges Channel

Author's Note

This book is about groups of people and the words used to describe them. Such words are always controversial. My intention is to dispel the concept of a single Celtic people, language or nation. There are Ireland, Scotland and Wales, as well as Cornwall, Brittany and the Isle of Man. They have never in any respect cohered as one entity and I regard lumping them together as Celts or 'the fringe' as distorting and dismissive.

However, since these peoples do share a language root and given that much of the book is about their joint relationship with England, I do refer to them as a group in the pre-historical period, using the term 'Celtic-speaking'. Otherwise their languages are classified as Brythonic or Gaelic, and then Welsh, Irish, Gaelic or Breton. In other words, I try to call people and their language whatever they call themselves.

The words Britain and Britons are more confusing. They used to refer to all the British Isles, then to 'Celtic-speaking' regions as distinct from the Germanic-speaking 'Anglo-Saxons', and then again to the island of Britain not Ireland. However, the word Britain is so often used as a convenience to refer to the whole of the British Isles, at least in early history, that this usage is hard to avoid. With the word 'Great' it nowadays formally refers to England, Scotland and Wales but not Ireland. Only since 1801 has there been a so-called United Kingdom, first of 'Great Britain and Ireland' and then, since 1922, of 'Great Britain and Northern Ireland'. In the possible event of Ireland reuniting, we must assume the UK will revert to GB.

This book is not an academic work but a history of an ongoing debate among scholars about the origins of the peoples of the British Isles and about their past, present and perhaps future relations. It does not carry notes, but works consulted and quoted are listed in the bibliography.

I have shown the text in whole or part to some of those closely involved in these debates, with whom I have conversed in the course of its preparation. They include Colin Renfrew, Barry Cunliffe, John Koch and Roy Foster. I thank them profusely, but they carry no responsibility for any mistakes I may have made, or for my conclusions. I have discussed devolution and independence over the years with too many to mention but have been helped in particular by Philip Stevens, Tom Jenkins, Tony Travers, my wife Hannah Kaye, and my assiduous editor Trevor Horwood. I would also thank my publisher Andrew Franklin and all at Profile Books.

Introduction

The most vivid account of the geography of the British Isles appears in the first volume of the *Oxford History of England*, published in 1936. It refers to the islands as created 'in two parts'. The western part is 'ancient, mountainous, rugged, broken, irregular, scrubby, sour-soiled and incommunicable' – in short, not a pretty place. The eastern part is a contrast, 'newer, softer, warmer, alluvial and fertile, attractive to invaders'. The authors of the *History* assured readers that, despite this distinction, the series would be 'all-encompassing'. It would narrate the story of the islands of Britain as a whole.

That promise was not kept, and is rarely kept in histories of the British Isles. Historians invariably direct their readers to the eastern half of the archipelago, the 'fertile, attractive' side called England. This bias is reflected in the attention given to the peoples occupying the two sides, notably to the conflicts between them leading to the supremacy of the peoples of the east. Britons are taught from birth the story of England, just England. They are taught little or nothing of the 'others' – notably the Irish, Scottish and Welsh commonly referred to collectively as the Celts.

The first part of this book explains why the word Celt is a misnomer. As we shall see, scholarship since the 1960s has struggled to dismantle long-held theories of how the British people came into existence. This dismantling is important because, to a remarkable extent, theories of Celticism continue to fuel many of the prejudices and misconceptions that divide the peoples of the British Isles to this day. They both distort history and demean the distinctive characteristics of the Irish, Scottish and Welsh nations.

First among those misconceptions is that a people called the Celts invaded Britain from continental Europe sometime in the second or first millennium BC. There has never been found a distinct people, race or tribe claiming the name or language of Celtic. The word *keltoi* first appears in Greek as applied generally to aliens or 'barbarians', assumed to be inhabitants of western Europe before the rise of the classical world. In Latin, the term used is *Galli* or Gauls. Nowhere in this period was any such term applied to the people of the British Isles. Excavations in the nineteenth century of Iron Age sites at Hallstatt in Austria and La Tène in Switzerland were declared evidence of a 'Celtic' civilisation, possibly even stretching from Asia Minor in the east to Portugal in the west. Its artefacts too were granted the designation 'Celtic', the style in use to this day.

As we shall see, early analysis of ancient DNA generally accepted that the peoples who occupied the British Isles dated back to a climatic migration northwards after the end of the last Ice Age. This migration occurred with global warming, primarily up the Atlantic coast of Europe from Iberia. On the eastern side of the islands, perhaps more recent DNA showed an occupation from continental northern Europe. There is little consensus on the balance between these two incursions, or when they occurred. Neither merits the title 'Celtic invasion'.

Probably in the late Bronze Age (*c.*2100–800 BC) these inhabitants of Britain came into contact with a variety of languages spreading across Europe that accompanied the growth of trade in metals. These tongues, loosely related to each other within the proto-Celtic Indo-European group, were assumed to have permeated every corner of the British Isles at least down to the period of the Roman occupation. That permeation is now doubted, with the eastern side of Britain thought possibly to have been speaking some version of the Germanic of northern Europe.

Certainly, two completely different language groups were in use in the British Isles by the second century after the withdrawal of the Roman empire. This was attributed to another misconception: a further mass incursion – this time of Saxons – in the fifth and sixth centuries, supposedly either wiping out the eastern Celtic speakers or driving them westwards across Britain. Like the Celtic invasion before it, this second one is also now discredited. While there are genetic signs of people migrating round the North Sea at the end of the Roman empire, there is nothing to indicate a wipe-out of its inhabitants and their total replacement throughout the length of eastern Britain. It is now thought possible that the many different peoples of the British Isles, east and west, evolved their own languages independent of any population movement. The east looked east and the west looked west.

This theory of a long-standing division, genetic and linguistic, between the peoples of the east and west of the British Isles remains controversial. What does appear to be the case is that the ancient geographical divide described in the 1930s by those Oxford historians became deeply embedded in the history of the peoples of Britain. It attended the cohesion of the easterners eventually into one nation, and the fragmentation of the westerners. It was reflected in the boundaries of the Roman province of Britannia and in the emergent identities of the Irish, Welsh and Scottish peoples. It was reflected in the supremacy of what became the first 'empire' of the English-speaking easterners.

A uniting kingdom

The second part of the book narrates the course of that

supremacy. Most European countries, however diverse their origins, tell their story as that of a nation state being fashioned from various tribal agglomerations and unions. If one dominant group emerges, it must hold the others in thrall through military might and/or cultural assimilation. In her book *Acts of Union and Disunion* the historian Linda Colley describes the leaders of these agglomerations as having to operate on two levels. They had to 'nurture a sense of belonging and allegiance' to secure the subservience of lesser groups. But to retain that allegiance they had also to 'acknowledge and protect [their] partial autonomy and separate rights and cultures'. They could never take those rights for granted.

It was on this basis that European states were formed. Prussians, Hanoverians and Bavarians became one nation as Germany. Burgundians, Gascons and Savoyards became French. Romans, Venetians and Sicilians become Italians. In turn, Alpine French, Germans and Italians became Swiss. They fashioned constitutions that would hold together their disparate components. Only a very few failed, most recently Yugoslavia and Czechoslovakia.

From the very start of their supremacy, the English failed to instil Colley's sense of 'belonging and allegiance' among the Celtic-speaking tribes of the west. Nor did they respond to the westerners' distinctive identities by granting them a degree of 'autonomy and separate rights'. The tribes occupying eastern Britain in the fifth century AD formed themselves first into seven kingdoms, then into three and then into one, England. By the eleventh century, under Anglo-Saxons, Danes and then Normans, England was among the earliest 'nationalised' states in Europe. It was an early 'union'.

Not only did the westerners never join hands and hearts with these easterners, they found little coherence either within themselves or between each other. Unlike those of England, few of the clans or 'kingdoms' of Wales, Scotland and Ireland behaved as if they were members of a collective whole. Their efforts at self-government came constantly to grief, with rulers no sooner succeeding in briefly uniting their peoples than they died in feuds and civil wars.

Over time, these westerners did combine sufficiently to be recognisably Irish, Scottish and Welsh, with distinctive languages and dialects. What they never did was unite against England. They did not speak a common language or acknowledge one leader. At the time of the Battle of Brunanburh in 937 against Athelstan's English, a Welsh bard did call for such an alliance, embracing even Cornwall, but it was never achieved. He did not use the word Celtic.

Despite frequent revolts and conflicts, England was never to have serious trouble holding its neighbours in thrall. The borderlands roughly of Offa's Dyke, Hadrian's Wall and the Irish Sea were to remain England's boundaries throughout history. Over time, the nations beyond them passed under English sovereignty, first by conquest and colonisation and then through annexation: Wales in 1536, Scotland in 1707 and Ireland in 1801. An 'English empire' was formed on the British Isles. But it was an empire of the most tenuous union, many of its members continuing to refuse to acknowledge themselves as 'British'.

Only in the seventeenth century did scholars begin to see the isles as possessing a collective 'Celtic' past, largely through the identification of a common linguistic root. In the eighteenth century England's domestic empire did form a sort of communality with the growth of an overseas British empire in which Scots, Irish and Welsh were prominent as soldiers, governors and migrants. By the nineteenth century a 'united kingdom' so-called was messily in place, at least under one monarch, one parliament and one flag. It was a union of convenience rather than of hearts.

A disuniting kingdom

The third part of the book asks how and why that union began
to dissolve. The answer lay primarily in Ireland, where for three
centuries London governments had dismissed with contempt
the Irish yearning for at least a degree of self-government. This
was in large part through English antipathy to the island's
dominant Roman Catholicism. The resulting rebellions and
repressions led finally to Irish secession in 1922. While treated
by most English with a careless shrug, it was described in the
1930s by the historian G. M. Young as 'the great failure . . . the
one irreparable disaster of our history'. I find it hard to quarrel
with that judgement.

Freed of Ireland, British politicians who were then starting to dismantle their overseas empire behaved as if the earlier
domestic one could now be taken for granted. The outcome
was as Colley predicted. The Scots and Welsh took a lead from
the Irish and a new spirit of nationalism emerged. At the end of
the twentieth century, the same pressures that had lost Ireland
were gaining traction in Scotland and even in Wales.

At no point in debates about home rule, whether in Ireland
or Scotland, was there any suggestion of a Celtic nation.
The Irish, Scots and Welsh remained passionate in their sep-
arateness. No attempt was made to form a 'Celtic' party or
grouping of MPs in the House of Commons. Only in Celtic
studies departments of universities was a sort of union recognised. Language remained the principal cohering characteristic
of Celtic-speaking regions, except that there was no one Celtic
language. Indeed language, while a token to nationalist politicians, was a side issue. To speak English does not make
someone any less Irish, Scottish or Welsh.

In the final part of the book I consider the argument for
small-state independence. It is impossible to deny that Ireland
has done well on its own and impossible to deny that this has
come about largely through its liberation from British rule and

in stark contrast to the experience of Northern Ireland as well as Wales and Scotland. Whether the same factors would play in the latter provinces of Britain is a matter of now-heated debate, but Ireland's experience should make every unionist pause.

I am half-Welsh and half-English and have tried to rid my analysis from either loyalty. But I do believe that any well-constituted state should be able to accommodate diversity and prosper from it. A country's politics, culture, society and outlook on the world should all benefit from such diversity. A Britain composed of England, Scotland, Wales and (once upon a time) all of Ireland must surely be stronger than one comprising England alone, particularly an England fast becoming a vast and dependent suburb of the London metropolis.

Yet to realise the benefits of such a union, England must change its political relations with the non-English peoples of Great Britain, if not of the British Isles as a whole. It must find stability and cohesion by devolving to them ever greater autonomy through new federal institutions. It has to change its outlook as well as its constitution. To this challenge, I return below.

Part One

The Myth of the Celts

1

How Ancient Were the Britons?

A group of Mesolithic people standing 8,200 years ago on the North Downs above what is now the Strait of Dover might have witnessed an astonishing sight. At their feet was an outlet into the English Channel of two great rivers, now the Thames and the Rhine. To their north lay a series of marshes, relics of the land bridge that had joined Britain to mainland Europe across what was known as Doggerland.

Our onlookers would have seen a cloud towering over the northern horizon above a wall of water possibly thirty metres high. This tsunami had been created by a landslip off the Norwegian coast that would become known as the first Storegga Slide. The resulting wave made landfall in north-east Scotland and left traces that can still be found thirty kilometres inland. It swept south, submerging Doggerland and carrying millions of tons of rubble and sand hurtling towards the downs on which our onlookers were standing.

The impact would have been seismic. The water burst through a valley in the uplands and out into what is now the English Channel. Underwater archaeology has revealed scouring marks as the debris was dragged along the Channel floor. What had been a peninsula at the western extremity of Europe was now the British Isles.

During the following millennia, the inhabitants of this now-maritime nation developed an agrarian economy, felling most of the virgin woodlands and evolving a social organisation sufficient to build boats, exchange goods by sea, lay out settlements and erect monuments. Their faces have vanished, their words are a mystery, only fragments of their artefacts survive. These were the indigenous people we used to call ancient Britons, ghosts flitting across the stage on which the drama of British history was later enacted.

The traditional narrative

The prehistory of the British Isles was long the preserve of one profession, archaeology, fashioning theories often in a fog of inherited conjecture and myth. One such theory held that the ancient Britons were subjected to an invasion by a newly arriving people during the second or first millennium BC, outlier of a great population sweep across Europe from the east. This was thought to originate in the steppes of Russia, the Caucasus or Anatolia, impelled by the arrival of horses and the discovery of copper and tin in the late Bronze Age.

These people were said to have occupied Europe before the rise of Greece and Rome, filling what scholars viewed as a vacuum in the prehistoric narrative. They were first mentioned as *keltoi*, a general term meaning little more than 'aliens', by the Greek historian Herodotus (*c.*484–425 BC) and later described by Julius Caesar as Gauls. Though sometimes given the names of individual tribes, these people were lumped together as 'Celts' or more often 'barbarians'. They were also assumed to have brought with them northern Europe's first lingua franca, a branch of Indo-European known as proto-Celtic. No one at that time placed the Celts in Britain, rather in Spain and France. The first mention of Britons is *c.*320 BC by the Greek geographer Pytheas of Massalia as *Pretani* or *Briteni*, implying that they were 'painted ones'.

The identification of people in Britain with Herodotus' Celts was suggested only in the seventeenth century, purely on grounds of language. A French priest, Paul-Yves Pezron, first identified as 'Gallic' the similar languages of his Breton compatriots and those of the western British Isles. He hazarded that they were at some time past the same people. This insight was developed by Edward Lhuyd (1660–1709), a Welsh scholar working in Oxford around the turn of the seventeenth century, who classified 'Goidelic' Irish and Scots Gaelic as Q-Celtic. He classified Welsh, Cornish and Breton as P-Celtic or 'Brythonic'. Lhuyd chose to group them collectively as Celtic rather than Pezron's Gallic, apparently as a patriotic – or non-French – gesture. All were assumed to have come to Britain from France.

Lhuyd's thesis became received wisdom. It joined similar 'foundation narratives' in nationalist France and Germany. Napoleon later imagined himself a latter-day Celtic emperor. German linguists and anthropologists hailed the Celts as the first Germans. The idea that this was all one people and one culture was reinforced by the archaeological discovery in the 1840s that Hallstatt, then and now a picturesque Austrian settlement, was a centre of salt mining and manufacture in the first millennium BC. This was followed by discoveries at La Tène in Switzerland. Their excavation yielded artefacts of elegance and charm from what became two eponymous material cultures, duly declared signs of a great Celtic civilisation.

Who these people were – or perhaps more intriguing had once been – remained a mystery. In 1956 a leading Lithuanian–American anthropologist, Marija Gimbutas, discovered a people called the Yamnayans who swept westwards from the Pontic and Caucasian steppes c.3300–2600 BC. They are supposed to have brought with them such wonders of Asian civilisation as the horse and wheel, ideal accompaniments to the emerging ages of copper and bronze. These incomers spread out across the Ukrainian and Hungarian plains, fusing their so-called 'steppe' DNA with that of indigenous peoples.

How far these Yamnayans fed into the Celtic narrative

is confused. The assumption is that *c*.2600 BC they mutated into the so-called Bell Beaker culture of the Bronze Age, permeating westwards across northern Europe and becoming in turn Herodotus' *keltoi*. This fitted neatly into the idea of a Europe constantly overrun and enriched by invaders. Hallstatt and La Tène demonstrated a status sufficient to threaten early Greeks and Romans, a threat that suggested a mighty people. To nationalist prehistorians, they were thus fitting ancestors of the later glory of France and Germany. By the 1920s the French historian Albert Grenier could declare the Celts nothing less than an empire, possibly 'the greatest power in Europe . . . inexhaustible in energy and human might'.

This concept of a Celtic empire continues to dominate maps and histories of 'Celtic Europe'. Geographers, like historians, cannot bear gaps. They seek links, commonalities, lines of invasion, influence and power. Whatever was west Europe's pattern of occupation – and DNA may yet clarify this – it had evaporated by the time of Rome's expansion northwards. By now 'the Celts' had become a people massively dispersed and reduced to 'tribes'. They had expanded – or possibly been driven by new invaders – to the extremities of the continent, clinging to the wild Atlantic shores of Spain, France and the British Isles. In the case of Britain they were portrayed as replacing the entirety of the population with their language and culture. With the decline of Rome, their old lands were now overwhelmed by new waves of intruders, Franks, Goths, Huns and Vandals. Thus the *Oxford History of England* was unequivocal. It described Britain as 'a refuse-heap on the edge of the ocean into which are swept the outworn relics of ethnic migrations.' Britain became the Celt's last redoubt.

2

The Celtosceptic Dawn

The narrative crumbles

Already in the 1960s this Celtic narrative was being challenged. The oft-cited 'empire' suggested by Hallstatt and La Tène was supported by no other imperial settlements. There was no evidence of people in Austria/Switzerland speaking anything like Celtic. Nor did historians regard it as plausible for entire peoples and languages to be obliterated by D-Day-style invasions, landings and genetic replacements. Ancient civilisations did not evolve in this catastrophic way.

Prehistory now became an academic confrontation. In 1966 the Disney Professor of Archaeology and Ethnology at Cambridge University, Sir Grahame Clark, was dismissive. He described the traditional Celtic narrative as 'suffering from invasion neurosis'. He objected to ancient Britons being seen as 'dimwits clad in druidical garb . . . figures of fun if not of scorn', needing to be taught a lesson in Bronze Age civilisation by incoming Celtic warriors. The inhabitants of the British Isles did not need conquerors to help them advance in trade and technology. There was no reason to posit any assault, wipeout or swamping just because a people appeared to acquire a new language. Clark's Oxford contemporary, the Anglo-Saxon scholar J. R. R. Tolkien, derided the whole idea as nothing but a 'fabulous Celtic twilight . . . a magic bag into which anything could be tossed and anything retrieved'. It was still one of which he made full use as a novelist.

Prehistoric archaeology was long a closed shop, confined to scholars of things, of mounds, walls, pots and jewels. In the second half of the twentieth century it was transformed by the arrival of physicists, chemists, pathologists, anthropologists and linguists. The radiocarbon dating of plants and organic matter revised chronologies. In the 1990s the application of ancient DNA (aDNA) genetics to human skeletons revealed their life cycles in extraordinary detail. Bones, teeth, skin, even faeces began to tell their tales.

The dating of Britain's oldest resident, the Red Lady of Paviland, in South Wales, was revised 30,000 years, from early Roman to before the last Ice Age. She turned out to be a Palaeolithic young man with a taste for fish. Stonehenge's Amesbury Archer of *c.*2300 BC was revealed as Swiss, with a tooth abscess and a gammy leg. His partner came from Kent. Science had revolutionised archaeology.

By the 1990s the sceptics were in full cry. The anthropologist Malcolm Chapman published his *Celts: The Construction of a Myth* in 1992, describing them as the mere 'others' of ancient Europe. They filled a gap in Europe's story with 'an apparent continuity and substance'. The word Celt had become so obfuscated that Chapman suggested it be banned from academic discourse. A British Museum archaeologist, Simon James, in 1999 likewise dismissed the Celts as an eighteenth-century invention. Calling them a specific people was 'a political falsification of history, dangerous in the hands of separatists'. It was as if history lay not in the mountains and seas of Britain but in the minds of feuding scholars.

In *The Discovery of France*, the historian Graham Robb wrote that to gather under one name the myriad peoples who once inhabited Europe was anyway a fallacy. They did not see themselves as such. They owed loyalty to a family or clan tradition and to the territory on which it had settled. As for 'ethnic identity', Robb pointed out that it been 'long eroded or at least delegated to the wizards of DNA'. That certain peoples once used a shared language to help communicate with neighbours meant nothing. English speakers do likewise without becoming English. The Celts were simply a myth.

The paths diverge: Celtic from the west

Faced with this blizzard of scepticism, the Celts' most ardent champion, Oxford's Barry Cunliffe, did not disown them. But he published two works, *The Ancient Celts* in 1997 followed in 2001 by another called *Facing the Ocean*, which were both firmly in the revisionist line. They drew on two influential insights into the study of prehistory. The first was the idea of the *longue durée* associated with the twentieth-century French historian Fernand Braudel (1902–85). He emphasised the slow passage of historical change, often unnoticed over time, warning in particular against imposing on prehistory a template of events-led upheavals familiar in modern times: a high-speed chronology of monarchs, conquests, invasions, revolutions and imported technologies. In particular Braudel objected to attributing every advance in human behaviour to an external agent. This was a reprise of Clark's 'invasion neurosis'.

Another insight was equally significant to the saga of the British Isles. This told ancient historians not to overrate contact by land compared with contact by sea. Before the advent of the horse, water was by far the fastest and most efficient means of communication. A journey that on foot could take weeks or months could be undertaken in hours or days by even the most primitive boat. It was by water that early contact was made and languages employed to facilitate it. This helped explain the swift advances of the riverine and insular cultures of the Egyptians and the Aegean islanders compared with their hinterlands.

Sea-borne mobility round the coast of Europe rose

dramatically in the second millennium BC with the burgeon-
ing trade in copper, tin, tools, pots, axes, ploughs, swords and
coins. Transport became an industry in itself. Families became
extended communities that needed to converse with strangers.
This concept of 'sea-as-land' viewed the peoples of the British
Isles not as English, Scots, Irish or Welsh, but as those of the
Irish Sea, the North Sea and the English Channel. The infertile
limestone ridge running from the Scottish Highlands down the
spine of England should thus be seen as not a bridge but a
divide.

According to Cunliffe, the peoples of the west coast of
Ireland would thus have felt more akin to those sailing the
Atlantic and touching the shores of Cornwall, Brittany and
Spain than they would to the peoples of eastern England. He
noted that western burials indicating 'elite behaviour mani-
fest in war gear and feasting accoutrements were similar from
southern Portugal to northern Scotland'. These people were
not invaders or conquerors, they were descendants of the tribes
that probably inhabited these shores far back in time.

Advances in genetic archaeology were now supporting such
a thesis, that the mass of the population of the British Isles
was probably stable throughout prehistory. Analysis of DNA
from ancient skeletons published in 1996 suggested that 70 per
cent of Britons alive at the turn of the twentieth century were
descended from the same people as had inhabited the British
Isles in the Mesolithic or Middle Stone Age. Much publicity
greeted the revelation that a local teacher in Somerset and three
of his pupils shared their DNA with that of a 9,000-year-old
skeleton found in the Cheddar Gorge. It also appeared that
their ancestors had mostly originated from a common source,
the Iberian peninsula.

This strongly supported Cunliffe's thesis that 'a very high
percentage of the British population, both male and female, are
descended from hunter-gatherer pioneers who arrived before

4,000 BC, and that the Atlantic littoral zone provided one of the major corridors of movement'. This movement occurred long before the arrival of any supposed Yamnayans or 'Celts'.

Language remained a conundrum. Mesolithic Europe would have contained an unknown number of tongues. As in today's Amazon or Borneo jungles, land-bound peoples needed only to communicate with their village and neighbourhood. Sea-going people had to deal with strangers and needed a common tongue. This had made the Mediterranean the prime conduit for the western diffusion of what was called Indo-European, supposedly out of Anatolia (Turkey) and the near east. A second route eventually yielded the Germanic languages that spread, it is believed more slowly, to the north across the Caucasus into eastern Europe.

In 1987 Cambridge University's Colin Renfrew set out a proposed timeline for the Mediterranean diffusion that reached Italy, southern France and Spain, as described by the Greek geographer Strabo in the first century AD. Renfrew suggested that proto-Celtic-speaking might have reached the Iberian peninsula as early as the seventh to sixth millennium BC. Here evidence was supported by pioneering research into Iberian-Celtic inscriptions by John Koch, an American linguist at the University of Wales based in Aberystwyth. This was supported by a large database of European Celtic place names and inscriptions assembled in 2006 by Patrick Sims-Williams, also in Aberystwyth. Celtic traces were concentrated in Iberia and western France but died out going east, though Sims-Williams favours France for 'Celtic' language origination.

Celtic as the lingua franca of Atlantic trade now took on a life of its own, detached from any necessary link to race, tribe or population migration. Cunliffe dubbed his 'Celts from the west' as merely users of a language that permeated northwards up trading routes from Portugal across the Bay of Biscay to the western extremities of the British Isles. He suggested this may have begun as early as the third millennium BC, associated with the spread out of Iberia of the so-called Beaker culture with the transition to the Bronze Age. In this case, Celtic might almost be called the 'language of bronze'. To Koch, the evidence of Iberian Celtic 'finally loosened the long-held spell of the Hallstatt and La Tène cultures on the origin of the Celts'. Cunliffe echoed Chapman in wondering if Celtic languages might better be named 'Atlantic'.

A 2006 survey of this genetic revolution by Stephen Oppenheimer in his compendium *The Origins of the British* confirmed the scepticism of prehistorians since the 1960s. There was 'no clear direct evidence, linguistic, archaeological or genetic, which identified [central European] cultures as Celto-linguistic homelands'. A steppe origin for Celtic Europe was 'one of the last remaining archaeological myths left over from the nineteenth century'. To Oppenheimer, 'it might almost be regarded as a hoax'. There was a Celtic group of languages, now identified as a common tongue carried north by Cunliffe's peoples of the sea. There were no Celts, just sociable sailors.

The steppe strikes back

Genetics had certainly transformed the debate on Celtic origins in the 1990s but it did not rest. By the late 2010s laboratories across Europe and America were studying a wealth of ancient genome material pouring in from European excavation sites. Initially this confirmed that the British Isles were originally peopled roughly two-thirds from Iberia and one-third from northern Europe. Iberian DNA was close to 100 per cent down the western half of the British Isles, but so-called steppe DNA rose to nearer 40 per cent towards the North Sea.

In 2015 a survey of the origins of the 'Peoples of the British Isles' provided a new X-ray of Britain's past. The survey did not undermine the earlier divergence of Iberian versus steppe origination but it did offer it a more fine-grained account of the occupation of the British Isles. Most intriguing was the mapping of genetic 'clusters'. This agreed with a marked difference in clusters between the west and the east. But the most noticeable feature was that those in the west seemed markedly diverse, while those in the east seemed synthesised over large areas.

It was as if genes were reflective of geography, perhaps not surprisingly. The 2015 survey found that, in the west, 'an Atlantic population that dates back to the Neolithic or even Mesolithic remains unchallenged'. These Celtic speakers appeared fragmented and isolated, forming tightly differentiated communities constant over time. They did not mix genetically or linguistically right down to the twentieth century. Other distinctions were even more specific. The Cornish clusters changed at the Devon border. The north Welsh were different from the south Welsh, Lancashire from Yorkshire and the Scottish Highlands from the Lowlands. Anyone who knows these regions today will recognise such divergences. A Devonian acquaintance told me he never felt comfortable in 'foreign' Cornwall, while a South Walian once described north Wales as 'Taliban country'.

Archaeogenetics now began to reveal patterns that were anything but straightforward. The distinction of male Y-chromosomes and female mitochondrial DNA suggested separate backgrounds, possibly between horse-bound 'alpha male' raiders going in one direction and female slaves in the other. Then in 2018 new material from the Reich genetics laboratory at Harvard began issuing a mass of new data. This appeared to confirm Gimbutas's thesis in the 1950s of a large-scale incursion of steppe males, her Yamnayans, across east Europe in the early Bronze Age, c.3300 BC.

More serious was the indication that this incursion subsequently led to substantial population replacement in Britain, some suggested by as much as 90 per cent. Generalisation was complicated by so much evidence coming from burial sites possibly of 'mobile elites', unrelated to underlying populations. This was somewhat like saying that the Amesbury Archer's Alpine origin proved that the Swiss built Stonehenge. But it revived a flurry of controversy, reinforced by a further Reich cache of skeleton material in 2021 supporting a later incursion into Britain in *c*.1200 BC, possibly from France. It was suggested in addition that these migrants could well have brought a form of Celtic language with them that was to emerge as Brythonic.

The debate was abruptly blown open. There were now advocates of Cunliffe's Celtic language reaching Britain from the ocean, but others of its arriving from the east and from the centre of Europe. In 2021 Cunliffe and Koch prepared a compendium of essays titled *Exploring Celtic Origins*. They accepted that much was changing. 'What seems now to have been an age of innocence,' they wrote, 'is overtaken by a deluge of aDNA . . . a glimpse of tantalising complexity.'

It still seemed implausible that there had been a 90 per cent replacement of Britons in the early Bronze Age or in the later Iron Age of the first millennium BC. To Cunliffe this would have required 'a genocide far outstripping the worst excesses of the twentieth century'. It was invasion neurosis gone mad. But he did admit to a new scepticism surrounding the evolution of Britons in the third to second millennium BC. New evidence was replacing old certainties, at least as far as the occupation of the eastern side of the British Isles was concerned. Prehistorians felt they were hanging on the words of lab technicians, awaiting each new email with trepidation.

The conundrum of language

What seems clear to a lay observer is that Europe in the Bronze Age of the third and second millennia BC was slowly emerging from a patchwork of hundreds of long-established tribal settlements. Links were formed by seagoing and then land-borne trade as people and their lifestyles were transformed by the arrival of metals. The population enclaves on the western side of Britain would have been hubs of this great economic awakening, possibly centred on the tin resources of Cornwall. It seems more than likely that these peoples would have become users of the Celtic-root languages spreading up the Atlantic coast with the trade in metals.

Linguists tell us that Celtic was once divided into some dozen tongues. So-called 'continental' Celtic may have covered northern Italy, much of France, Spain and Portugal. It has all but vanished. The six 'insular' Celtics still found in the British Isles and Brittany were divided into two distinct groups, to the west Goidelic, and to the east Brythonic. A reasonably robust consensus is that Goidelic travelled the Atlantic routes north from Iberia, touching the outer rim of Ireland and western Scotland. Brythonic kept closer to the French shore, crossing the Channel to Cornwall and south-west Britain and extending north to Wales and much of the north. Whatever their trajectories, Goidelic and Brythonic each fragmented into different languages and dialects, mostly incomprehensible to each other, though Cornish and Breton claim to be as close as Danish and Swedish.

It remains extraordinary that this fragmentation never healed. Centuries of English-speaking evolved a common tongue, but 'Celtic' never did. This was despite its core language having apparently served as a trading lingua franca, as later did Latin and English. To be 'Celtic-speaking' was merely a classification, never to have felt the need for a linguistic bond. To speak a Romance language is not to be a member of a Romance people. The same is surely true of 'Celts'.

3

The East Side Story

Europe by the start of the Iron Age (*c*.800 BC) was seeing the emergence of a linguistic divide between the various branches of Indo-European. One of two such branches, possibly the older, was the proto-Celtic that has been traced to the shores of the western Mediterranean. Another was the proto-Germanic of Scandinavia and northern Europe. These two language groups appear to have met somewhere across the great European plains of the Danube and the Rhine. That meeting was to divide peoples down the ages of Europe's subsequent history.

Whether such a linguistic watershed reflected any great genetic or tribal difference we cannot as yet tell, though prehistorians are dying for a massive pan-European DNA census. What we do know is that, at least by the first millennium AD and almost certainly earlier, some version of this linguistic divide was to run down the spine of the British Isles. This would not have been surprising, given that both sides were occupied by people close to opposing seas, some to the Atlantic and others to the North Sea. But while those to the west have now been given a plausibly coherent narrative – 'Celtic from the west' – those to the east are revealed as having a more complex and indeed frequently changing background. Amid a fog of conflicting theories, all that does appear to be the case is that their ancestry does in large part reflect the so-called steppe origins of the peoples of the North Sea.

These peoples remain a mystery. The Iron Age settlements

down the coast of East Anglia and round Kent to Sussex were known by the Romans as the 'Saxon Shore'. Once assumed to imply a shore threatened by Saxons, it is now taken possibly to mean the opposite, a shore inhabited by 'Saxons'. The television archaeologist Francis Pryor has identified Saxon forts from Brancaster in Norfolk round to Roman Porchester near Portsmouth, 'with all the hallmarks of civilian settlements'. This supports the theory that many would have been settled, possibly for a very long time, by Germanic-speaking migrants across the North Sea from the continent.

It must be significant that all Celtic languages have cognates of 'Saxon' for their neighbouring, usually hostile, Britons to the east: Sassenach, Sasanach, Sowsnek, Saison and Saozon. It would be odd if all referred simply to one small German tribe across the North Sea. More likely is that it was the name given by Brythonic speakers, for whatever reason, to the peoples who had long occupied lands down the east coast of Britain. As such, it would indeed be the case that a Germanic tongue, a precursor to the Anglo-Saxon language sometimes called Old English, might go back deep into the Iron Age and possibly before.

Since this was before the age of writing, linguists must grasp at straws. They have established that the earliest traces tend to lie in the names of natural features, especially rivers. Crucial markers for trade and travel, rivers rarely change their names. Exhaustive research has revealed that very few rivers in the east of England have Brythonic names, possibly some using *aber* as mouth of, *tame* as dark water and *ouse* for swamp. In 1953 British Celtic-languages expert, Kenneth Jackson, divided England into two areas. One, roughly east of a line from Southampton to Yorkshire, has rivers almost all of whose names have Germanic roots. Moving west, his second area finds Celtic-named rivers more common.

The same roughly goes for place names. The language scholar Richard Coates has found just thirty-five names he regards as Brythonic down the eastern side of Britain among hundreds that are Germanic. When Londoners vacated their city on Rome's departure in the fifth century, it was not in some Celtic suburb that they settled but in the ancient Auld Wych, or old port in Anglo-Saxon. I find it hard to believe London's Aldwych was ever 'Celtic'.

The search for an eastern tongue that might have preceded Anglo-Saxon has been a major academic undertaking. It was called by another scholar of this subject, Margaret Gelling, 'the obscurest question in the whole of English history'. The geneticist Peter Forster, basing his research on the Anglo-Saxon saga *Beowulf* (*c.*700), proposed a Germanic language, possibly unique to eastern Britain, with an 'English' vocabulary related to Norse as well as German. The Dutch linguist Peter Schrijver has likewise championed an ancient English lingua franca, perhaps related to Old Frisian across the North Sea. This can only be called work in progress.

Amid this uncertainty we can offer at best a tentative picture of the people of Britain at the time of the Roman invasion. Those to the west and north of a line roughly up the central limestone ridge were mostly long-established, predominantly of ancient Iberian extraction. On most of the island of Britain their speech was Brythonic Celtic, from the south-west up through Wales and the valley of the Severn to the Midlands, Lancashire, Cumbria and the borders, and to the Clyde and the Forth. Goidelic Celtic took hold in Ireland, Man and the Highlands and Islands of Scotland.

The peoples of Britain's east and south-east, however, had long been subject to Belgic, Germanic and Scandinavian spheres of influence and settlement. They probably spoke some long-lost predecessor of Old English, though they may have been familiar with Brythonic as a language for trade – indicated in the scatter of Brythonic river names. This, I have to stress, is a conjectural but to me plausible resolution of the 'Celtic Britain conundrum'.

4

Enter the Romans

Defining Britannia

The impact of the Roman invasion on the peoples of Iron Age Britain is hard to assess for the simple reason that they never told us. Apart from a few inscriptions, they wrote nothing down and kept no Homeric record of their past. For three and a half centuries we have only the limited documentation of their occupiers. That conquest, at least after the initial (and indubitable) invasion, appears not to have involved mass slaughter, enslavement or population replacement. Life for most Britons under the Romans must have continued much as before. In the century since Julius Caesar's probing expeditions of 55 and 54 BC, there developed extensive trading contacts with Gaul. Cornish tin had made its way as far as Italy. Apart from that, Caesar had written, 'no one goes to Britain except traders'. It had little strategic significance to the empire.

Resistance to Rome was short lived. In AD 43 the emperor Claudius's troops under Aulus Plautius landed in Kent under the pretext of aiding pro-Roman tribes in the south-east against the aggression of the Catuvellauni. Possibly Belgic in origin, the Catuvellauni were located from around St Albans into the Midlands under their chief, Caratacus. His early defeat at the Battle of the Medway in 43 effectively secured the south-east of Britain for Rome.

Conquest did not lead, as so often in European conflict, to mere elite replacement and the payment of tribute. It saw the creation of an extraordinary infrastructure, of towns and roads, forts and markets, temples and villas, the defining lifestyle of this still new empire. Rome also created a new politics, the concept of *civitas*, an ordered society of settlements under delegated local government and civil law. In its train came writing, entertainment, design and religious faith, at first pagan and later Christian. Imperial culture was remarkably uniform. A tiled floor in a Cotswolds villa was the same as one in Libya.

What we do not know was who occupied this conquered territory. Soldiers and merchants came from across the empire and would have spoken 'vulgar' Latin. Colonists were regularly imported and even granted Roman citizenship to stabilise communities. Soon there emerged an assimilated 'Romano-British' population, benefiting from the new regime and its economy and loyal to Rome. There are few records of armed resistance to the empire, at least in the south-east, throughout the period of occupation.

Within two decades Roman authority had reached as far west as the River Exe at Exeter, the land of the Dumnonii people of Devon and Cornwall, while to the north, a headquarters was built in 71 at York in the territory of the extensive Brigantes tribe. So far only the Welsh offered serious resistance, notably the Silures in the south and the Ordovices in the centre and north. After the Battle of the Medway the Catuvellauni king Caratacus retreated to lead the Silures against the Romans, to be defeated in 50. He fled north but was betrayed to the Romans by the Brigantes.

The Ordovices in north Wales remained troublesome until in 60 a Roman army under Suetonius crossed Snowdonia and besieged them in Anglesey. Virtually the sole chronicler of the early empire, Tacitus, described scenes of Druids and 'black-robed women with dishevelled hair like Furies brandishing torches', who initially terrified the Roman soldiers. The Ordovices were defeated and the Romans went on to build two of their most impressive camps on the Welsh border, at Caerleon in Gwent and at Chester. Caerleon indicated extensive Romanisation in south-east Wales. Both bases boasted imposing amphitheatres that still survive.

During this Welsh uprising, the previously compliant Iceni of East Anglia revolted under their queen, Boudicca, protesting a broken treaty with her late husband, her flogging and the rape of her daughters. Before Suetonius could recall his troops from Wales, Boudicca attacked London, Colchester and St Albans, reputedly (and improbably) butchering 40,000 civilians. She was defeated and committed suicide in AD 61. Hers was the only serious insurgency of eastern Britons against the Romans and it had been sorely provoked. Britannia now hosted the Roman empire with little of the rebelliousness seen in Germany or France. London became probably the largest Roman city in northern Europe, but as a trading centre rather than a military base.

How far across the British Isles the empire should extend was not decided. In 80 the governor Agricola embarked on an expansion north out of the Brigantes' territory to the line of the Forth and Clyde estuaries in Scotland. He sailed round the Orkneys and down Scotland's west coast, where he settled a naval base with the intention of advancing on Ireland.

All did not go well. Hostility from the Highland tribes compelled Agricola to advance to a new base at Stirling, eventually defeating the Caledonians in a set battle in 83 or 84 at Mons Graupius near Forfar. The Caledonian king Calgacus was alleged by Tacitus to have addressed his troops before battle: 'To robbery, slaughter and plunder they give the lying name of empire: they make a desolation and they call it peace.' It was to be the motto of imperial resistance down the ages.

Agricola requested military reinforcements from Rome but did not get them. In 85 a sceptical emperor Domitian ordered him to retreat and any further conquest of Scotland, let alone of Ireland, was abandoned. Tacitus, Agricola's son-in-law, described him as angry at being summoned home. Caledonia was '*perdomita et statim omissa*', no sooner conquered than let go. Even Trajan, the most expansionist of emperors, had no interest in Scotland, declaring a boundary with what Rome regarded as unstable territory.

The Picts, as the Caledonians came to be called, were left alone, as were Ireland's tribes, some confusingly named the Scotti. Agricola's ventures marked the effective limit of the Roman empire in the British Isles, though northern raids into Roman territory became a frequent occurrence. A border wall was ordered from the Solway Firth to the Tyne that would rank among the most spectacular relics of Roman empire anywhere. It was named after Trajan's successor, Hadrian, who personally walked its entire seventy-three-mile length on a visit in 121. The barrier comprised sixteen forts, a ditch and a twenty-foot wall. Where it still runs along the Whin Sill escarpment it remains a monument to the resistance of indigenous Britain to Europe's greatest empire. It also scarred into the landscape an emotional boundary between the English and their northern neighbours.

Along the northern and western areas of Britannia, forts were steadily established and bases garrisoned with troops drawn from tribes friendly to Rome elsewhere in the empire, including from what is now Germany. These bases were linked by metalled roads along which soldiers, goods and messages could travel with unprecedented speed. It is said that not until the railways could news travel faster than by horseback on a Roman road. Order was maintained and trade prospered.

By the end of the second century the British colony had been divided into Britannia Superior, embracing most of the south, East Anglia and Wales with its capital in London, and Britannia Inferior, governing the north from York. The former developed the more sophisticated communities, populated with Latin-speaking officials and landowners. Villas and towns housed merchants, craftsmen, servants and slaves. When Gerald of Wales visited Caerleon in the twelfth century he was amazed at the 'immense palaces formerly crowned with gilded roofs . . . a town of prodigious size, with hot baths, temples and amphitheatres'. Caerleon was probably the biggest town in Britannia outside London.

While Britannia Superior was mostly peaceful throughout the Roman period, the rest became less so. The Welsh tribes remained remarkably loyal, treated by Rome as a bulwark against Irish raiders. But to the north Hadrian's Wall was a severe drain on imperial resources, estimated to consume two-thirds of the province's military strength. In the 140s, within a dozen years of the wall's completion, the governor of Britain, Quintus Lollius Urbicus, was faced with a Caledonian rising. He was ordered by the then emperor, Antoninus Pius, to build another wall to the north along the Forth–Clyde line. Neither wall proved effective. The Antonine Wall was gradually abandoned and even Hadrian's Wall was partly destroyed. In 208 the emperor Severus ordered Hadrian's Wall rebuilt and arrived personally to oversee it. It was clearly to the Romans a significant imperial boundary. There were no more Agricolas and the Scots were firmly left as 'barbarians'.

We thus see under the Roman occupation a strengthened emergence of the two Britains, east and west, noted earlier. The peoples of the south-east, the Midlands and south Wales became known as Romano-Britons. They were politically stable, secure and loyal to a regime that had long ordered and blessed them. Their lingua franca was assumed to be a version of Latin, but as for what they spoke 'at home' we can only guess. I prefer to imagine it was a long-standing Old English tongue of their forebears. Meanwhile, to the north and west, tribes continued their Iron Age lifestyle communicating in their various Celtic tongues.

The decay of Roman Britain

The story of the British Isles under Roman rule was told by Tacitus and others as that of a mostly benign empire operating at the limit of its geographical authority. The bargain was Roman security and civilisation in return for tribal obedience and sometimes tribute. As the fourth century progressed, this bargain began to fray. Detached Britannia was dubbed 'the cradle of usurpers' for the frequency with which its commanders and armies mutinied. Some generals even declared themselves emperor on location, as did Constantine the Great in York in 306. Britain was no longer a secure colony. Garrisons along its frontiers were frequently depleted to serve elsewhere and its coasts fell vulnerable to raids from cross-border tribes, both from non-Roman Britain to the north and from Germanic tribes across the North Sea.

In 367 these raids saw a significant development. A grand alliance was formed to assault the Roman province between the Picts of the Scottish Highlands, the 'North Welsh' of Strathclyde and Cumbria, the Scotti of Ireland and an unidentified tribe known as the Attacotti. They were believed to have colluded with tribes across the North Sea. It was what the Romans termed the Great (or Barbarian) Conspiracy. Wales was not included and stayed loyal to Rome.

At the start of the uprising, the garrison on Hadrian's Wall mutinied and joined the rebels. This left the eastern and western seaboards open to attack. Britannia was undefended and armed bands roamed as far south as the Thames, even threatening London. For the first time non-Roman Britain was uniting on the warpath against a weakening Roman empire, much as had Arminius's Germans on the Rhine frontier. But there was no co-ordination within the alliance. No single rebel leader emerged to exploit the moment. The raiders returned home with such booty as they could collect.

We can assume that the Romano-British inhabitants of the

south-east were horrified by the uprising, viewing the incursion as a barbarian menace. A year later, in 368, a Roman commander named Theodosius was sent to restore imperial authority, executing rebel leaders and re-garrisoning Hadrian's Wall. A Spanish-born general accompanying him named Magnus Maximus briefly became Rome's western emperor (r.383–8). Under the name of Macsen Wledig, he was reputed to have acquired a Welsh wife, Helen. His background in Celtic-speaking Spanish Galatia and his reputed garrisoning of Armorica (Brittany) with Welsh troops brought him heroic status in the world of Welsh mythology and legend.

Maximus's celebrity indicates the confusion and obscurity that overcame all accounts of the state of Britain at the turn of the fifth century. We know that in 410 the occupants of the British *civitates* appealed to the emperor Honorius to send troops to protect them against persistent raids. Honorius faced Germans rebelling on the Rhine and Huns threatening Rome and refused all help. He told the Britons in a clear-cut letter that they were now a free country and should look to their own resources. Britannia was no longer defensible.

The British Isles after 410 disappear from official Roman records. History customarily depicts them as descending into a 'dark age' of anarchy, decline and foreign invasion. For many Romano-Britons, it must indeed have been traumatic. But commanders and magistrates are thought to have stayed in post, sometimes as local 'tribunes'. Soldiers remained on Hadrian's Wall. Many villas and settlements were gradually abandoned, for reasons that remain obscure. The familiar detritus of Roman occupation, weapons, inscriptions, coins and legionary relics, disappeared. But archaeology offers few signs of violence or destruction. There was no evident crisis, indeed the reverse.

A surviving church, a living faith

A significant sign of continuity came from Rome's new faith, Christianity. Over the course of the fourth century this came to replace polytheism among the Roman population and Druidism among the Britons. Of the latter we know little. A lack of evidence left the Druids to be richly mined for myth and imitation by revivalists. A scholar of Druidism, Miranda Aldhouse-Green, judiciously places them somewhere between loveable nature-worshipping shamans and blood-sacrificing savages. Unlike the Romans, they built no surviving temples to their gods. Stone circles and henges are thought long to predate them, despite the theories of modern Druidical revivalists.

The Christian church was one institution to leave some record of its activities after the departure of Rome, and they extended well outside the boundaries of Britannia. As early as the third century a Roman scholar, Tertullian (c.155–220), was reporting on 'the places among the Britons unpenetrated by the Romans that have come under the rule of Christ'. This is assumed to refer to Ireland. After the official recognition of Christianity by the emperor Constantine in 313, records show Britain already sending bishops from York, Lincoln and London to the Council of Arles held in 314. This must imply an already established religious community. It flourished alongside paganism in Britain into the seventh century, when Penda of Mercia (r.626–55) was said to be the last pagan British king. Though Druidism died out, what was later dubbed 'Celtic Christianity' saw peripatetic priests described in one text as 'saints and Druids'.

In 380 a British priest named Pelagius visited Rome, where he publicly disputed with no less a figure than St Augustine. The bone of contention was Christianity's proclaimed surrender of free will to a preordaining God. This, said Pelagius, stripped humans of choice and thus of moral responsibility. For challenging the interpretive authority of the Roman church – a foretaste of Luther – Pelagius was declared a heretic, at one point even a Druid. His ideas none the less were sufficiently popular in Britain for the Roman church to despatch Bishop Germanus of Auxerre in 429 to suppress what must have seemed a serious dissent. Britain was by then beyond the boundary of imperial authority and it is intriguing that the Roman church should already have been presuming to a similar outreach. It was, as Hobbes later wrote, 'the ghost of the deceased Roman Empire, sitting crowned on the grave therof'.

Germanus proved effective, not only as a charismatic preacher but also as a former soldier. In the second role he diverted from his mission to head a so-called Christian army against Pictish and 'Saxon' raiders who had reached as far west as the Mold river on the Welsh border. His triumph there in c.430 was allegedly sealed by his adopting the Hebrew biblical call 'Alleluia' as a battle cry. Its echo round the hills terrified the enemy. When Germanus returned home to France, his biographer reports that 'this very opulent island found peace and security on several fronts'.

Heresy or not, Christianity had taken hold among western Britons. While Germanus was struggling against Pelagianism, the church was growing in strength in Wales, Ireland and Scotland. An early figure was the son of a prosperous family in north-west England named Patrick (385–461). Kidnapped by Irish raiders and sold in Dublin as a slave, he eventually escaped and made his way to a monastery in Brittany. From there he returned, possibly via Wales, to arrive as a missionary in Ireland. Patrick's energy and erudition came to define the Irish church. Though never formally canonised, he became and remains Ireland's patron saint.

The concept of a Celtic Christianity remains controversial. Its following among western Britons when easterners were still consorting with Germanic paganism gave it a status almost independent of Rome. That is now considered dubious. What is certainly the case is that the Celtic-speaking territories of the western British Isles were visited by a missionary movement known as the 'age of saints'. Contemporary with Patrick in Ireland was Scotland's St Ninian (c.360–432), who founded Britain's first known monastery at Whithorn in Galloway, begun in 397. He went on to lead a mission to the Picts.

The age of saints appears at its most vigorous, or at least lasting, in Cornwall and Wales. In Wales wandering priests travelled incessantly, setting up crosses and attracting worshippers to shelters of wattle and daub, sometimes founding 'colleges' or *clasau* for their followers. To the historian Wynford Vaughan-Thomas, 'each with his bell, his well and his special powers over birds and beasts and nature, seem[s] to carry some faint trace of old pagan Celtic practices . . . of old Celtic magic'. The prefix *llan* for a holy site lives on in dozens of Welsh place names, and is even applied to earlier Druidical stone circles. A later missionary in the sixth century, St Columba, was known to call Christ 'my Druid'.

Of secular rulers in this period we know of only one, Vortigern (c.394–455). His story is so enveloped in folklore as to be near-impenetrable. He clashed with Germanus – allegedly over his wish to marry his own daughter – but also featured in fighting off many raids round the British coast. He is believed to have sponsored the move of a chief named Cunedda in c.420 from the lands of the Welsh-speaking Gododdin in North Britain down to Gwynedd in Wales to guard against the Irish. Vortigern ended his life in Wales, where he dissolved into myth, supposedly founding a dynasty and bequeathing the nation his emblem of a red dragon.

5

The Myth of the Saxons

When invasion is not invasion

As we have seen, the origins of the peoples of eastern Britain remain obscure. The traditional history is unequivocal. These people arrived from overseas, like the Celts before them, reputedly as violent intruders from the plains of north Germany. They allegedly killed or evicted the indigenous Celtic population and imposed on the land a wholly new language, Anglo-Saxon. Such a thesis dates back to one near-contemporary source, a fiercely 'anti-Saxon' Welsh monk named Gildas, from whom all later authorities took their lead.

Gildas's tract, *The Conquest and Ruin of Britain*, written *c.*540, describes the Saxons as 'a multitude of whelps come forth from the lair of this barbarian lioness [Germany]', followed by 'a larger company of her wolfish offspring to join their bastard-born comrades'. First invited as mercenaries to protect the British from other such raids, these intruders were said to have devastated Britain. Multitudinous landings saw tens of thousands slaughtered, raped, enslaved or driven off their land and herded west, to be replaced by incoming Angles, Saxons, Jutes, Frisians and others. England was reduced to a wilderness of emptied towns, smashed altars and corpses covered in congealed blood, corpses, said Gildas, 'licking even the western [Irish] ocean with their red and savage tongue'.

This history offered a military climax to its invasion, a battle between the Saxons and the indigenous Britons at an unknown location called Mons Badonicus in *c*.500. A victorious British general named only as *dux bellorum* halted the Saxons and established half a century of peace. Gildas's book was blatant propaganda, a howl of Welsh pain at the misdeeds of the inhabitants of eastern Britain later pressing west towards Wales in the sixth century. It clearly suited him to portray his enemies as foreigners. For want of an alternative narrative, this went on to inform all later accounts of the period, notably those of the Venerable Bede in the eighth century and of another Welsh monk, Nennius, in the ninth.

It was Nennius who identified the victor of Mons Badonicus as 'King' Arthur, the name lauded by Geoffrey of Monmouth (*c*.1095–1155) as a figure of legendary British glamour and saintly personality. Arthur and his entourage of Guinevere, Merlin, Lancelot and others were subsequently to be claimed by Cornish, Welsh and, most emphatically, Breton romantics. They became the toast of the Plantagenets and Hollywood romantics ever after. All of England (and much of France) was to have its Arthur.

Gildas's fifth-century Saxon invasion remains a toxin in the history of what are controversially termed Britain's Dark Ages (*c*. AD 500–700). Histories down to the present day still take what Gildas wrote at face value and repeat it uncritically. Scholars have sought to explain the received wisdom in all its implausibility. Given the rapid spread of the Anglo-Saxon occupation and its linguistic supremacy – it had to be validated by suggestions of mass slaughter, mass eviction or at best mass enslavement. All traces of a Celtic/Brythonic culture had to have been obliterated, place names changed, settlements vacated and demolished.

From Bede onwards, scholars thus saw their task as to explain how the Saxon invasion happened, not ask whether it happened. The Saxon invasion of fifth-century Britain became a study in confirmation bias. To the Germanophile Victorians in particular, the Saxon arrival took on the aura of a second coming, an ethnic refreshing of Romano-British Celts grown indolent on the fat of the Roman empire.

This stance has changed. Most contemporary scholars of this period now accept that, while there was certainly considerable Germanic raiding and some migration across the North Sea at the ending of the Roman empire, there was no formal incursion or population eradication. There are no archaeological remains of mass graves or gutted settlements. There are no Welsh sagas of tribes fleeing north and west. British huts continued to be built round, not rectangular as in Germany. At Berinsfield in Oxford, a fifth-century grave was filled with Germanic goods – continental trade was voluminous – but its human contents showed long-standing local DNA.

It stands to reason that the population replacement of eastern Britain – of Brythonic speakers by Anglo-Saxon speakers – in a matter of two to three generations is inconceivable. Various models have been proffered, such as apartheid settlements and 'elite replacements'. The incoming Saxons could have banned Brythonic in the east, though such bans are never total. In reality, as the historian Jared Diamond has pointed out, ethnic/cultural eradication on such a scale was unknown before the age of 'guns, germs and steel'. Even the imperial eradication of aboriginal tribes in Australasia, Africa and America was never this complete.

The most thorough demolition of the theory of a mass Saxon incursion comes from Cambridge University's Susan Oosthuizen in *The Emergence of the English* (2019). She did for the Saxons what Cunliffe had done for the invading Celts. She found no genetic markers or changes in land ownership or burial practice. She found no evidence of 'a political take-over by Anglo-Saxons of existing communities or the foundation of new Germanic kingdoms by immigrant elites'. Saxon pedigrees tracing back to royal houses on mainland Europe were mostly fantasies, such as Wessex kings claiming descent from the god Woden.

To Oosthuizen, the post-Roman era in the British Isles appears to have been one of relative peace. Romano-Britons and their western neighbours did indeed have to adjust to occasional new arrivals from Europe, but evidence suggests that 'enough Roman stability survived from four centuries of occupation for [Britain] to evolve and adapt at least for the first two post-imperial centuries'. As for 'a substantive invasion, settlement or conquest of Britain from north-west Europe in the fifth century', it simply did not happen.

There is little doubt that northern Europe in the fourth and fifth centuries saw considerable population upheaval. The migrations successively of Goths and Huns from the east caused considerable disruption, though how much of it led to population displacement rather than assimilation is much debated, informed by a constant flow of new DNA evidence. The consensus is that such migration did contribute to British DNA, but only minimally and over a period of time rather than traumatically.

This would seem to confirm the thesis outlined in previous chapters, that people long called 'Saxons' by westerners had, for whatever reason, been long-standing occupants of the eastern side of the British Isles. Their probable use of a Germanic Old English language would have been reinforced by the many thousands of German veterans, settled in Britain by the Romans and loyal to them, who were part of what were called the empire's *foederati* (allies). Max Adams, in *The First Kingdom* (2021), also suggests that by the fifth century these 'Saxons' might well have reacted against their Roman past by favouring a Germanic tradition. He posits a 'culture war' of east Britons as against those in the west, one that included a spasmodic revival of paganism and a favouring of Germanic gods such as Woden and Thor, giving their names to English days of the week. It is perhaps intriguing that, until the twentieth century, the North Sea was widely known on both its sides as the German Ocean.

The Old English question

The most crucial evidence for the settlement of any territory is the language spoken by its people. After the fall of the Roman empire in the west, Germanic peoples – Visigoths, Vandals, Burgundians, Franks, Vikings, Ostrogoths and Lombards – are known to have moved west into France and on into Spain, Portugal and even north Africa. Though traditionally presented as invading hordes, under *longue durée*, these movements should rather be seen as migrations of herdsmen and hunter-gatherers, moving with the seasons. What is significant is that, in every case west of the Rhine, their presumably Germanic tongue was lost in the process of assimilating with the prevailing Latin lingua franca.

Yet Saxon invasion theory asks us to believe that when these same tribes migrated to Britain, uniquely in Europe no trace of any indigenous Celtic tongue survived their arrival, beyond barely a dozen 'loan' words. Instead we find, as by a miracle, that a Germanic language is in a matter of a century being spoken everywhere across eastern Britain and indeed deep westwards. Anglo-Saxon was crowded with traces of Latin, but no Brythonic.

This conforms to the evidence described in the last chapter from river and place names. To this can be added virtually the only written evidence we have from this period, inscriptions gathered in University College London's 'inscribed stones' project (1999). This listed hundreds of Celtic-language inscriptions from the Roman and post-Roman period across the British Isles. Virtually all are in Ireland, Scotland and Wales. None are in eastern England, where all are in Latin.

It must also be significant that the sixth-century law books of kings Ethelbert of Kent (r.589–616) and Ine of Wessex (r.689–726), which delve deep into local customs of marriage and property, were written in Old English. There are no such records in Brythonic. The same applies to the earliest English creative literature, *Caedmon's Hymn* (c.670) and *The Dream of the Rood* (c.700), both in Old English. We have sagas in Welsh, but they hail from the Brythonic-speaking regions of north and west Britain, none from the east.

As for how far west the borderland of Old English might have gone, we cannot tell. The archaeology of place names, inscriptions and burials hints at somewhere along Kenneth Jackson's line from Yorkshire to Southampton, dividing what might be called 'greater' south-east England from the rest of Britain. It seems that the long-established 'Saxons' of the east were moving west well before the end of the fifth century. Later battles between 'Britons' and 'Saxons' are recorded throughout the sixth and seventh centuries, but none is in the east and almost all are somewhere down the central spine of England.

Other clues are at best fragmentary. Gildas's Battle of Mons Badonicus, believed to have been somewhere at the southern end of the Cotswolds, possibly in Wiltshire, was said to have marked the westward limit of Saxon 'invasion'. By the seventh century Saxons appear to have progressed to the valley of the Severn. Here the diary of a Welsh monk, St Beuno (d.640), specifically mentions his fear on hearing 'a strange-tongued man across the river shouting at his dog'. The language cannot have been Brythonic or Latin, which Beuno would have known. It must have been Anglo-Saxon.

One day I am sure these questions will be settled. For the time being I prefer to repeat that a divide between a Brythonic-speaking west and an English-speaking east must most plausibly have been the result not of conquest or invasion but of long-standing settlement. The 'Welsh' never occupied eastern England and were never evicted from it. Indeed, in the twelfth century, the chronicler Gerald of Wales remarked on 'how everyone in Wales entertains this illusion' of a once-Welsh 'British' empire of which they were brutally dispossessed. A medieval chronicler in 1316 was more direct. He described the 'long-standing madness of the Welsh, as formerly called the Britons, that they were once noble, crowned over the whole realm of England, but were expelled by the Saxons and lost both name and kingdom'. Yet still Celtic departments set essays on 'Why do the English not speak Welsh?' The answer must be because they speak English and always have.

6

The Shaping of Western Britain

The Cornish axis

Across Europe in the sixth century new political landscapes were emerging. Local power structures built on ancient tribes began to re-form. Most prominent of these was the empire of the Franks, based in what is now Belgium, led by Europe's first expansionist warrior since the fall of Rome, Clovis of West Francia (r.481–511). In Britain, and despite Gildas, the chief conflicts in the sixth and seventh centuries were between local kings seeking to divide the legacy of Roman rule. This led to the cohering of the seven kingdoms of what was later called the heptarchy. These were Wessex, Mercia and Northumbria up the centre of what became England, and the smaller East Anglia, Essex, Kent and Sussex in the south-east. Omitted were Cumbria and Scotland to the north, Wales and the West Country to the west.

While ostensibly on the periphery of the British Isles and mostly beyond the borders of Romanised Britannia Superior, the peoples outside the heptarchy would not have considered themselves subordinate. The western trade routes through the Irish Sea were active. Settlements were cosmopolitan and burials filled with manufactures from across Europe. Churches and monastic communities were closely connected with each other and movement between them was intense. There seems little trace in the west of the paganism that flourished in eastern Britain after the Roman departure.

Hence probably the migration of many of the Dumnonii tribe of Cornwall to Armorica (Brittany), probably in the fifth century. The Cornish regarded the Armoricans as 'cousins', and to this day two Breton districts are named Domnonée and Cornouaille. The Gaulish once spoken in Brittany might have been similar to Cornish Celtic. Today, Breton and Cornish are the closest related of the six Celtic tongues, though not the same. For much of its history Brittany was as proudly semi-detached from France as was Cornwall from Britain.

The Cornish migration to Brittany is as yet unexplained and may have been the result of Wessex pressing westwards, though it seems to have preceded any such pressure. It was not until 577 that the Wessex king Ceawlin won a significant victory over the forces of the south-west at Dyrham east of Bristol. In this battle three Brythonic kings, Commagil of Gloucester, Condidan of Cirencester and Farinmagil of Bath, are all said to have died. The victory took Wessex's domain to the banks of the Severn and was considered critical in 'dividing the Welsh' – from Saxon *wealh* for 'foreigner' – those of Dumnonia in Devon/Cornwall from those of South Wales.

West of Dyrham, the Dumnonii put up stern resistance to Wessex expansion. There is the relic of a substantial earthwork, Wansdyke, stretching from Wiltshire down to the Maes Knoll hill fort in Somerset, sign of a major undertaking of collective defence. Dorset and Somerset did not fall to Wessex until almost a century later in the 650s, with Devon following later still, in 822. The *Anglo-Saxon Chronicle* records that, after the fall of the Devonians, Cornish hostility towards them intensified. Cornwall finally fell to Egbert of Wessex (r.802–39) at the Battle of Hingston Down in 838, despite having turned to the Vikings for assistance. The last king of Cornwall, Dungarth, died c.875, though this did not end Cornwall's long-standing resistance to English rule. It continues to this day.

The birth of Wales

The Romans initially regarded the six tribes of Wales, notably the Silures in the south and the Ordovices in the north, as unreliable. But once conquered they were not treated as inhabiting a separate province; indeed, they were part of Romanised Britannia Superior from the third century onwards. Wales's location made its stability crucial to any ruler of Britannia. It was needed by the Romans as a bulwark against raiders from Ireland and points north, and thus merited the two impressive military bases at Caerleon and Chester. Forts and roads were built, with villas extant at least in the south. Wales's loyalty to Rome was often mentioned. After Rome's fifth-century withdrawal, Cunedda's kingdom of Gwynedd in the north was described as so pro-Roman that, when it was finally overrun by Edward I in the thirteenth century, the historian James Campbell joked (I assume) that 'a strong case can be made for [Wales] as the last relic of the entire Roman Empire, east and west, to fall to the barbarian'.

That said, it was significant that Wales did not later evolve, as did Brythonic-speaking Cornwall and Cumbria, into just another part of England's western flank. Instead Wales's former tribal lands mutated, like England, into a Welsh heptarchy: Gwent, Brycheiniog, Glywysing and Dyfed in the south, Ceredigion and Powys in mid-Wales and Gwynedd in the north. Each was to feature in Welsh history throughout the Middle Ages and thus contribute to a distinctive Welsh identity.

Wales had naturally been long in contact with Ireland, some of it welcome, some hostile, with extensive Irish settlements in Pembroke. The name of Breconshire (Brycheiniog) is traced to an Irish chieftain, Broccan. The most remarkable relics of such contact is the number of inscribed memorial stones in the early Irish lettering called Ogham. This has an alphabet of upright strokes and crosses, and is unlike any other known form of writing. Some 400 such inscriptions, mostly of names, have been found in southern Ireland and Pembrokeshire. They are extraordinary and form a unique Celtic script.

A reason for Wales's distinctiveness could be the valleys of the Severn and the Dee as defensible frontiers with England, while upland Wales limited the fertile country to narrow strips in the north and south. In *c*.630, a century after the Battle of Dyrham, a Wessex army did attempt to cross the Severn and conquer Gwent, only to be beaten back by the Welsh. The historian John Davies wrote that 'this victory ranks among the most important events in Welsh history', marking the limit of English advance into Glamorgan. It stopped the English in perpetuity from penetrating across south Wales to Pembroke and the route to Ireland.

To the north, the kingdom of Powys straddled the land between the upper Wye, the upper Severn and the Dee. Its rulers found themselves divided in their loyalty between the 'pure' Wales of Gwynedd and English Mercia to the east. This clash was further complicated in the seventh century by frequent conflict between Mercia and Northumbria as both sought mastery of northern England. Around 615 a Powys army was defeated at Chester by the Bernician (later Northumbrian) king Aethelfrith (*r*.567–616). Though a pagan, he reputedly slaughtered 1,200 Welsh monks after hearing that they had prayed for his defeat. His son Edwin (*r*.616–33) was later vanquished by the first celebrated king of Gwynedd, Cadwallon (*r*.625–34), who drove him across England to Doncaster, declaring his ambition 'to exterminate the English race'. It was at least the ghost of a Welsh presence in Saxon country.

For all this activity, Wales remained a land apart. Its churches survived and prospered independent of those to the east. St Sampson (490–565) was a celebrated founder of sixth-century monasteries in Wales, Ireland, Cornwall and Dol in Brittany. Many similar institutions became *clasau* or collegiate missions, such as those of St Illtud (*c*.450–*c*.530) at Llantwit

Major and St Dubricius (*c*.465–*c*.550) at Llandaff. The latter was noted for curing leprosy and supposedly crowning King Arthur. Such was the pride of the Welsh that when their bishops met Augustine of Canterbury in 603 and were asked to submit to Rome's authority, they dismissed him for failing to show them sufficient respect. Wales was the last British church to accept the authority of Rome in 768.

Critical to Wales's security throughout this period were its relations with Mercia, named for the 'march' or border with Wales. Mercia's king in the eighth century was Offa (*r*.757–96), the first English monarch to dominate the southern half of Britain. By 771 Offa was overlord of the Midlands as well as of East Anglia, Kent and Wessex. He established early *burhs*, or towns, at Hereford, Oxford and Stamford, and even opened diplomatic relations with the pope and the emperor Charlemagne. When his ecclesiastical authority was challenged by Canterbury, he lobbied the pope in 787 to make his base at Lichfield a separate archbishopric, which briefly it was.

After early conflicts with the Welsh, Offa reached a border settlement with Powys, to be marked by the eighty-two-mile long dyke and rampart that bears his name. This ran two-thirds of the distance from the Dee in the north to the mouth of the Severn. Its course suggested that it was not a defensive structure but a negotiated boundary between existing Welsh and English settlements. While parts of Powys later disappeared into Mercia's Shropshire, Offa's Dyke brought stability and continuity to the border between Wales and later England that has survived ever since.

The Old North and the Scots

Throughout the early Middle Ages the land described as Welsh extended far to the north of England, to the so-called Hen Ogledd or Old North. This embraced Brythonic-speaking

Cumbria and Strathclyde, stretching east to the Firth of Forth. These were known to the Welsh as the *cymru*, or fellowship, the word surviving both in the Welsh word for Wales and in the Lake District's Cumbria, with its now extinct dialect of Cumbric. Gerald of Wales viewed this language as purer and less 'Irish' than that of Wales itself.

At the start of the sixth century a patchwork of such northern kingdoms comprised Rheged in Cumbria and Elmet in north Yorkshire, with, to their north, Strathclyde and Cunedda's old land of the Gododdin on the Forth. These ancient kingdoms had a genuine affinity with the people of Wales. The sixth-century Welsh poets Taliesin, Arthur's legendary bard, and Aneurin, author of the saga *Y Gododdin*, were both active in the Old North.

Rheged passed into childhood fantasy as the domain of Old King Cole, Coel Hen in Welsh. Beyond it lay the kingdom of Strathclyde, ruled from its Clydeside citadel of Dumbarton Rock. The rock now rises dark and uninviting over the Clyde, shorn of the glamour of its sovereign past, recalled in Norman Davies's *Vanished Kingdoms*. The Cumbric dialect is currently subject to an attempted revival. It produced a charming numbering of its sheep, recited to me by my (half Yorkshire) mother as *yan, tyan, tethera, mether, pimp*. My father would counter with the Welsh *un, dau, tri, pedwar, pimp*. I once suggested to Scotland's then first minister, Alex Salmond, that Edinburgh airport should not be greeting visitors in English and Gaelic, as it does, but in the Gododdin's original tongue of Welsh. He was not receptive.

The kingdom of Strathclyde sustained its independence remarkably from the fifth century to the eleventh. Other northern kingdoms such as Bernicia and Deira were less fortunate, falling early victims to the expansion of the Northumbrians. In *c.*600 Aethelfrith, later the curse of the Welsh, defeated the Gododdin at the Battle of Catraeth (Catterick), after which only their bard was reputedly left alive to tell his people of their loss. Aethelfrith also defeated an army of the Scots under their king Aedan at the Battle of Degsastan in 603. Brythonic Elmet (round Leeds) was crushed in c.616. The North Welsh clearly made poor warriors. Legend held that the Gododdin at Catterick were so drunk they could hardly hold their swords.

Aethelfrith's Northumbria had now completed the separation of another 'Wales', the Old North from Gwynedd. His domain stretched from the North Sea to the Irish Sea across what is now Yorkshire and Lancashire. Yet though both Mercia and Northumbria had by the eighth century been able to cohere their own kingdoms, neither had been able to breach their ancient borders with Wales and Scotland. Brythonic speaking appeared to have retreated into three separate territories – Cornwall, Wales and Cumbria/Strathclyde – but there it appeared secure.

Sometime in the fifth century the people of Ireland, the confusingly named Scotti, established a kingdom called Dalriada in south-west Scotland. This appears to have been a formalising of a long-standing infiltration from northern Ireland along Scotland's west coast. Northwards, it touched the islands where the Norwegians still exercised sovereignty, embracing Orkney and Shetland. Dalriada spoke Irish or Goidelic Gaelic, the name of its mainland territory Argyll meaning 'east Gael'. In 574 a meeting at Drum Ceat in Ulster reputedly divided Dalriada into two kingdoms, Irish and now Scottish.

The Dalriadan kings proved determined expansionists. They soon came into conflict with the Picts, formerly Caledonians, of what was then called Alba, still a romantic name for Scotland. These people occupied a very different country from the lowlands to the south, mountainous and cold, its coast long settled by the Scandinavian Norse. Caledonians had caused Agricola much strife and were forerunners of the Vikings as raiders of southern Britain. Their DNA suggests a strong Scandinavian component, overwhelmingly so in Orkney and Shetland. Experts disagree as to whether their language was Celtic Gaelic, Brythonic or possibly a version of Germanic/Norse.

In 685 these Picts won a crucial victory over the Northumbrians at the Battle of Nechtansmere, probably in the eastern Highlands. This ended Northumbrian ambitions in Scotland, and thus any wider English expansion north of the Forth. Like the Welsh victory on the Wye in 630, Nechtansmere is one of those little-known battles that were to prove crucial in determining England's borders with its Celtic-speaking neighbours. Had the Picts lost, England might well have extended northwards to the Forth–Clyde line, rendering Gaelic Scotland little bigger than Brythonic Wales.

A Christian Ireland

Ireland is rarely mentioned in Roman histories of the British Isles. Yet in the Bronze and Iron Ages, its position on the Atlantic trade routes kept it in the European mainstream. The Irish Sea was to the peoples of its coasts what the North Sea was to the eastern English. The ancient Neolithic Hill of Tara in Meath long served as the legendary seat of Irish kings. Their leading dynasty was Ulster's Uí Neíll (O'Neill), descendants of a fifth-century 'Niall of the Nine Hostages' and reputed king of Tara.

This Uí Neíll pre-eminence was contested through much of Ireland's history, not least by the rival kingdoms to the south of Connacht, Munster and Leinster. The island hosted a reputed 200 recorded clans, or *tuath*, with associated kings, Druids and bards. Feuding was endemic. A leader would emerge and dominate his surrounding country but then swiftly die, either while leading his soldiers into battle or through vendetta. The plethora of prehistoric hill forts suggests a land rarely at peace with itself.

From earliest times the Irish were avid emigrants. Archaeology indicates prehistoric Irish settlements in Cornwall, Wales and Scotland. In the fourth century AD the Déisi of east Ireland resettled in south Wales, possibly relocated by the Romans as a defensive move against other Irish. Most significant was Ireland's continued role in the dissemination of early Christianity. Following the primacy of St Patrick noted above came the formation of an early sisterhood by St Brigid of Kildare (451–525), the daughter of a Pictish slave and known as 'the Mary of the Gael'. For their part, the northern Irish Dalriadans exported to Scotland the remarkable St Columba (c.521–97), who in 563 founded an abbey on the island of Iona. Like Germanus, Columba was a military commander as well as a missionary. He led the Dalriadans in their conflict with the Picts, defeating such mysterious Pictish kings as Aedan the False and Eochaid the Venomous. On his Highland travels, Columba reputedly confronted a monster infesting Loch Ness, apparently deterring it from an attack.

The power of this early church is shown in its outreach into parts of the British Isles as yet not subject to the disciplines of Roman rule. Ireland appears to have developed a religious community and a missionary zeal in advance of England's. A later Irish missionary, St Aidan, moved in 634 from Scottish Iona down into Northumbria at the invitation of King Oswald. There he founded Lindisfarne abbey and with it a tradition of Irish/Celtic scholarship and art. Oswald's brother Oswy went on to found another Ionan monastery at Whitby in 657.

This Irish missionary zeal was to reach out across Europe, with visitations recorded in Ukraine, Italy, Germany, Denmark and Iceland. It also reached deep into England, a southernmost outpost surviving on the Essex coast in St Peter-on-the-Wall at Bradwell, built c.654. Alone and deserted in its coastal meadow, it is as evocative a site of Celtic Christianity as any hut on the west coast of Ireland.

So-called Celtic Christianity did not long outlast the determined diplomacy of the Roman church. It met its demise at the Synod of Whitby in 664, at which the eloquence of Bishop Wilfrid of Ripon brought victory to Canterbury. The defeated monks left Whitby and retreated to Ireland, reputedly in disgust. A saying held that 'the Celtic church gave love, the Roman church gave law'. At Whitby law triumphed, but love produced the more lasting art. The Ionan monks who remained at Lindisfarne went on to produce one of the most exquisite works of art in early medieval Europe, the *Lindisfarne Gospels* (*c.*710–15). Their Irish compatriots a century later produced the *Book of Kells*. Churchmen such as Patrick and Columba wrote vivid accounts of their lives at a time when the English were still tongue-tied. It is through them that we can perhaps see the sixth and seventh centuries in the British Isles as Celticism's finest hour, a beacon across Europe of what was briefly a coherent culture.

Wilfrid's triumph at Whitby was critical in the unification not just of an English church but of England itself. The old Roman province of Britannia had combined from heptarchy to the four kingdoms of Northumbria, Mercia, Kent and Wessex. When Bede wrote his *Ecclesiastical History of the English People* in 731 he referred to that people in the singular, at least in their adherence to Rome. The cathedral of Canterbury now 'ruled' them all, under one episcopal leadership and a combined corps of educated clergy. The English church was established as what might be termed a national government in waiting.

In 669 Theodore of Tarsus arrived to establish fourteen territorial bishoprics under the archbishopric of Canterbury. The kings of Kent and Wessex were told to write legal codes based on those in use throughout the papal domain. These stipulated the separation of church and state and exempted the church from all civil dues and duties. These significant liberties sowed the seeds of many later disputes between European monarchs and Rome. But it brought to England the outline of a new unity. As for the ancient Celtic church, so long a beacon of religious dynamism, it retreated into itself, fragmented and disorderly.

Still no place called England

Whatever may once have been the true extent of Celtic-speaking across the British Isles, by the end of the eighth century it had retreated before the indubitable advance westwards of the Anglo-Saxon-speaking kingdoms. These kingdoms were not yet stable. While Clovis and Charlemagne were establishing a new Frankish empire on continental Europe, England was still afflicted with what Milton called the 'wars of kites or crows flocking and fighting in the air'. Of the three now-dominant nations, Northumbria had led during the seventh century and Mercia during the eighth, but by the ninth century Wessex was moving into the ascendancy. The victory of Egbert of Wessex (r.802–39) over the Mercians in 825 moved England's political centre of gravity emphatically south to the Wessex capital of Winchester. His successor, Alfred the Great (r.871–99), was to lay the foundations of a new English statehood. His founding of the *Anglo-Saxon Chronicle* as a record of past and present events at last drew back a curtain on the history of England.

Celtic-speaking Britain now faced a new reality. To the east, monarchies, courts and aristocracies were forming. Cities were growing. Bishops were acquiring an authority recalling that of Roman Britannia. At Whitby these bishops had established loyalty to a collective church, template for a new nation. But this emergent statehood was not that of the British Isles as a whole. The rugged geography of the west remained a secur-ity, a borderland of separation for England's neighbours. It impeded any move towards their coherence, but it was also their protection.

When, in Shakespeare's *Richard II*, John of Gaunt spoke of an England 'whose rocky shore beats back the envious siege . . . and serves it in the office of a wall', he was confusing England with the British Isles. The 'office of a wall' in truth described the Welsh mountains, the Irish Sea and the Highlands of Scotland. The wall they formed was against the English.

7

Viking Intermission

Fiery dragons and Sons of Death

In 789 three Viking longships came ashore on a Wessex beach. A local official is said to have welcomed their occupants and assumed they were there to trade, inviting them to meet his king. They killed him on the spot. Four years later another longship landed on the island of Lindisfarne and stripped its monastery of its treasure. Similar raids then began round the coast of Britain east and west almost every year, primarily in quest for booty and slaves. A shoreline long vulnerable to seaborne raiders now faced annual visitations of the 'angry menace of the oars'. The *Anglo-Saxon Chronicle* described, 'whirlwinds, lightning, storms and fiery dragons flying across the sky'. To the settled Christian inhabitants of Bede's Northumbria, the arrival of the Vikings was the wrath of God let loose. It was widely seen as punishment for some collective sin.

The period from the start of the ninth century to the mideleventh is referred to as the Viking era of British history. For the most part raids down the Irish Sea originated in Norway and those down the North Sea originated in Denmark. Pushed by Scandinavian overpopulation and pulled by tales of wealth for the taking, men took to longships in their thousands. They developed an extraordinary skill in ship design and navigation. Their ships could travel fifty miles in a day across some of the world's roughest seas. Alistair Moffat estimates the journey from Shetland to Norway in a fair wind at thirty-six hours in ships carrying sixty warriors up rivers drawing just three feet of water. When they came ashore, the so-called *berserker* fighters were violent and merciless. Herbal narcotics coupled with a belief in a riotous afterlife generated a ferocity that terrified its victims. It was alleged that when Vikings could find no one to kill they killed each other. The *Chronicle* described them as Sons of Death.

From the 790s Viking raids became regular and apparently planned. They did not discriminate between western and eastern targets. Monasteries were first ports of call for their reserves of treasure and potential able-bodied slaves. Lindisfarne was attacked by Danes in 793 and again in succeeding years, its precious metals looted, its monks killed or enslaved and what must have a wealth of manuscripts destroyed. In 794 the monastery of Iona was reduced to rubble. Bangor in Wales was another victim. Many women were taken to the Norse settlement of Iceland, where DNA still shows British traces.

The York scholar Alcuin, in service at Charlemagne's court in the 790s, wrote that 'never before has such terror appeared in Britain as we have now suffered from a pagan race. The heathens poured out the blood of saints around the altar.' Sceptics of the putative Saxon invasion of Britain can compare the copious evidence for the real Viking one.

The Vikings in the north

Most concerted were the Norse (Norwegian) attacks on Ireland, suggesting it was a particularly rich source of plunder. The first came in 795, followed by twenty-five raids of increasing severity in as many years. Prime targets were monasteries as bases for local clan rulers and their supporters. These included Cork, Wexford and Limerick. Even the island hermitage of Skellig Michael on its almost inaccessible sea-girt rock was attacked. The scale of these operations is indicated by a report of no fewer than sixty Norse longships sailing up the Shannon and Bann rivers in 837.

In time, the invaders set up trading bases on Irish soil, the most notable being Dublin, founded in 841. These bases made the Vikings vulnerable to counter-attack, leading the Irish to form collective defences. In 849 Norse Dublin was sacked by local Irish kings, as at various times were Wexford, Waterford and Limerick. The kingdoms of Meath and Munster in the south and Connacht and the O'Neill lands in the north formed alliances which, while they did not halt the raids, rendered the Norse settlements insecure. Perhaps as a result, the Vikings grew more attuned to settlement and trade, merging into the local population. Eventually they converted to Christianity, learned Irish and created what came to be called a 'Hiberno-Norse' culture.

Dublin was ideally located midway on the route from Spain and Biscay north to Scandinavia. Manufactures and metals from the south and skins and spices from the Baltic and Russia passed through its quaysides, which also boasted west Europe's principal slave market. Irish burial grounds were filled with objects originating in central Europe and the Mediterranean. Dublin was eventually surrounded by walls and a wide protected zone of ramparts and ditches called the Pale – from Latin *palus*, or stake. This colony extended over much of what became Louth, Kildare and Meath, later to be known as the 'obedient shires'.

The Vikings also established colonies on islands and coastal settlements round the west and north of Scotland. The Kingdom of the Isles, from the Hebrides south to the Isle of Man, came under varying degrees of Norwegian overlordship throughout the early Middle Ages. Of 126 village names on the Isle of Lewis, ninety-nine are of Norse origin. The leading Hebridean clan, the Macleods, is named from the son of a Viking named Lod while Macaulay derives from Mac-Olaf.

The islands remained Norwegian, or at least Norse-Irish, until claimed by Scotland in the thirteenth century.

Of the southern islands, Man held the key. Located in the middle of the Irish Sea, it was in many ways the hub of the Celtic-speaking world. From its highest point at Snaefell, Wales, England, Scotland and Ireland can all be seen. The island was settled largely by the Irish but at various times was ruled by Norwegians, Welsh, Scots and Northumbrians. From 892 the king of Man was the Norse Earl of Orkney, owing fealty to the kings of Norway. The local Tynwald founded in 930 claimed to be the earliest post-classical parliament in Europe, predating Iceland's Althing. The Manx language was closest to, though not the same as, Irish Goidelic. Its last native speaker, Ned Maddrell, died much recorded and celebrated, in 1974.

To the far north, DNA evidence gives modern Shetland an almost 50 per cent Norse ancestry. Orkney was reputedly a year-round base for attacks on Ireland, while the name for the adjacent Scottish coast was, and remains, the land not to the north but to the south, Sutherland. Orkney passed to Scotland only in 1472. Norse territory in Britain is estimated to have extended over some 3,000 square miles.

Scotland's capacity to resist Viking attack was crippled by the same clan conflict as afflicted Ireland. There was no leading tribe or charismatic tradition. Forming a fighting force from local warriors sworn to lifetime vendettas against their neighbours was never easy. In the mid-ninth century a king of Dalriada did manage to coalesce most of the clans. Kenneth MacAlpin (r.843–58) claimed the Pictish throne through his mother's line and thus the title of 'King of the Scots'. He settled his royal capital at Scone in Perthshire, and when he died in 858 only English-speaking Lothian in the south-east was not under his domain. By then Viking attacks on Scotland were infrequent, whether through diplomacy or the exhaustion of plunder is unclear.

MacAlpin's suppression of Pictish rebellion marked the end of the Picts as a separate people. The fate of their language is subject of much academic debate. Contact with Dalriada appears to have led to the replacement of whatever was Pictish, possibly by Brythonic, Scots Gaelic or Old English in the south. Even in southern Scotland Graham Robb in his travelogue of the border country, *The Debatable Land*, claimed to have found in one small range of hills overlooking Liddesdale 'whose names are derived from Cumbric, Old English, Old Norse, Middle English and Scots'. Language remains the most elusive of archaeologies.

The Vikings in the south

Elsewhere, the pattern of Viking attacks varied widely, the distinction between raiding and settling, thieving and conquering never quite clear. Place names and genetic markers occur on both east and west coasts. In the Lake District Buttermere refers to a Viking named Buthar. The Welsh coast has Norse names such as Anglesey, Bardsey, Skomer and Swansea, the suffix -*sey* being the Norse for island. Swansea was Svein's island.

Wales was at least able to unite against the threat. The traditional supremacy of Gwynedd was cemented in the ninth century as Rhodri Mawr (*r*.844–78) extended his overlordship to Powys and Ceredigion. This enabled him to raise an army against a Viking attack on Anglesey in 856, when he killed the Norse leader, Gorm. After Rhodri's death his son Anarawd paid homage to the Wessex monarch King Alfred and in 893 joined him to defeat a substantial Viking incursion that reached the upper Severn at Welshpool.

Down England's east coast it was the Danes who were active. In 845 a warlord, Ragnar Lodbrok, came ashore in Northumbria, but locals threw him into a dungeon filled with vipers. This was unwise, and Lodbrok's sons, Halfdan and

Ivar the Boneless, needed no further encouragement. From 850 raids took place almost annually until in 865 a 'great heathen army' arrived in East Anglia, stayed over winter and carried all before it, capturing York in 866. Halfdan declared it his capital and himself king of Northumbria.

Danes were now roaming free over most of Mercia, Yorkshire and East Anglia. England's rulers seemed powerless to combine and confront them. That same year a Norse army sailed out of Dublin and destroyed Dumbarton, capital of the old Brythonic kingdom of Strathclyde, reputedly departing with 200 ships laden with treasure and slaves. A devastated Strathclyde now fell under the control of the western Scots, though the sagas claim that many Brythonic-speakers went south to join what they saw as their kinsmen in Gwynedd.

Only as the Danes moved south towards Wessex did they encounter serious resistance. In 878 a substantial Danish army confronted Alfred of Wessex (r.871–99), who defeated its commander, Guthrum, at the Battle of Edington in Wiltshire. The peace terms were hardly onerous, requiring that the Danes become Christians and depart from Wessex north of London's River Lea. Eastern England now fell under what was termed the Danelaw, formally established in 884. This embraced East Anglia, the East Midlands, Yorkshire and Lancashire as far as the border with Northumbria. Danish control now covered almost half the land area of what is now England, with York as the Danelaw capital. England might have halted the Viking conquest but it was cut in half.

These Viking attacks constituted an assault on the British Isles unlike any since Rome. The scale of any population inflow is unclear, with genetic research suggesting some 6 per cent of British ancestry as of Scandinavian origins, but over an uncertain period of time. Immigration appears mostly uncontentious. The *Anglo-Saxon Chronicle* for 876 reports that Danes had arrived 'to plough and support themselves'. They seem to have integrated and assimilated, as they did throughout the Viking diaspora across Europe. They arrived in terror but settled in peace.

The Danes established new patterns of government in the Danelaw, dividing the land into ridings and weapontakes. 'Boroughs' were founded at Derby, Lincoln, Nottingham and Stamford. Many places acquired Danish names distinct from English ones, ending in -thorpe, -by and -gill. Though originally pagan, the Danes converted to Christianity, indicated by the number of Kirkbys or 'church towns'. Studies of the Northumbrian Geordie vocabulary reveal many traces of Old Norse – yet none of Celtic. Danish words including sky, window, law and hustings entered the English language.

Brunanburh: an English empire is born

By his defeat of Guthrum at Edington, Alfred of Wessex was established as the leading monarch of what remained of non-Viking 'England'. He ruled southern England from Cornwall to Kent and north through the western half of Mercia. He repaired Roman roads and set up military bases known as *burhs*, thirty-three in number. He formulated a code of law, welcomed scholars from Europe and recruited a clerical civil service. Hankering after the classical culture of Charlemagne's Aachen, he visited Rome and was received by the pope. Alfred's Wessex was a new Britain, in tune with both the European church and the classical values of Greece and Rome. He was dismayed to find that no one in his kingdom could write Latin.

Of the Brythonic-speaking kingdoms one at least was happy to join him. Rhodri Mawr's grandson Hywel (*r.*920–50), based in Dyfed, found himself ruler by marriage also of Gwynedd and Powys. Only Morganwg (Glamorgan) and Gwent were outside his domain. Like Alfred, he went on a pilgrimage to Rome, and he also minted the first Welsh coins, albeit in

Chester. Hywel drew up what was seen as the most advanced law code in Britain. This was rooted in the liberal principle of reparation rather than retribution, expressed by Hywel as 'rather to ensure reconciliation between kinship groups than to keep order through punishment'. To John Davies, the code 'was among the most splendid creations of the culture of the Welsh, for centuries a powerful symbol of their unity and identity'.

Above all, Hywel was pragmatic towards Wessex. He paid tribute to Alfred's grandson Athelstan ($r.924$–39) and visited his court, where he was addressed, presumably by virtue of his language, as 'king of the Britons'. By the turn of the tenth century Wales had established not just a stable eastern boundary but an alliance based on realpolitik with its most powerful neighbour. Hywel was rewarded with the epithet of Dda, the Good.

Athelstan was set on enforcing Wessex's pre-eminence among the kingdoms of the British Isles at least outside the Danelaw. In 927 he went north to meet the kings of Wales, Scotland, Strathclyde and non-Danish Northumbria. The site of the conclave was Eamont Bridge near Penrith in Cumbria. The Irish were not present. At this meeting Athelstan's sovereignty over the other monarchs was acknowledged by all present and Eamont Bridge is therefore said to mark the 'foundation' of England. The chronicle recorded that he 'ruled all of England singly, which prior to him many kings had shared between them'.

The accord did not hold. Five years later Athelstan complained that Constantine II of Scotland had broken faith and invaded Scotland as punishment. The Scots' response was dramatic. In 937 Constantine sought help from his fellow kings in raising an army against the new England. He won support from Owain of Strathclyde and from the Irish under the Norse king of Dublin, Olaf Guthfrithson. However, Hywel of Wales did not join him, despite a bard in St David's declaring that 'the

Irish of Ireland, Anglesey [sic] and Scotland as well as the men of Cornwall and Strathclyde . . . shall be made welcome among us'. Hywel disagreed. He was an ally of Athelstan and would remain so. The bard's mention of Cornwall is intriguing, suggesting it was now the last redoubt of Brythonic identity in the West Country.

The Battle of Brunanburh took place in October 937, possibly at a site in the Wirral, between what was briefly a genuine, if partial, Celtic alliance and an English force composed primarily of Wessex and Mercia. It was one of few confrontations in history between the English and an alliance of Celtic-speaking neighbours. The struggle lasted all day and the Irish and Scots were annihilated. Constantine's son was killed as well as 'five Irish kings'. Athelstan won what the *Anglo-Saxon Chronicle* called 'the greatest battle fought on English soil' with improbable reports of 34,000 deaths. It left Athelstan's Wessex as the undisputed kingdom of non-Danelaw England, and with military superiority over the British Isles.

Superiority in battle is not supremacy and Athelstan was unable to bring even Strathclyde into his fold. It was from Strathclyde that the Welsh poet Taliesin is believed to have written his 'Prophecy of Britain' *c*.940, reflecting frustration at Hywel Dda's non-appearance at Brunanburh. He predicted that Athelstan's victory would be avenged by a new and greater alliance of the 'Old North', Irish, Wales, Cornwall, Brittany and, for good measure, the Vikings. The implied bond must rank as a high point of any putative coalition of Celtic-speaking peoples, notably with England weakened by the Danish incursion. But there was no one leader or country to take up the cause. The coalitional dismantled while the Danelaw ended with the eviction of Eric Bloodaxe as king of Northumbria in 954.

Wessex's leadership of England was reasserted in the long-postponed coronation of Athelstan's successor Edgar (*r*.957–75) at Bath in 973. Afterwards, in a symbolic ceremony,

Edgar was 'rowed in homage' on the River Dee at Chester by eight kings, including those of Wales, Scotland, Cumbria, Strathclyde and Ireland. The *Anglo-Saxon Chronicle* declared Edgar as holding 'the land as emperor . . . over all the kings and the Scots and the Welsh'. For the first time the outline of an English nation and an English empire could be envisaged. England was not just coming into existence as a nation but doing so in a context of acknowledged sovereignty over the whole British Isles.

Edgar's successors could not live up to this role. Viking raids resumed, and in 1013 Ethelred 'the Unready' (r.978–1016) was overwhelmed by a Danish army and fled into exile, to be succeeded by the Danish king Cnut (r.1016–35). England had barely come into being before its king was toppled and it fell to a foreign power. Cnut (or Canute) might be treated as a figure of fun in English textbooks – for supposedly trying to resist the tide – but in reality he brought to the British Isles stability and relief from further attack. Had he secured his succession, he might well have founded a new Anglo-Scandinavian empire round the shores of the North and Baltic seas. Instead, Cnut's England plunged into conflict on his death and its throne eventually passed to his Anglo-Norman stepson, Edward the Confessor (r.1042–66), followed by the Anglo-Dane Harold Godwinson, Harold of England.

Turbulent statelets

England's Celtic-speaking neighbours failed to flex any but the puniest of muscles during the century in which an alien Scandinavian power dominated England. Their politics was fragmentary and their feuds seemingly eternal. Scotland and Wales rarely enjoyed a stable monarch. In Ireland there was constant conflict between the dominant O'Neills and the kings of the south.

The Irish conflicts culminated in the Battle of Clontarf in 1014, the result of the elevation of the Munster leader Brian Boru (r.1002–14) to High King of Ireland. This was challenged by the Irish-Norse lord of Dublin, Sigtrygg Silkbeard (r.989–1036), in alliance with leaders of the Orkneys and other islands. The battle took place at Clontarf outside Dublin, and though Boru and his son and grandson were all killed, the Munster army was victorious. Clontarf illustrated the depth of Norse penetration of Irish leadership. Sigtrygg was a king in the mould of Alfred, devout in his Christianity and founder of Dublin's Christ Church cathedral. But virtually his entire reign was spent fighting for or against other kings. He was forced to abdicate and died in 1042.

Across the Irish Sea, Welsh policy continued to be defined by relations with England. Hywel Dda left a largely united country and a unique framework of law, but once again a hereditary monarch could not bequeath a stable succession. In 950 Hywel divided Wales among his offspring with disastrous consequences. The Welsh chronicle records that over the following century thirty-five Welsh rulers died at each other's hands and 'a further four were blinded'.

Only one stood out as remarkable, the aggressive Gruffydd ap Llywelyn of Gwynedd (r.1055–63). He succeeded in uniting Wales with Glamorgan, meaning that for seven years Gruffydd was one of the few Welsh kings ever to rule the entirety of Wales. However, he recklessly involved himself in English border politics and duly incurred the wrath of Harold Godwinson. Though he defeated two English armies, he was murdered by his own people and his head was sent to England in triumph. Harold married Gruffydd's widow in an attempt to reconcile England and Wales.

In Scotland the heirs to MacAlpin of Dalriada consolidated their hold over the Pictish lands. Lothian was overrun by the Scottish king Malcolm II in 1018, thus advancing the notional

Scottish border south to the River Tweed and the autonomous town of Berwick. Adjacent Strathclyde had long been allied to the Scottish crown, but in 1034 its heir, Duncan, also inherited MacAlpin's Scottish throne. Reigning from 1034 to 1040, he at last brought Brythonic Strathclyde fully into Scotland's embrace.

This merger marked the demise of Strathclyde as the Hen Ogledd, though its Cumbric language was to continue in use in the Lake District, possibly into the thirteenth century. It lives on in such 'Welsh' place names as Glasgow (green hollow), Carlisle (Lisle's castle) and Penrith (chief ford). But once more, unification did not put an end to feuding. Duncan's assumption of the Scottish crown was challenged by a rival, Macbeth (r.1040–57), who eventually toppled and killed him.

Macbeth was an efficient and stabilising monarch who ruled Scotland for seventeen years. He undertook a pilgrimage to Rome, where he was reported to have 'scattered money round the poor like seed'. Macbeth was eventually killed by Duncan's son Malcolm III (r.1058–93), supposed ancestor of the Stuart dynasty. Macbeth subsequently fell victim to artistic politics as Malcolm's descendant was Shakespeare's patron, James I of England. Macbeth duly joined Richard III in getting the Bard's thumbs down and is unlikely ever to recover.

The ingénue nations of the British Isles at the end of the Anglo-Saxon era now had borders that are more or less recognisable today. They formed a geopolitical identity and were threatened only by the Danes. Danish monarchs regarded the English crown as their inheritance from Cnut. It was in this cause that in 1066 Harald Hardrada invaded England to march on York, only to be defeated by Harold Godwinson at Stamford Bridge. Harold had little time to savour his victory. He promptly had to march south to face another former Viking with a claim to his throne, this one far more deadly, William of Normandy.

8

Norman Arrival

A new England, a new Scotland

William the Conqueror was a child of Danish imperialism. He was the direct descendant of the Viking warlord Rollo, who had been granted Normandy in 911 by the French king as a protection against other Viking raiders. However, William's invasion need not have concerned the Celtic-speaking regions of Britain. It was the English throne that he claimed and won at the Battle of Hastings in 1066, and none other.

To secure the support of his barons for an enterprise which they regarded as beyond the bounds of feudal duty, William had to promise great rewards to any who joined him. Rather than merely seize England's crown and revenues, he visited on the Saxon aristocracy and church possibly the greatest theft of wealth in Europe's pre-revolutionary history. In the years after the conquest, some 95 per cent of England's productive land was confiscated and transferred to the Norman aristocracy and church.

William's policy was tactical. As he marched across England, he carefully avoided London, negotiating with the City's aldermen and merchants to leave their wealth and liberties intact. He promised, 'I will not suffer any man to do you any wrong.' The rest of England enjoyed no such generosity. The slightest sign of opposition was suppressed. Rebellions in East Anglia and the north, said the chronicle, saw William 'yielding to his worst impulses, setting no bounds to his fury'. One result was the 'harrying of the north' begun in 1069. The later Domesday Book indicated that 75 per cent of the north-eastern population of England was killed, starved or driven from its land.

The response of the Scots and Welsh was initially ambivalent. Malcolm III, slayer of Macbeth, was married to Margaret, sister of Edgar the Atheling, rightful claimant to Harold's English throne. Malcolm had been raised in London, and when Margaret arrived in Scotland she brought English customs and religious practices to the Scottish court. She also rebuilt the monastery of Iona. After the Battle of Hastings, Edgar had fled north to join his sister, meaning that Scotland was now harbouring a rival to the Conqueror's throne.

After five years, and under pressure from belligerent courtiers, Malcolm in 1071 threw caution to the winds. Relying on arousing northern opposition to William's monarchy, he led a Scottish army south over the Lothian border, demanding nothing less than the throne for his brother-in-law, Edgar. An angry William promptly invaded Scotland and forced Malcolm to pay him homage at Abernethy, near Perth.

Malcolm died in another raid south in 1093 and there followed a quarter-century of internecine strife, as Scotland fought over who should be its ruler. Malcolm's most damaging bequest to his country was to have nine sons, all ambitious for kingship. Not until 1124 could the Norman-educated ninth son, David I (r.1124–53), attain the one prerequisite for success among Scottish monarchs, survival. He was to rule Scotland for thirty years roughly coterminous with the reign of Henry I of England (r.1100–1135).

David's pragmatism recalled that of Hywel Dda: at all costs to avoid war with England. He had been brought up in Henry's court said William of Malmesbury, 'with his manners polished from the rust of Scottish barbarity'. His domestic policy was one of Norman assimilation, inviting Norman courtiers north to take baronial land in Scotland and in effect to become its aristocracy. A favourite was Walter FitzAlan, whose father had been steward to the bishops of Dol in Brittany. FitzAlan was granted much of Renfrewshire and other estates and adopted the name of Steward from his family's Breton occupation. The later spelling of the house of Stuart was a French innovation of Mary Queen of Scots, there being no 'w' in French.

David thus pre-empted the emergence of an indigenous Lowlands ruling class. Where the old Scots court had probably spoken Gaelic (or possibly Pictish), it now spoke French, though the capital was moved from Scone south to Edinburgh in English-speaking Lothian. New bishoprics were founded, with monasteries at Kelso and Melrose, David adamantly refusing to bring his church under the authority of York. Fifteen royal burghs were established, with the right to hold markets and promote trade. The Lowlands became a miniature England in what historians have called the Davidian revolution.

Old habits died hard. When England's politics were destabilised by the murder of Thomas Becket in 1170, David's successor, William, sought to seize territorial advantage by invading Northumbria. He was roundly defeated by Henry II at the Battle of Alnwick in 1174 and forced to sign the Treaty of Falaise. This put Scotland in formal homage to the English crown and its clergy under the Archbishop of Canterbury. English garrisons were placed in castles at Roxburgh, Berwick, Jedburgh, Stirling and Edinburgh. The treaty was revoked when Richard I came to the English throne, but it foretold a historical pattern of Scottish recklessness provoking English overreaction.

Scotland remained a disparate territory. The Lowland southeast was Normanised, but the Highlands and the western isles remained lands – and languages – apart. The islands intermittently embraced Man, old Dalriada, Skye and the Hebrides, but were contested by Irish-Norse kings. The half-Norse, half-Irish ruler Somerled (*d*.1164) in the twelfth century established the kingdom and lordship of Argyll and the Isles with legendary magnificence. When Scotland finally gained sovereignty over the Isles in the fifteenth century, Somerled's MacDonald family retained their overlordship. A reputed half million Scots claim MacDonald as their genetic forebear.

The rape of Wales

Scotland under the Normans at least acquired the foundations of a ruling establishment. Wales did not. Its kingdoms had cohered into four, Gwynedd in the north, Powys in the east, Deheubarth (Dyfed) in the south-west and Glamorgan in the south-east. Their kings saw them as independent monarchies, even if a Rhodri Mawr or a Hywel Dda had occasionally contrived to lead them as one. Wales was not ruled as a united realm and its fragmentation could hardly have been regarded by the Conqueror as a threat. But, like the Romans, he saw Wales as too close to home for comfort.

The Conqueror needed two things of Wales: a security zone to contain Wales's lawless interior and land to bestow on his barons. Both were obtained by establishing the so-called Welsh Marches, the kingdoms encircling ancient Gwynedd to the south and east. William duly granted three 'Marcher lordships' to his closest allies. Hugh d'Avranches was made Earl of Chester, Roger de Montgomerie Earl of Shrewsbury and William FitzOsbern Earl of Hereford. There was no single governor over the Marches. Each lord was granted so-called palatine powers, with authority 'sicut regale', like a king. It was a licence for territorial aggrandisement and anarchy.

FitzOsbern built a magnificent castle at Chepstow at the mouth of the Wye and advanced west, occupying Caerleon and the old Welsh kingdom of Gwent before seizing the entirety of Glamorgan. He died in 1071, but his son Roger joined a Midlands rebellion against William, which led to him being stripped of his lordship. It took another decade for Norman control to cross south Wales to the extremity of Pembroke. Here the Normans resettled large numbers of Flemings over the course of the twelfth century, in part to deter Irish raids. The Landsker Line across Pembrokeshire still marks the boundary of this settlement, indicated in English place names to its south.

In mid-Wales, Roger de Montgomerie advanced into the upper Severn valley and beyond, penetrating as far as Ceredigion and seizing land for his family and friends as he went. In the north, Hugh of Chester moved along the coast to Anglesey, his cousin Robert of Rhuddlan reaching Caernarvon in 1081. Here the ancient Welsh kingdom of Gwynedd was never going to submit lightly and conflict was persistent. Hugh earned himself the unflattering epithets of the Chester Lupus (wolf) and the Fat Hunter (Gros Veneur). The terms were commemorated by his descendants in the Grosvenors' west London estates.

The lack of coherent authority in the hands of either the kings of Gwynedd or the Marcher lords was to bedevil Wales for four and a half centuries. The lords were drawn into alliances and feuds with local Welsh kings. In a typical such confrontation, the Battle of Mynydd Carn near St David's in 1081, a Deheubarth army with Irish and Danish support confronted an army of Glamorgan and Powys with Norman support. The victory for Deheubarth briefly strengthened Wales against the Normans. It led William I to march to Pembroke and visit the Welsh shrine of St David's, signing in 1081 a treaty with the local king of Deheubarth, Rhys ap Tewdwr (r. 1078–93).

Nowhere was Wales stable for long. The Normans' armoured knights could overwhelm Welsh infantry in open battle but were vulnerable to guerrilla attacks. Their motte-and-bailey castles made the March one of the most fortified frontiers in Europe. Archaeologists have identified eighty-five mottes in Shropshire, thirty castles in Glamorgan and some

400 Norman forts in Wales as a whole. They are vivid memorials to Welsh nuisance value.

The most persistent opposition to the Normans came from the kingdom of Gwynedd, where Gruffydd ap Cynan (r.1081–1137) regularly drove Norman intruders from his land. To the south the Cadwgan clan continued in control of much of what is now Ceredigion and parts of Powys. Even the Vikings returned, with the Norse king Magnus Barelegs (d.1103) – so named for his liking for the kilt – becoming king of the Scottish islands, taking Man and Dublin and even landing on Anglesey in 1098. He thought in the words of the *Chronicle* 'that he would conquer all England'. He eventually died in Ireland.

The fate of individuals caught up in the Welsh anarchy was not confined to kings. Princess Nest (c.1085–c.1136), daughter of Rhys of Deheubarth and descendant of Hywel Dda, was carried off after a battle by the Normans under William Rufus (1087–1100). Startlingly beautiful, she captivated the king's son, the future Henry I, appearing with him in an illuminated manuscript together in bed and both wearing crowns. Nest was later wife to Gerald, custodian of Pembroke Castle, was kidnapped by Owain Cadwgan, returned to marry the Sheriff of Pembroke and then the Constable of Ceredigion. Two of her sons, Maurice FitzGerald and Robert FitzStephen, went on to lead the Norman invasion of Ireland and found Irish dynasties. She has been plausibly dubbed 'the Helen of Wales'.

Over the course of the twelfth century Wales settled into two halves. The north, known as Pura Wallia, centred on Gwynedd, with contested portions of Ceredigion and Powys. The south was the March, or Marcia Wallia. There were none of Scotland's boroughs, rather fortresses with market settlements round their gates. The old Welsh *clasau* or monastic colleges decayed and the Welsh church was reordered under Norman bishops at St David's and Llandaff. This was despite pleas for Welsh ecclesiastical independence from the diarist

Gerald of Wales, one of Nest's many grandsons. His longing for a bishopric was never satisfied, denied, so he said, from his being both insufficiently English and insufficiently Welsh, a curse on self-styled half-castes down the ages.

To whom goes Ireland?

Ireland was different again. The Irish Sea remained a vigorous trading corridor. William's son Rufus allegedly planned a pontoon bridge from Scotland to Antrim. But the Conqueror was happy to let sleeping – or at least brawling – dogs lie. Ireland was seen as no threat to England. It was not until the arrival of the Plantagenets under Henry II (r.1154–89) that circumstances altered.

The Marcher lord of Chepstow at the time was Richard 'Strongbow' de Clare (1130–76), Second Earl of Pembroke. Disinherited by Henry II for having supported King Stephen against his mother, Matilda, Strongbow formed an alliance with the king of the wealthy Irish province of Leinster, Dermot MacMurrough. He too had been dispossessed of his land, by the high king of Ireland, Rory O'Connor, following a matrimonial dispute. In a private deal, Richard offered to help MacMurrough regain his kingdom if, in return, he could marry MacMurrough's daughter and succeed eventually to the kingship itself.

Strongbow was joined in this private venture by two other Marcher grandees, Nest's sons Robert FitzStephen and Maurice FitzGerald, and by four of her grandsons, to be known collectively as the Pembroke Circle. Such was the confusion of loyalties that they spoke French and went into battle against the Irish saluting the Welsh 'Sainte David'. All were to become Irish lords and Nest was dubbed 'queen-bee of the Cambro-Norman swarm'. Since her brother Gruffydd was ancestor to the Tudor dynasty of England, her Rhys family of Deheubarth towered over the history of Celtic-speaking Britain. No one involved seems to have spoken English.

The invasion of Ireland in 1169–70 was the first arrival of English – or rather Norman/Welsh – soldiers on Irish soil and one that was never to be forgotten. It was an act of private enterprise, or perhaps banditry, by a group of Marcher barons unauthorised by their king, Henry II. Strongbow's soldiers proved invincible, taking not just Leinster but also Dublin, Wexford and Waterford. They were followed by a gold rush of Norman adventurers eager for Irish land, who in turn were followed by Welsh settlers. To this day Walsh (or Welsh) is among the most common surnames in Ireland.

Henry II disapproved of Strongbow's invasion. He wanted no powerful warlords in control of territory on both sides of the Irish Sea. Strongbow was allowed to keep his Irish estates but on condition that he surrendered his English and Welsh ones. Henry personally visited Ireland for six months in 1172, the first (and almost the last) English king to do so in a spirit of peace. In return, Strongbow acknowledged Henry as his liege and as lord of Dublin. The king held a grand feast of 'unknown English dishes' for the Irish 'kinglets'. How many attended is not known, but the clear implication was that the English crown was now asserting its sovereignty over Ireland. England acquired its Irish empire, as was said of its Indian one, 'in a fit of absence of mind'.

The historian of this 'first English empire', as he called it, Rees Davies, argued that such an advance into Ireland was only a matter of time. Ultimately, no English ruler could ignore the Irish Sea. To Davies, the western trade conduit was 'the highway of power in this zone – the means to a more than local or regional supremacy'. As yet, no formal homage was paid to any Norman monarch by 'kings' in Ireland, by the O'Neills of Ulster or the Connachta of Connaught. But since Strongbow was bidding to join their ranks, Henry could not tolerate a semi-independent power emerging on his western flank. Besides, his attention at the time was focused on a greater empire across the Channel in France and Aquitaine.

In 1177 Henry duly made his younger son John (the future king) 'Lord of Ireland', firmly under his authority. Hugh de Lacy he made Lord of Meath. He also declared that no part of Ireland be called a kingdom. Normans were now arriving in Ireland in strength, but behaving quite unlike those who took titles and estates in David's Scotland. While the latter remained essentially Anglo-Norman courtiers, the Irish settlers married and integrated into the existing Irish establishment. In Scotland, they spoke French and then English; in Ireland they spoke French and then Irish. Whereas in Scotland they might aspire to remain good Normans, in Ireland they aspired to become good Irish.

The fumbling for a new Britain

Under the Plantagenets the ambition of William's original conquest of England had been fulfilled. The Norman seizure of England's land and church and the insertion of a new elite and government laid the foundations for one of medieval Europe's most coherent states. This was in stark contrast with the preceding Anglo-Saxon instability. Only round the edges was the political landscape ragged. Here the power of London exerted its sovereignty through military might and declarations of homage. There were no treaties or constitutions, no titles or coats of arms, no councils or assemblies. To Henry II, whose domain embraced the Angevin empire of his father and the Aquitanian empire of his queen, Eleanor, this domestic empire might have seemed small change. Yet it was a constant distraction.

After enforcing on Scotland the Treaty of Falaise in 1174, Henry the following year enforced the same homage on the king of Connacht as premier Irish ruler. In Wales he was aided by a period of stability under Rhys ap Gruffydd of Deheubarth (*r.*1155–97), whom he made justiciar or governor of south-west Wales. But while the separate rulers of Gwynedd and Powys would declare their homage to Henry, they would not do so to Rhys. The ever observant Gerald of Wales wrote that by these moves Henry was able 'to include the whole island of Britain in one monarchy'. But it was not really one monarchy, rather a portfolio of monarchies, bound together by force of arms and oaths of allegiance. Wales, Ireland and Scotland retained their own disparate rulers, courts, laws and assorted militias. In each of them, succession was accompanied by fierce argument if not civil war.

Such a moment came during the turbulent reign of King John (*r.*1199–1216). Wales, after a bitter succession struggle, was ruled by Gwynedd's Llywelyn the Great (*r.*1195–1240), whose relations with John were initially good. Llywelyn married John's natural daughter, Joan. But in 1211 a Powys border dispute led to a Welsh uprising in which Llywelyn sided with John's increasingly powerful baronial enemies. Likewise in Scotland John's weakness led to its king, William, again seeking possession of Northumbria, and being again refused. This initiated what was to become a Scottish instinct when trouble brewed with England, an attempted alliance with the English crown's enemy, Capetian France, based in Paris.

This coincided with a parallel invitation from John's barons to Prince Louis of France to invade and help topple him. As John approached his doom, in 1216 a Scottish army marched south across England to coincide with Louis's invasion in support of the barons. The new king of Scotland, Alexander II (*r.*1214–49), even paid Louis formal homage at Dover. The seeds of an 'auld alliance' between Scotland and France were sown. Scotland and Wales were now both acting alongside dissident barons against the English crown. Helpful though it might have been to undermine John, the precedent for all concerned was ominous.

John's death in 1216 meant England now passed to Henry III (*r*.1216–72), a passionate Francophile. The young king married the thirteen-year-old Eleanor of Provence, and became obsessed with his equally Francophile hero, Edward the Confessor, rebuilding Edward's Westminster Abbey in the French style. As for Wales, Scotland and Ireland, Henry saw them as simply a resource for the enrichment of his courtiers.

Wales was unimportant to Henry. The 1247 Treaty of Woodstock with Llywelyn the Great's successor, Llywelyn ap Gruffydd (*r*.1246–82), reduced Pura Wallia to the status of an English lordship, inciting the English Benedictine monk Matthew Paris to write that 'Wales has been reduced to nothing'. As his reign weakened, in 1267 Henry reversed Woodstock with the Treaty of Montgomery, finally acknowledging Llywelyn as Prince of Wales. This was the first formal acceptance by England of a single integrated Welsh nation.

Scotland was treated with greater respect. Its kings, Alexander II and Alexander III (*r*.1249–86), were initially preoccupied with gaining control of their western isles from the Norwegians. This was achieved after the Battle of Largs in 1263 and the subsequent Treaty of Perth. Scotland's sovereignty now expanded to embrace the previously anarchic Highlands and islands. At Alexander III's coronation his genealogy had been recited to the assembled gathering in Gaelic, and he carefully did not pledge homage to the English crown.

On Henry III's death an observer might have concluded that Wales and Scotland could demonstrate relatively stable monarchies. Both had features of medieval states in embryo, in homage to the English crown much as France's dukedoms were to Paris. Ireland was some way behind but with the advantage of an island of its own. Though all these countries had experienced subservience to England, this had not imposed on them the apparatus of imperial rule, whether constitutional, judicial or fiscal. They were de facto self-governing. The trouble was the absence of any procedure for settling disagreements. There was only the battlefield. England's emergent rule was therefore to be enforced through the sword.

Part Two

English Empire in Embryo

9

Edwardian Rule

The architecture of hegemony: Wales

Henry III's successor was his son Edward I (*r*.1272–1307), a king who combined the military aggression of a Norman warlord with an enthusiasm for legal nicety. He was for his time a giant, six foot two inches tall, intelligent, legalistic, a brilliant soldier but with a bad temper. As a young man he had in 1265 rescued his father from Simon de Montfort's rebellion. When he returned from a crusade to take power in 1274, he was brimming with confidence. He codified English law in the Statutes of Westminster and demanded a census and warrants of feudal entitlement from landowners across the country. When Earl Warenne, lord warden of the Scottish Marches, was challenged for his warrant by royal inspectors, he flourished the rusty sword his ancestors had wielded at Hastings and declared, 'This is my warrant.'

In Wales the warrant that mattered was Henry III's Treaty of Montgomery. It lay in the homage Llywelyn paid to England on behalf of Wales, but it was homage as a newly independent nation, not a subject province. And while it might apply to Pura Wallia, it did not apply to the Marcher lords. Their most powerful voice was that of Gilbert de Clare of Glamorgan, now erecting Britain's grandest castle at Caerphilly. De Clare was not an ally of the princes of Gwynedd. To him, Wales was in no sense one country. It belonged to England.

Llywelyn had married de Montfort's daughter, tactically

83

shrewd under Henry III but a serious handicap when his son Edward was on the throne. Edward considered Llywelyn unreliable and demanded he 'bend the knee' in his king's presence. Llywelyn declined to do this, leading Edward to call him a 'rebel and disturber of the peace'. Submission was demanded and declined. The outcome undid all the progress made in Anglo-Welsh relations over the previous century. It rendered the Treaty of Montgomery null and void.

Edward now paid Llywelyn a different kind of compliment, invasion with main force. His campaign in Wales in 1277 was the costliest military adventure seen in the British Isles since the Norman Conquest. It was gratuitous and cruel, setting the rules of engagement for an emergent Edwardian empire. In July an army of 15,000 seasoned troops assembled at Chester, composed of English and Welsh mercenaries and soldiers of the Marcher lords. In addition, there were many 'King's Welshmen', all with grudges against Llywelyn. They included his brother Dafydd and the Lord of Powys, Gruffydd ap Gwenwynwyn. As so often in his domestic conflicts, Edward divided to conquer. He was supported by baggage trains, road engineers, castle builders and off-shore naval support.

When Edward's ships occupied Llywelyn's supply base on Anglesey, the Welsh immediately surrendered, but the conditions of settlement stored further trouble. It allowed Llywelyn to retain Gwynedd, but only with an intolerable fine of £50,000. His brother Dafydd turned rebel and in 1282 rose against Edward, supported by lesser princes. They shamed Llywelyn into joining them.

Edward's reaction was swift and savage. By 1283 Llywelyn's head was off and posted on the Tower of London alongside that of his brother. The latter was all that remained of Dafydd after the first recorded case of a new and terrible punishment for treason: hanging, drawing and quartering. To castles at Aberystwyth, Builth and Flint, Edward now added Conwy,

Beaumaris, Criccieth and Harlech. Most spectacular of all was Caernarvon, its design based on the walls of imperial Constantinople. They together formed the grandest symbol of medieval conquest in Europe, yet supposedly within one kingdom.

As well as being military assets, Edward's Welsh castles were imperial 'shock and awe'. They were designed by Master James of Savoy, builder of crusader forts in the Levant, and recorded as costing £80,000, a stupefying sum for its day. Surrounding each castle was a French-style fortified town, from which the Welsh were excluded from living or trading. New Marcher lords were appointed, answerable solely to the king. The son of Edward's ally Gruffydd ap Gwenwynwyn of Powys changed his name to de la Pole to sound more Norman.

Edward now declared Wales 'united and annexed' to the English crown. His first-born son would be 'Prince of Wales', the infant being crowned in Lincoln to add to the shame. Pura Wallia was shrunk and dubbed a principality, formed of just four counties now called 'the king's lands', Anglesey, Caernarvon, Merioneth and Flint. Under the 1284 Statute of Rhuddlan, Wales had to adopt English common law, largely replacing the code of Hywel Dda.

Every one of Edward's ordinances fuelled a Welsh sense of oppression that lasted throughout the late Middle Ages. To mark the settlement, Edward staged a spectacular banquet at Nefyn at the end of Wales's Llŷn peninsula. He had 'reburied' King Arthur at Glastonbury and decided that he, not any Welshman, was to be Arthur's descendant, the banquet being served on a round table on Arthurian lines. Celt, Saxon and Plantagenet were to be fused into one imperial myth. When I chided a Welsh tourism minister for the poor promotion of his Welsh castles, his reply was, 'Why should we promote such symbols of English oppression?' Old resentments die hard in Wales.

The architecture of hegemony: Scotland

The death in 1286 of Alexander III of Scotland led to his succession being disputed in a 'great cause' between Robert the Bruce and John of Balliol. Both were descended from Anglo-Norman settlers, le Brus and de Baliol. Both would have probably spoken French. Edward I backed Balliol (r.1292–6) as the more compliant contender, providing that Balliol pay him homage and other demeaning tributes. These included donating much-needed levies for Edward's French wars. Balliol refused, declining to acknowledge Scotland as a vassal state. In 1295 he and his barons, mostly Normans, duly revived Alexander II's alliance with France, with each agreeing to support the other in conflict with England. No move was more likely to infuriate Edward.

With Wales already under his belt, the English king secured the homage of Balliol's rival, Bruce. He then advanced into Scotland in 1296, sparking what became the first war of Scottish independence. He sacked Berwick and marched through Edinburgh, Stirling, Perth and Elgin with an army of 11,000 mostly Welsh mercenaries. Balliol, though lawful king of Scotland, was ritually stripped of his knightly regalia and taken to London as a prisoner. The Stone of Scone, historic seat of coronation of Scottish kings, was removed to London and placed under the English throne in Westminster Abbey, to remain there until 1996. Scotland was left with an English governor and garrison, effectively a colony. When Edward wanted to consult its parliament – which, unlike Wales, it did possess – he summoned it south to Berwick.

Nothing was gained by this oppression. With clans feuding, claimants dying and English bases in Scotland vulnerable to guerrilla attack, the country descended into chaos. A year later a young knight, William Wallace – the name meant Welshman, probably a native of old Strathclyde – killed a sheriff in a brawl over a woman and raised the flag of revolt. He wiped out an English force sent against him at Stirling Bridge in 1297 and famously made his belt of a tax-gatherer's skin. Edward marched north to confront Wallace. A measure of his intent was shown in his taxation of Ireland for supplies for this campaign. The levy was enormous: 500 cows, 1,000 pigs and 1,000 tuns of wine.

Wallace was defeated and went on the run for seven years, to be captured in 1305 and hanged, drawn and quartered in London. He became a lasting Scottish nationalist hero, his persona glorified by the actor Mel Gibson in the 1995 film *Braveheart*. Wallace sent a letter in 1297 to the merchants of Lübeck requesting trade, as 'the Kingdom of Scotland, God be thanked, has been recovered by war from the power of the English'.

Scotland now reverted to type. Robert the Bruce's grandson, also Robert (r.1306–29), feuded with another royal claimant, John Comyn, killing him in a fight and crowning himself king of Scotland in 1306. This Bruce proved a remarkable figure. Despite their Norman background, Scottish barons were clearly ever ready to support their king against the English. Edward in London murdered every Bruce relative he could find and knighted 300 noblemen if they joined another Scottish campaign. In 1307 he once again marched north, but in Carlisle at the age of sixty-eight he fell ill and died. He was eulogised as 'a great and terrible king . . . a conqueror of lands and a flower of chivalry'. On his grim tomb in Westminster Abbey is one inscription: 'Edward hammer of the Scots lies here'.

Edward's effete son Edward II (r.1307–27) was not the man to fight on. When he did come north in 1314, he was ambushed at Bannockburn outside Stirling and his army was humiliated. Two-thirds of his soldiers died in what was the worst defeat for an English army on home soil since Hastings. North of the border it was a victory to echo down the ages as Scotland's Agincourt. Edward was seen escaping on a horse for his ship at Dunbar.

Bannockburn restored Scottish morale after the fall of Wallace. Robert the Bruce's barons in 1320 presented him with the Declaration of Arbroath, a letter in Latin addressed to the pope, still regarded as arbitrator of European kingship. It stated, 'As long as but a hundred of us remain alive, never will we on any conditions be brought under English rule. It is in truth not for glory, nor riches, nor honours, that we are fighting, but for freedom – for that alone, which no honest man gives up but with life itself.' They added that they would be loyal to Bruce, but their superior loyalty was to Scotland. If he were to 'yield Scotland or us to the English king or people' they would dethrone him. Arbroath was Scotland's Magna Carta.

This was followed in 1328 by the Treaty of Edinburgh, when Edward III (r.1327–77) made a formal acknowledgement of Scotland as a sovereign nation and 'our dearest ally and friend'. This meant that in 1329, when Bruce died at the age of fifty-three, he could boast that for a quarter-century he had been the undefeated monarch of an independent European state. This state of grace did not last. Bruce was succeeded by the five-year-old David II (r.1329–71), surrounded by disputing claimants to the regency, with David opposed by a Balliol claimant in open alliance with England's Edward III.

Edward now regarded Scotland as a dangerous ally of his impending foe, France, with whom in 1337 he began what was to be the Hundred Years War. He was right in this regard. In accordance with Scotland's 'auld alliance', a Scottish army in 1346 recklessly marched south at French bidding to avenge Edward's victory over France at Crécy. It was crushed at the Battle of Neville's Cross, where the young David was captured. He was held prisoner for eleven years in London and Hampshire, later admitting it was a preferable residence as king to being north of the border. He particularly appreciated his new mistress.

When able at last to negotiate a treaty with Edward,

David II was to prove one of Scotland shrewdest monarchs. He first sought the confidence of Edward III, culminating in the 1357 Treaty of Berwick. In return for promising a large ransom to the impecunious English king, David was returned to Scotland. When his Scottish parliament predictably refused to pay, he 'bequeathed' Scotland to Edward, knowing well that the Scottish parliament would again overrule him. None the less, David died in 1371 after a forty-two-year reign leaving his country as independent as had Bruce before him. He was succeeded by Robert Stewart, descendant of the Norman Lord High Stewards of Scotland, starting a new era in Scotland's history.

The architecture of hegemony: Ireland

In 1315, just a year after his victory at Bannockburn, Robert the Bruce had taken his fight against the English to Ireland, in response to an O'Neill invitation to help oppose the overbearing English. His agent in this venture was to be his brother Edward, claiming Irish antecedence through his mother. Edward wrote to 'the Irish chiefs' a letter (in Latin) that stands as a seminal, if rare, document in the canon of pan-Celtic – or perhaps Irish–Scottish – dealings:

> Whereas we and you and our people and your people, free since ancient times, share the same national ancestry and are urged to come together more eagerly and joyfully in friendship by a common language and by common custom, we have sent you our beloved kinsman, the bearer of this letter, to negotiate with you in our name about permanently strengthening and maintaining inviolate the special friendship between us and you, so that with God's will our nation [*nostra nacio*] may be able to recover her ancient liberty.

This remarkable plea for Scots–Irish bonding worked in Ulster, with its long-standing affinity with the western Scots. The Irish chief, Domhnall O'Neill, justified his alliance to the pope, pointing out that 'the Kings of Lesser Scotia all trace their blood to our Greater Scotia and retain to some degree our language and customs'. The reference to ancient Dalriada at least had historical validity. Whether the southern Irish would see the Bruces as liberators or merely allies of the O'Neills was less certain.

The language used in such documents shows that, although pan-Celtic sentiments like these are rare, they did lie somewhere below the surface of national feeling in medieval Britain. As Rees Davies puts it, they served as 'eloquent testimonies to the individual identities and, in small degree, to the shared sense of oppression of the non-English peoples of the British Isles'. A shared enemy is at least a fair-weather friend.

Edward Bruce landed at Larne in Ulster in May 1315 with an army reputedly of 6,000 men. The O'Neills declared him king of Ireland, with significant talk of extending the campaign against the English back across the Irish Sea into Wales. Given the weakness of Edward II's throne at the time, such a co-ordinated uprising had a plausible chance of success.

In the event, the manner of Bruce's march south cost him all hope of support. He sacked towns and killed inhabitants that showed any loyalty to the Anglo-Irish ascendancy. In November 1315 he defeated the former Marcher lord, Roger Mortimer, now Lord of Meath, and burned the town of Kells. Soon the countryside from Connacht south to Munster was under his control, but by 1317, with Ireland locked in a famine, Bruce was reduced merely to ravaging the countryside outside the Dublin Pale.

Most of southern Ireland soon regarded Bruce's oppression as worse than England's. One tract referred to 'Scottish foreigners less noble than our own foreigners'. At the Battle of

Faughart near Dundalk in 1318 Bruce was finally brought to heel by an English army. He was killed and his body parts distributed across Ireland. His treatment of the Ireland he claimed to rule had been counterproductive and he was not mourned.

This was no basis on which to build a united Scots–Irish front against England. Even so, by the fourteenth century English sovereignty in Ireland had shrunk to the Pale round Dublin, from Kells in the north to the Wicklow mountains in the south. A rudimentary Offa's Dyke was built to mark it. The Pale was governed by English earls such as those of Desmond, Ormond and Kildare, but even their loyalty to England was not reliable. Outside the Pale, records suggest that the use of the English language (often meaning French) was diminishing. Ireland spoke Irish.

Under Edward III, English rule within the Pale was strengthened in 1366 by the Statutes of Kilkenny, their provisions similar to Edward I's Rhuddlan treaty with the Welsh. The document complained, in French, that many English in Ireland 'forsaking the English language, manners, mode of riding, laws and usages do now live and govern themselves according to the manners, fashion and language of the Irish enemies . . . and England laws there are put in subjection and decayed'. The old Norman families were said to have become 'more Irish than the Irish themselves'. The word 'enemy' to describe the Irish was instructive, as was the words English language for French.

The Statutes of Kilkenny rank among the classic texts of English imperial rule. They banned the use of the Irish language (though not the French) 'by the English'. They banned Anglo-Irish intermarriage, joint worship, fostering of Irish children by English parents and any exhibition of Irish culture, storytelling and songs, all on pain of land expropriation and transfer to English ownership. The Irish sport of hurling was to be replaced by archery and lancing. The measures were to be enforced by the king's second surviving son, Lionel of

Antwerp, 1st Duke of Clarence and Earl of Ulster, who arrived as England's viceroy and remained in Dublin just a year before leaving in disgust. A giant of nearly seven feet, he left for Italy, marriage to a Visconti and death two years later. Like Rhuddlan, far from abating local hostility, Kilkenny fostered it.

Was this an empire?

The Llywelyns in Wales and the Bruces in Scotland and Ireland demonstrated the capacity of England's neighbours to cause trouble if treated with sufficient hostility. But in no case did they threaten Plantagenet England's existence or its crown. Edward I's grandfather, King John, had lost most of his French empire and Edward had no intention of seeing his English one shrink any further. But his response was out of all proportion to the threat, and his solution of personal homage was tenuous. Wales was now divided between the Principality and the March and suffering the lash of the Treaty of Rhuddlan. Ireland ended the fourteenth century in tenuous subservience under the draconian Kilkenny statutes, which would today be termed apartheid. Scotland remained two countries, the Lowlands and the Highlands, still a patchwork of fiefdoms under the dubious thraldom of Edward III's Treaty of Berwick.

Of the three, only the last treaty was opposed. The result was a sort of standoff, Scotland's monarchy alone of the three nations commanding a critical political mass. Edward's empire had no formal constitutional status. The three nations were annexes and protectorates rather than colonies, stumbling from one crisis to another under what appeared to be the Plantagenet motto, that of the emperor Caligula, *Oderint dum metuant* – let them hate so long as they fear.

Had England at the start of the fourteenth century handled this empire otherwise, the British Isles might have emerged from the Middle Ages on course to becoming a unitary state of one realm rather than four. Other formerly Celtic-speaking territories such as Northumbria, Cumbria and Cornwall were being assimilated into England. Similar assimilations were taking place across Europe. It needed only diplomacy and compromise to achieve consent. Instead, the borders originally sketched by Agricola and Offa became ever more entrenched barriers to a singular identity.

Ireland became more detached, the old Norman settlers merging into the Irish population and even changing their names. Nest's descendant Gerald FitzMaurice became Gearóid Iarla. John Bermingham became Sean Mac Feorais. In Wales, the Llywelyns' incipient nationalism was snuffed out but Edward's ban on bardic culture saw a defiant flowering of Welshness. The poet Dafydd ap Gwilym (c.1315–50) became one of medieval Europe's most vivid erotic poets in the tradition of Petrarch. He wrote an ode to a seagull as his messenger of love and another in praise of his penis. Dafydd was sadly hidden from wider fame by his writing in the Welsh tongue.

10

Agony of Roses and Thistles

The apotheosis of Owain Glyndwr

Over the course of the fourteenth century, the population of the British Isles fell for the only time in its history, possibly by as much as a third. The causes were famine, the Black Death and the enormous cost of England's Hundred Years War with France. The result was a relative calm in relations between England and subordinate Wales, Scotland and Ireland. Only as the century drew to a close did Henry Bolingbroke's revolution of 1399 and his toppling of Richard II (r.1377–99) as Henry IV (r.1399–1413) offer a familiar invitation to border instability.

In 1400 a London-educated Welsh lawyer disputed a legal judgment with a local baron concerning land in Powys. The lawyer's name was Owain Glyndwr (c.1359–c.1415), who, incidentally, claimed descent from the kings of Gwynedd. He raised the flag of revolt against the crown in collusion with two currently rebelling foes of Henry IV, the Percys and the Mortimers. Glyndwr grandly proposed that on Henry's defeat he would be content to rule Wales, while they could divide England between them.

The Percy/Mortimer conspiracy failed, leaving Glyndwr uncomfortably on his own. He initially achieved some success, uniting Wales to the same extent as had Llywelyn a century before him. He captured Harlech castle in 1404 and summoned Welsh parliaments there and at Machynlleth. He wrote to the king of Scotland reminding him of their common antecedents

– as Bruce had written to O'Neill – hoping to stir a joint uprising against England. A Scottish bard's reply was that 'Britons shall flourish in alliance with the Alban people/ The whole island will bear its ancient name . . ./ The Britons with the Scots rule their fatherland./ They will rule in harmony and quiet prosperity/ Their enemies expelled.' Poets make fine warmongers.

As before, this was a faint hope. The nearest Glyndwr came to obtaining outside help was by invoking Scotland's old alliance with France. He detached St David's cathedral from the authority of Canterbury and proposed two Welsh universities. But Glyndwr's strategy was unclear. He could do little beyond attack any Welsh property that sided with Henry and win skirmishes with the aid of a small French force that landed at Milford Haven. When the French troops eventually saw Henry's full army outside Worcester they fled home. After 1405 the Welsh cause was hopeless.

Henry IV's son, the future Henry V, was commander of the English response. He turned from battles to blockades and Welsh bases began to surrender, Anglesey falling in 1406 and Harlech in 1409. Glyndwr's last plea to France, in the Pennal Letter of 1406, so named after the village in which it was written, even offered to bring the Welsh church under the Avignon papacy in return for help. It went unanswered and the Welsh took to the hills and guerrilla war. By 1412 Glyndwr had disappeared into Celtic legend, becoming the most desperate and appealing of Welsh heroes. Shakespeare described him in *Henry IV, Part 1* as 'a worthy gentleman, exceedingly well-read . . . Valiant as a lion and wondrous affable'. But his boast that he could 'call spirits from the vasty deep' was met with Hotspur's dismissive reply, 'Ay, but will they come when you do call?' They did not.

The Glyndwr revolt was a disaster for Wales. In 1402 it saw a reversion to Edwardian repression and penal laws. The Welsh could not bear arms in public, hold public office, serve on juries or marry an English person. If they did so marry, the progeny could not be regarded as English; nor could any Englishman be convicted on the word of a Welshman. Welsh bardic ceremonies and assemblies – even Welsh poetry – were again banned. A Welsh economy, struggling to recover from the recession of the fourteenth century, collapsed. Harvests were destroyed, towns wrecked and markets suspended. Divisions between rebel and loyalist factions became deep and lasting.

Glyndwr's rebellion, like Llywelyn's, was essentially one of personal pride fuelled by national identity. Henry V (r.1413–22) did posthumously pardon Glyndwr but the penal laws were not repealed. A country with a long history of being on good terms with England came to identify as a nation of 'others', specifically not English. Nothing was more likely to drive a wedge between Wales and the English.

A Highland tragedy

As Wales was paying England's price for Glyndwr's rebellion, Scotland was seeking a different route to peaceful coexistence. The death in 1371 of David II, the last of the Bruces, left the country under the Stewarts in the mildest of homage to the English crown. When the third Stewart, the twelve-year-old James I (r.1406–37), finally took the Scottish throne in 1424 it was after eighteen years as a hostage in the royal court in London, much as David had been. He was determined to modernise his new domain. But he began with a brutally medieval gesture. He executed his former regent, Duke Murdoch of the Stewart dynasty, as well as Murdoch's two sons and any potential rival on whom he could lay his hands.

James's next priority was to bring unity to a country long divided between the Lowlands and a northern hinterland in which clan rivalries and local wars were still embedded. Here the MacDonalds, the Macleods and the Mackenzies, the 'Spartans of the north', ruled the deep lochs and islands of the west

Highlands. The Mackays and the Gordons controlled much of the north-east. A chronicler wrote, 'There was no law in Scotland but the great man oppressed the poor man, and the whole country was a den of thieves . . . justice was sent into banishment.'

Such anarchy was not confined to the Highlands. The border country, the territory of the Armstrongs and Douglases, had long been a no-man's-land of scrub and moor. This was inhabited by bandit families known as 'reivers . . . broken men, clanless loons'. As a defence against smuggling they were informally licensed by both English and Scottish authorities in the sixteenth century 'to rob, burn, spoil, slay, murder and destroy all and every person and persons, their bodies, property, goods and livestock . . . without any redress to be made for the same'. All building was banned over a stretch of fifty square miles of the Solway Firth known as the Debatable Land.

In his history of Scotland Fitzroy Maclean argued that the Highland clans were in no sense part of any Scottish nation. They saw 'kings or parliaments or officers of state from the south . . . only as potential allies or enemies in their own personal struggles for power'. These struggles regularly turned to civil war. In 1411 at Harlaw, 10,000 Highlanders took to the battlefield as MacDonalds fought Mackays allied to Stewarts. This was followed by a failed attempt to sack Aberdeen. Later, in 1480, at the Battle of Bloody Bay off Mull, Angus Og set Macleans against each other as well as against MacDonalds and Macleods. The orgy of killing ended only when a harpist laid down his instrument and slit Og's throat. Conflicts even went international. In 1388 the Douglases fought the English Percys across the border at the Battle of Otterburn (or Chevy Chase), leaving 1,800 English dead.

Whatever James had learned in London, it was not diplomacy. He summoned the feuding Highland chiefs to a parliament, arrested forty of them and either executed them or stripped them of office. In retaliation, the survivors marched on Inverness and burned it to the ground. In 1437 James suffered a taste of his own medicine. Three clansmen whom he had offended decided to hack him to pieces in front of his wife. She had them tortured to death. The next king, James II (*r*.1437–60), was barely an improvement. Learning of a Douglas vendetta against him, he invited the chief of Clan Douglas to meet him under safe conduct and personally stabbed him to death at the dinner table. It was known understandably as the Black Dinner.

Scotland's relations with England remained poor, but they were those of a nuisance neighbour. It failed to pay ransom for aristocratic Scottish hostages, who now crowded London in a novel form of English taxation. Scotland's continued siding with France in the Hundred Years War infuriated the English court, with Scots appearing alongside the French on battlefields against the English. Henry V remarked on his deathbed that the Scots were 'a cursed nation. Wherever I go I find them in my beard.'

A Tudor consolation for Wales

In 1453 the Hundred Years War with France ended in England's defeat at the Battle of Castillon, a defeat ignored in most English histories against the earlier victory at Agincourt. No sooner was the war resolved than England embarked on its most divisive civil conflict since the days of King John. This was a succession struggle between Lancastrian and Yorkist descendants of Edward III caused by the crowning of Henry VI. From this War of the Roses the Scots and Irish mostly held aloof. The Welsh did not. They divided, with the Marcher lords predominantly Yorkists while Lancastrians rallied in the south-west under Jasper Tudor, Earl of Pembroke, uncle and guardian of his five-year-old nephew, Henry.

The Tudor child had been born to Edmund Tudor by Margaret Beaufort when she was just thirteen. This gave him a tenuous claim to the throne through Margaret's forebear, John of Gaunt. In 1471, as rival claimants to the throne fell in a ceaseless round of battles, Henry came into ever greater prominence and danger, and Jasper took him for refuge to Brittany. He was a quarter Welsh, and it is intriguing to wonder in what language his retinue conversed.

By the 1480s the Wars of the Roses culminated in Richard III of York (r.1483–5) taking the throne. Sensing their moment, Jasper Tudor and the now twenty-eight-year-old Henry in 1485 returned from exile, landing at Milford Haven in south Wales. With an army part French and part Welsh, they marched across Wales towards the Midlands. Richard's Welsh governor, Rhys ap Thomas (1449–1525), had promised that any invader would have 'to march over my belly'. He honoured the promise by carefully lying under a bridge as Henry's army passed above. Henry rode into battle at Bosworth Field under the red dragon of Cadwaladr of Gwynedd and it was Rhys who reputedly killed the un-horsed Richard.

Richard's defeat by Henry Tudor at Bosworth ended the long Plantagenet repression of the Welsh. As Henry VII (r.1485–1509), he his supporters, granted Jasper Tudor, Rhys ap Thomas and other Welsh grandees leading roles in Wales's government. Discriminatory laws went into abeyance and a middle-class of Welsh gentry and officials – the so-called *uchelwyr* – replaced most of the Marcher lords. Welshmen now crowded the streets of Windsor and Westminster, eager for preferment. One was Dafydd Seisyllt, founder of the Cecil dynasty as Lord Salisbury. The humiliations of Llywelyn and Glyndwr could be laid to rest. A part-Welshman was on the English throne.

A comic opera: Simnel and Warbeck

Henry VII's monarchy was not uncontested. Two imposter claimants soon arose and found ready sympathisers among any dissidents eager to capitalise on a still divided England. In 1487 an Irish uprising in favour of the ten-year-old Lambert Simnel was sponsored by the Anglo-Norman grandee Gerald FitzGerald, Earl of Kildare. The child was purported by his backers to be one of the princes imprisoned in the Tower of London by Richard III. Kildare crowned Simnel as king and financed an army to invade England. This army marched to link up with the ever-rebellious Percys and reached Nottingham before being halted by Henry. A measure of Henry's diplomacy was that he formally pardoned Kildare and employed Simnel as a kitchen boy.

Less sympathy was shown three years later in 1491 following a more determined bid by another pretender, Perkin Warbeck (c.1474–99). A Fleming, he also claimed to be one of Richard III's murdered princes. Again he won support, initially in Ireland, and then in Scotland from James IV (r.1488–1513), and from Henry's foes on the continent in Spain and elsewhere. Though James was to prove among Scotland's ablest monarchs, he followed in the reckless steps of his predecessors and tried, unsuccessfully, to invade England in 1496. He turned back after four miles on news of an English army sent to oppose him. James lost confidence in Warbeck, who moved on to try pastures new.

Warbeck completed what might be termed a truly remarkable Celtic circuit. In 1497 he took a Breton ship in search of support among another people dissatisfied with the English – the Cornish. They had recently staged a bizarre uprising against a tax imposed by Henry to raise money for his recent army against Scotland. The Cornish had traditionally donated tin taxes to the Crown through their Stanneries parliament and been excused other imposts. They objected strongly to this one and staged a rare Cornish revolt.

Two thousand angry Cornish miners banded into an army and in 1497 marched across southern England to Blackheath, outside London. There the spirit failed them and they were overwhelmed by the London militia. Their leader, Michael an Gof ('the smith'), known also as Michael Joseph, was hanged, drawn and quartered. None the less, back in Cornwall the survivors greeted Warbeck as their rightful king, crowning him as Richard IV on Bodmin Moor. He was possibly the only king of England to be crowned in a Celtic tongue. He was later arrested and eventually executed.

Scotland escaped lightly from the Warbeck episode. It had in James IV a Stewart capable of achieving a degree of stability. In 1503 he married Henry VII's daughter Margaret Tudor, sealing a so-called Treaty of Perpetual Peace with her father. It was intended to be 'good, real, sincere, true, entire and firm . . . to endure forever'. James was desperate to end Highland feuding. He was the last Scottish king to learn Gaelic and the first to visit the western islands. He secured a sort of calm by rewarding the Gordons and the Campbells at the expense of the Macleods. He built castles, appointed sheriffs and brought a degree of authority to parts of the Highlands and Islands.

The Irish were treated with no such leniency. Already under the lash of the 1366 Statutes of Kilkenny, in 1494 Ireland was further punished for supporting Warbeck by the appointment as Henry's deputy of Sir Edward Poynings, armed with what became Poynings' Law. This certified that 'no parliament be holden in this land [Ireland] until its proposed legislation had been approved both by Ireland's lord deputy and privy council and by England's monarch'. Ireland was to be utterly subservient to England and to disagree was treason. The repressive tenor of Poynings' Law was to last into the twentieth century.

The Simnel and Warbeck uprisings were mere pinpricks on the English state, yet they illustrated how tenuous was consent to the former Plantagenet empire in Scotland, Ireland and even

Cornwall. They showed how instinctively rebellion sought common cause among most of the Celtic-speaking peoples, but how futile was any likelihood that they would then unite. The only message given was one of ongoing instability in their relationship with the English authorities in London, and of ongoing intolerance in London's response.

11

An Empire Under Strain

Rough wooing and the France of the north

By the end of the fifteenth century the two sides of the British Isles had been confirmed in their differences. The east had cohered into a political entity, the centralised state of England. The west remained fragmented, though its various peoples had at least begun to form themselves into recognisable and distinct nations. They shared little beyond a vague sense of cousinage and their reluctant membership of England's domestic empire.

Scotland was by far the most mature in its emergent nationhood. James IV was more than a clan peacemaker. As fifteenth-century England fought its Wars of the Roses to a standstill he brought to a still-feudal Scotland some of the institutions of a Renaissance state. He reformed the law courts and welcomed Scotland's first printing press. He founded or enhanced universities at St Andrews, Glasgow and Aberdeen. Edinburgh followed in 1583. Medieval Scotland now had more universities than did England. Their colleges would go on to produce an enlightened middle class that was to serve Scotland well in turbulent times ahead. By these innovations James showed that a subordinate member of the English empire could progress under its own initiative even in advance of England.

Yet nothing, it seemed, could induce a Scottish monarch to renounce that old curse, the alliance with France. To Henry VII's youthful and self-confident successor in London, Henry VIII (r.1509–47), that alliance amounted to rebellion. In

1513 Henry embarked on a display of regal virility by invading France and capturing the town of Tournai. In support of his French allies, James in Scotland felt obliged to invade England. He duly assembled a glamorous army of 43,000 men and, with his barons in full battle array, marched down the well-trodden but suicidal path across the River Tweed into Northumberland. A furious Henry pointed out that, as king of England, he was 'the verie owner of Scotland'. James owed him homage not war.

An English army marched north to meet James at Flodden Field in what was to be the biggest Anglo-Scottish encounter in history. Though the Scots outnumbered the English, the battle was a catastrophe for Scotland. Its pikes were no match for English longbowmen, while its artillery took twenty minutes to load each round. James accorded with clan tradition and led his troops into battle. He was duly killed along with his son, nine earls and countless lords, bishops and gentry. Unusually no prisoners were taken for ransom. The pride of Scotland's aristocracy was wiped out.

James was the last British king to die in battle. All that he had achieved in twenty-five years of rule was ruined by another Scottish impulse to arms. His country was plunged into a succession war over another infant king, James V (r.1513–42) and for the rest of Henry VIII's reign and that of his daughter Elizabeth, Scotland was at odds with the English crown. Conflict was further inflamed by Henry's 1530s Reformation, in which Scotland initially stayed loyal to the Catholic church, estimated to own half of Scotland's wealth.

Scotland's child king was now offered, under the auld alliance, to a French princess named Madeleine. When she died in 1538 the boy was married to another French aristocrat, Marie de Guise, ostensibly setting the Scottish monarchy on an emphatically Francophile path. Maturing into an accomplished musician, poet and playwright, the young James V continued the Renaissance tradition of his father. But, like him, he could not resist infuriating England's Henry. When in 1542 James accepted an invitation from the Irish barons to resume Edward Bruce's kingship of Ireland, a furious Henry VIII in London had instantly to send a force to halt him at Solway Moss, a defeat that is said to have driven James to distraction and an early death.

With James on his deathbed, his daughter and heir was born and christened Mary, soon to be proclaimed the infant Queen of Scots (r.1542–67). Henry VIII at once demanded the baby marry his five-year-old son, the future Edward VI (r.1547–53), hoping that such a marriage might end Scotland's alliance with France. The baby's mother, Marie de Guise, refused, leading to constant negotiations between Edinburgh and London, attended by frequent border skirmishes. It was later dubbed, by Sir Walter Scott, Henry's 'rough wooing' and escalated into eight years of open war with Scotland.

Marie de Guise removed the six-year-old Queen Mary to France and betrothed her to the Dauphin, heir to the French throne. The French king was said to have 'leaped with blitheness' on the news and declared 'France and Scotland to be one country'. In London the privy council ordered an English army into Scotland to 'put all to the fire and the sword . . . burn Edinburgh town, so razed and defaced . . . as there may remain forever a perpetual memory of the vengeance of God'.

Scotland was now riven not just by national loyalty but by religion. The vigour of its new universities bred contact with early Lutheranism on the continent. Scottish opinion had converted to Henry's Reformation in England, but the Catholic church in Scotland remained rich and powerful, favoured by Marie de Guise as regent for her daughter Mary, now living in France. As such she decided to suppress all manifestation of Scottish Protestantism, requesting a French fleet to that end. A number of prominent Protestant divines such as Patrick

Hamilton and George Wishart found themselves burned at the stake.

For Tudor England this was unacceptable. Far from being a subordinate country paying homage to a Protestant England, Scotland was now a sovereign adjunct of Catholic France, the most powerful nation in Europe. However, on the Protestant Edward VI's premature death in 1553, England veered to being ruled by the ardently Catholic Mary Tudor (r.1553–8). Catholic Marys were everywhere dominating the turbulent scene. Scotland was now in open revolt against Marie de Guise. While in England Protestants were being burned at the stake, Scottish Protestants were smashing and looting Catholic churches.

In 1557 a group of nobles led by the Campbells of Argyll formed the Lords of the Congregation. They defied Marie de Guise and broke Scotland emphatically from Rome and 'its congregation of Satan', putting the Scottish church under a 'presbytery' of elders. The following year the formal marriage of Mary Queen of Scots to the Dauphin took place in Notre Dame cathedral and a year later the Dauphin took the throne as Francis II of France. Scotland and France were now one monarchy and declared their citizenships joint. This was an English nightmare.

There was no *longue durée* about Tudor England. England's monarch had changed yet again with the death of Mary in 1558. A new English queen, the Protestant Elizabeth I (r.1558–1603) came to the throne. At the same time a group of virulent Protestant preachers took to the pulpits of Scotland under the lashing tongue of a Calvinist from Switzerland, John Knox. His diatribe against 'the monstrous regimen of women' found Marie de Guise isolated, with a Scottish church assembly inviting Elizabeth to send an English army north to oppose her. A small French fleet sent to her aid was defeated at the Siege of Leith outside Edinburgh. The outcome was the 1560 Treaty of Edinburgh, officially ending the Scottish alliance with France. Marie died shortly afterwards.

This treaty, together with the assembly the same year of a so-called 'Reformation parliament', ranked as a foundation moment in Scotland's history. Members declared the nation's official faith to be Protestant and called for the withdrawal of all English and French forces from Scottish soil. It was a rare triumph of Anglo-Scots realpolitik, reached not by proud and egotistical monarchs but by Elizabeth's counsellor, Lord Burghley, a Welsh Cecil by background, with members of the Scottish parliament.

By the end of 1560 Francis II of France was dead, leaving the nineteen-year-old Mary Queen of Scots as a widow returning to her Scottish throne in Edinburgh. She wisely accepted that she was now queen of a Protestant country, but in 1561 she denounced the Treaty of Edinburgh with England and its break with France. Even by Stewart standards, what followed was extraordinary. Mary in 1565 married Henry Stuart, Lord Darnley, her cousin (possibly), by whom she had a son. The family spelling changed to Stuart. In a reputed fit of jealousy, Darnley killed Mary's Italian secretary in her presence and was himself killed by Mary's allies in return. In 1567, at the age of twenty-four, Mary entered on a third marriage, this time with the Earl of Bothwell, a young admiral suspected of Darnley's murder, leading an exasperated Scottish parliament to demand she abdicate.

After further adventures, much to the delight of later biographers, Mary escaped to England, where she was now first in line to her cousin Elizabeth's throne. Her son was crowned as yet another Scottish infant monarch, James VI, left in the care of a remarkable tutor, George Buchanan (1506–82). He was to write a first history of Scotland and had been tutor successively to Montaigne and his new charge's mother. He regularly thrashed the young king to give him 'a deep respect for learning', one that the king later acknowledged.

As courtiers feuded over who should be regent, Mary,

imprisoned in England, was in 1587 accused by her English enemies of plotting Elizabeth's death. Enough was enough and she was executed at Fotheringhay Castle.

A new Wales – or a new England

By the time Henry VIII came to the throne in 1509, his father's part-Welshness was inconspicuous. In title he was lord of the Principality and of much of the March, but the old Marcher families had largely dispersed or died in the Roses wars. There was no governor or government of Wales as a whole. Henry decided in effect to incorporate it into England, declaring significantly 'this realm of England is an empire'. The initial vehicle of incorporation was an Act of Union of 1536 introduced by Henry's chancellor Thomas Cromwell, himself of Welsh descent. Another followed in 1543.

These acts stated that Welsh 'rights, usages, laws and customs be far discrepant' from those of England, and people 'do daily use a speech nothing like or consonant with the mother tongue used within this realm' of which 'some rude and ignorant people have made distinction'. Wales should therefore 'be incorporated, united and annexed to and with this realm of England'. This was not initiated by any act of Welsh rebellion. It was seen as a matter of tidiness and convenience.

From now on, counties became the standard unit of local government throughout Wales. Flintshire was divided between Welsh Flint and English Flint, remaining so into the twentieth century. Local JPs were appointed as magistrates 'of their own nation', a significant use of the word. Boroughs and landed gentry would be represented in the English Parliament, commencing in 1542. The Welsh language was banned from administration and the courts. Wales became in effect joined to and part of England.

In addition, the reformed Church of England would

embrace the church in Wales, while the Welsh monastic houses such as Tintern, Valle Crucis and Strata Florida were dissolved. The monasteries were hardly missed. Thirteen Welsh Cistercian abbeys had just eighty-five monks between them. By 1603 a religious census showed 200,000 communicants for the Anglican church, against just 800 listed as Catholics. A mere fifteen Welsh clergy refused to change loyalties. The monasteries mostly passed into the hands of the Welsh gentry and landed aristocracy, the Tudor *uchelwyr*. They included the Wynns and Vaughans in the north, the Herberts of Pembroke and the Somersets (later Beauforts) of Raglan. For the next two centuries these families represented what passed for Wales's aristocracy.

All that remained distinctive of Welsh government was the Council of Wales in Ludlow, supposedly representing the Prince of Wales and supervising the conduct of the law and the judiciary. This was, to John Davies, 'a successful experiment in regional government, administering the law cheaply and rapidly'. It proved so popular that the 'oppressed poor flocked to it'. For convenience the former Marcher counties of England such as Shropshire and Herefordshire were brought under its remit.

In Scotland and Ireland such unionist measures and suppression of national identity would have led to violent protest. In Wales there was none. The realpolitik of Hywel Dda ruled the day. The old Norman March was gone, and to that extent a sort of Welsh coherence was realised. Despite official emphasis on the English language, there was no attempt at linguistic eradication, as there had been of Irish in Ireland.

Christian worship remained in Welsh and an act passed under Elizabeth I in 1563 authorised the translation of the Bible into Welsh. This was executed and published by Bishop William Morgan in 1588. It was ordered to be placed in every church in Wales, as was a Welsh prayer book. The Irish did not have a bible in Irish until 1690, or the Scots in Gaelic until 1801. Records show that between 1546 and 1660, 108 books were published in Welsh, as against eleven in Irish and eight in Scottish Gaelic. One thing that survived union was Welshness.

The union was widely welcomed in Wales. Apologists argued that it at last brought to the Welsh the freedoms enjoyed by the English. Since there had never been a formal Welsh parliament, none was missed. Welshmen arrived at Westminster, apparently pleased that to be Welsh was as good as to be English. A Carmarthen vicar was recorded as telling an English visitor, 'Offa's Dyke is extinguished with love and charity . . . our green leeks, somewhat offensive to your dainty nostrils, are now tempered with your fragrant roses . . . God give us grace to dwell together.' A new nation, officially 'England and Wales', came into being as one political and statistical entity. It had no border and no ongoing quarrel. In that form it was to last four and a half centuries.

Strangely, a less easy relationship existed between England and Cornwall. The county had briefly appeared on England's political stage with the rise of Perkin Warbeck, and in 1549 it took the opposite route from Scotland in rejecting the Henrician Reformation and Cranmer's new prayer book. In what was called the Prayer Book Rebellion, a letter was sent to Cranmer stating that 'we Cornishmen, whereof certain of us understand no English, utterly refuse this new English'. As local people took up arms, the cry was 'kill all the gentlemen'. An English army had to be deployed to suppress them, leading eventually to the deaths of reputedly a devastating 5,000 Cornish.

The Cornish language was now in retreat, confined largely to the western Penwith area beyond Truro and lacking a bible or a prayer book in Cornish. Despite the hold Methodism eventually took on the county, its Catholic recusancy was to prove lasting. I recall a sign outside the Anglican parish church in St Ives in the 1990s telling visitors, 'Some people will tell you that at the Reformation England ceased to be Catholic and became Protestant. Do not believe them.'

Irish ghosts begin to stir

Henry VIII was to find Ireland as troublesome as he did Scotland, but his response could not have been more different. London retained a measure of respect for Scotland. It was a separate kingdom with a separate monarch and an educated establishment. Ireland was regarded as politically immature, at least outside the Dublin Pale. Henry VII had subjugated it with Poynings' Law and left it to its own devices, under a rough-and-ready oligarchy of earls led by the FitzGerald earls of Kildare, known as the Geraldines. Such colonial devolution, as was seen during the Simnel uprising, was unreliable.

This was evident in 1534, when the then Earl of Kildare's twenty-one-year-old son, acting as deputy in his father's absence in London, raised the flag of revolt against Henry's Reformation, affirming his and Ireland's loyalty to the Catholic faith. Despite pleadings for caution from the Dublin establishment, FitzGerald summoned sufficient support to 'go Irish'. He laid siege to Dublin Castle and swore death to all 'born in England'. He went so far as to offer a loyally Catholic Ireland to the pope and the Holy Roman Empire. The rising was a fiasco, and within a year FitzGerald was pardoned and offered safe passage to England. When he arrived he was hanged and drawn but, 'in view of the pardon', not quartered.

Henry suspended the Kildares as royal deputies and declared himself king of Ireland. A privy council in Dublin would henceforth rule the island under an appointed deputy. More radically, Henry enforced oaths of loyalty on all Ireland's extensive landowners. Land belonging to clan chiefs was to be surrendered to the king. It would only be 'regranted' under oaths of adherence to English law and administration. The central purpose was to stifle Catholicism. In the case of any resistance, land would be seized and granted to Protestant incomers from Britain. A new Irish parliament was also packed to ensure a Protestant majority under a 'Protestant ascendancy'.

This first so-called 'Irish plantation', initiated in 1541, was insensitive. Its intention was to remedy what were seen as weaknesses in the Statutes of Kilkenny and Poynings' Law. According to London, if 'our Irish enemies', be they O'Neills of Ulster, O'Donnells of Tyrconnell or Kavanaghs of Wexford, would not become Englishmen, then Englishmen would replace them. It was as if England had decided to replace the Scottish MacDonalds with English Smiths and Joneses. It did not succeed. The few 'planted' settlers were greeted with such hostility the majority returned to England.

Eventually, most Irish lords submitted their allegiance and continued as before, ameliorated with the offer of dissolved monastic land. The O'Neills became Earls of Tyrone. But assimilation was a different matter. Ireland was universally Irish-speaking, including the old Anglo-Norman aristocracy. When Henry's coronation had been announced in Dublin's parliament in 1509, translators had to be summoned as virtually no one understood English.

Despite its failure, the Protestant plantation resumed under Elizabeth. The arrival of English on confiscated farms was again opposed and rarely lasted. The most extensive settlements were in Munster, including land granted to Sir Walter Raleigh, who sold it to the Boyle family, later Earls of Cork. Plantations were met with revolts in Leinster and the south-west 'kingdom' of Desmond (Irish for south Munster). Here they led to the Desmond Rebellions of 1569 and 1579, led by local Geraldines. Some 30,000 Irish died of starvation following England's scorched earth policy and much of the land was resettled by the soldiers responsible.

In sixteenth-century Ireland the subversive role played by

France in fourteenth-century Scotland was replicated by Spain, with Madrid eager for a second front in the Anglo-Spanish wars. Following the Desmond Rebellions, the pope formally excommunicated Elizabeth and declared that Irish Catholics should treat her as an illegitimate monarch, inflicting on millions of Irish a loyalty divided not just by nationality but also by religion. London seemed wholly blind to the domestic realities of Ireland. The country reacted to Elizabeth's anti-Catholicism with the shock of a nation brought face to face with its subservience.

The response now became endemic to Ireland's response to English rule. It was that of rolling rebellion. Hugh O'Neill of Tyrone and Rory O'Donnell of Tyrconnell secured rare unanimity from as much as 80 per cent of their fellow clan leaders in defying the English crown. In 1593 the O'Neills declared a full-scale revolt against the 'English conquest', a revolt that was to pin down 18,000 English troops in guerrilla warfare across Ireland. What became the (Irish) Nine Years War was largely fought in Ulster. The English were hampered by difficulties of supply and the Irish refusal of set-piece battles. The Irish were hampered rather than aided by their Spanish allies.

Finally, an ageing Elizabeth allowed her favourite, the young Earl of Essex, to take command and cross the Irish Sea. He merely appeased O'Neill with concessions and returned to London to conspire to topple Elizabeth. He was executed, and the O'Neill rebellion ended in defeat at the Battle of Kinsale in 1601. Under Elizabeth, the English death toll from battle and disease was put at 30,000, the Irish at 100,000.

With James I on the English throne, policy switched to one of moderation. There was a flurry of Irish pardons and compromises, but Irish Catholicism was still to be suppressed. The result of the defeat at Kinsale was the so-called 'flight of the earls' in 1607, led by O'Neill and O'Donnell in person. The pride of Ireland's aristocracy emigrated, some for adventure, most to seek help in Catholic Spain, many never to return or regain their lands. The flight denuded the land of leadership and the country of any ruling establishment.

Ireland was now to endure a century of reinvigorated plantation, a policy of population replacement unlike anything attempted so far in the British Isles. Replacement on the basis of religion replicated what the Holy Roman Empire's Catholic armies were inflicting on Protestant Bohemia, to hypocritical protests from British leaders. In 1608 Protestants from Scotland and northern England were invited to expropriate Catholic-owned land to the north-west of Ulster and Donegal, so far the most 'native' and un-Anglicised region of Ireland. Unlike the north-east's Antrim and Down – which had links with Scotland since the days of Dalriada – this land had been in local clan ownership since time immemorial. It was considered ideal for resettlement as its earls had mostly fled in 1607. Up to three-quarters of the north of Ireland was to pass to what London now called 'British' settlers.

These newcomers were not rich English aristocrats, as in the case of Elizabeth's attempted plantation of the south. They were smallholders who were required only to speak English, worship in the Anglican faith and bring with them Protestant labourers. Those who could not afford the expense were subsidised by liveried companies of the City of London. These subsidies were generous, even funding a complete rebuilding of the town of Derry as Londonderry. Similar colonies at the time were being settled in Virginia and New England.

Some 20,000 British – half English, half Scots – are estimated to have settled in Ulster between 1608 and 1620, rising to a possible population of 100,000 by the century's end. This compared with the estimated 80,000 Britons who crossed the Atlantic in the wake of the *Mayflower* under the early Stuarts. The newcomers concentrated on the better land round defended towns. The indigenous Irish did not, as London hoped, vanish.

1. Wild west shores
Ireland: Innishmurray; Scotland: Scara Brae;
Wales: St Govan's hermitage

longtam venuge: qui souffrra de porta seulemet vng
lac de soye a vng ymage de sainct george pendat a icellui
Auffi se ledit colier doit auoit besoing de reparacion il pora
eftre mis en la main de sommer iusques a ce quil soit
repair. Lequel colier auffi ne pourra eftre enrichy de
pierres ou daultres chofes referue led ymage qui pourra
eftre garniy au plaisir du chenalier. Et tausi ne pourra
eftre ledit colier vendu engaigte domie ne aliene pour
necessite ou cause quelconque que ce soit

Alexander Rex Scotor   Lewellin princeps Wallie

2. Edward's empire
Caernarvon Castle; Edward I in Parliament

3. Resistance
Battle of Bannockburn; Ireland's Brian Boru; Owain Glyndwr

4. English caricatures
Welsh harpist in despair; Bonnie Scots piper;
Irish leprechaun; John Bull satisfied

5. The flight into exile

Ireland flees its famine;
Highland clearance

6. Forms of revival
Perth station in high season; Klondike
comes to Merthyr Vale; Rhondda ladies

7. Faces of dissent
Henry Grattan; Charles Parnell; Keir Hardie; David Lloyd George

8. Divided not ruled
Bloody Sunday graffiti in Belfast; A disuniting kingdom

They sought refuge on poorer land, often in adjacent settlements, sowing the seeds of future discord.

The resulting hostility was to echo through the folk literature of Ireland. There were Irish tales of 'foreign tribes', of an 'arrogant impure crowd' driving the Irish off their land by 'force and legal chicanery'. The plantation of Ulster was the invention of courtiers, clergy and officials living in London and ignorant of the land they were presuming to rule. They did not visit it and cannot have imagined the communities they were upheaving, or those they were seeking to create. It was the worst sort of absentee imperialism.

12

The Wars of the Three Kingdoms

Scotland and the twin monarchies

While the bonds of England's Irish empire were thus being refashioned, the spotlight returned to Scotland. In 1485 a part-Welsh dynasty, the Tudors, had been prevailed upon to rescue England from a disputed succession. Now it was Scotland's turn. In truth, candidates for the English crown had always been of mixed blood, but the Tudors and the Stuarts were considered sufficiently 'native' by their respective nations of origin as satisfactorily to dilute the English monarchy.

With the execution of Mary Queen of Scots in 1587, the succession to the English throne passed to Mary's son, James VI of Scotland, as great-great-grandson of Henry Tudor. The new king had been tutored in the bloodstained Scottish court under the tutelage of various regents. Perhaps surprisingly, he had matured into a competent, even erudite ruler. On assuming the English throne as James I (r.1603–25), his progress south to London was a much-ridiculed cavalcade of 'coarse and beggarly Scotsmen'. He exercised his prerogative as he went, hanging some victims without trial and conferring knighthoods on all who asked, even reputedly (and improbably) on a side of beef as 'sir loin'.

In London, Elizabeth's tired Puritan regime was galvanised by the newcomer from Scotland's Renaissance court. London society came to life. Entertainment was raucous and bisexual. Shakespeare's previously modest South Bank troupe became

The King's Men. James built an exquisite Italian palace at Greenwich, the Queen's House, designed by Inigo Jones, for his Danish wife, Anne. London's view of Scotland as a place of dour Calvinists was transformed.

James was the nearest an English monarch had come – or perhaps ever would come – to an intellectual and a diplomat. His determination to end Elizabeth's long and costly war with Spain bore early fruit in the Treaty of London of 1604. He tried to steer a middle way between continuing Catholic tendencies in the Church of England and the more extreme Puritans. His chief handicap was to enjoy arguing with everyone, not least with parliamentarians in Edinburgh and London. This was complicated by his belief in the royal prerogative as a divine right, on which he wrote a book. He was also fascinated by witchcraft, an interest to be honoured by his house dramatist William Shakespeare in *Macbeth*.

James was the king separately of Scotland but ex officio of Ireland and Wales. He personified the 'union of crowns', and in 1606 invented the union flag composed of the crosses of St George and St Andrew. There was much argument over which should be on top of the other, with St George winning. James wished also to see constitutional union with Scotland, in what might be called the Welsh solution. Citing the Almighty, he told the London Parliament, 'Hath He not made us all in one island, compassed with one sea and of itself by nature indivisible?'

The Scottish assembly was ready to agree with James, but the English one was not. A union of crowns was one thing, of parliaments and governments another. London MPs still regarded Scotland much as had the Romans, a land of northern barbarians and unfit to send members to Westminster. One MP said of the Scots, they had 'not suffered above two kings to die in their beds in two hundred years', though a similar accusation had not excluded the Welsh. James was rebuffed and had to remain king of two separate nations. His fixation on the union was at least commemorated in calling the national flag the Union Jack after his nickname.

A similar and more delicate distance was established in matters ecclesiastical. The Scottish Presbyterians shared none of James's enthusiasm for bishops, regarded as England's quasi-Catholic episcopal hierarchy. Conflict was to continue throughout James's reign. Presbyterianism had taken deep root in Scotland and any confrontation would merely lead to conflict. As long as both countries at least were Protestant, James diplomatically let the matter rest.

In the event, the king did not return to Scotland for fourteen years, ruling by letter from London. As king of Scotland he governed, he said, 'with my pen . . . which others could not do by the sword'. When he did return it was to grapple with the severest blot on the country's politics, and one that had defeated his predecessors. This was the continuing clan anarchy in the Highlands and Islands. Massacres and vendettas continued. At the Eigg massacre in 1577 the Macleods suffocated 350 MacDonalds by trapping them in a cave and lighting a fire at its mouth. In 1603 the MacGregors killed over 140 Colquhouns in cold blood at the Battle of Glen Fruin.

James employed familiar methods, including imprisonment, summary execution and land expropriation. He even banned the notorious MacGregors from using their own name. Determined to lift the Highlands into the modern age, he demanded that the clan chiefs' male heirs be educated in Edinburgh. Under the Statutes of Iona, bards, beggars and fugitives were banned – as was the sale of wine and whisky 'other than to chiefs and gentlemen'. This was true Highland emasculation.

Central to James's policy was the grant of ever more power to the Stuarts' ancestral allies, the Campbells of Argyll. Like the Stuarts, the Campbells were not long-standing Highlanders. According to Alistair Moffat, they took their name from the Gaelic for 'crooked mouth', meaning foreign sounding.

Their origins were probably in Brythonic-speaking Strathclyde. Either way, in 1607 the Campbells were granted the peninsula of Kintyre from the MacDonalds and the island of Islay from the Macleans, assuring them the lasting enmity of both. Unlike the great castles built by the English against the Welsh, the castles of Scotland were built by Scotsmen against each other. Inter-clan violence did not cease but its scale drastically diminished.

Where James had debated and negotiated with Presbyterians, his son Charles I (r.1625–49) would have none of them. As king of Scotland and notionally of its church, he was determined to bring the Kirk into line with the English church, notably on bishops, governance and liturgy. When he visited Scotland to be crowned its king in 1633, he came accompanied by his conservative Archbishop Laud, complete with candles, crucifixes and genuflection. He ignored the Presbyterian assembly and enforced Laud's new prayer book on churches throughout Scotland.

This was religious provocation of a high order. When the new prayer book was read in Edinburgh's St Giles's cathedral on the first Sunday of the new regime, there was a riot, sparked in part by a female activist, Jenny Geddes, throwing a stool at the minister. The Bishop of Brechin conducted Sunday services with a pair of loaded pistols ready on his pulpit. The prayer book proved unusable and the bulk of the Scottish aristocracy and establishment said so, forming a committee of opposition known as the Tables. By 1638 Scotland was in a ferment not seen since the days of Mary Queen of Scots.

Charles in London was wholly unmoved, demanding all dissent be punished. The Scottish response was a new National Covenant drawn up by the Tables and approved by the Scottish parliament. It honoured Scotland's loyalty to the king in matters secular but not religious. Here loyalty should be to Christ and the Bible. Protestantism was the faith of Scotland and the Covenant was described as 'the great marriage day of this nation with God'. It was carried to towns across the Lowlands and signed by thousands, the first great petition in British history. Only Royalist pockets round Aberdeen declined to sign.

This Covenant was to be of deep and lasting significance to Scottish identity. As the Irish were steeling themselves to a divorce from London on Catholicism, so were the Scots on Protestantism. Both saw widespread popular uprisings against an English central authority utterly resistant to compromise. To the Scots, the Henrician Reformation had toppled the pope but merely replaced him with the king. The Scots wanted no pope, Roman or English. The Covenant was a cry 'against our poor country being made an English province'. Scottish clergymen who failed to read the Covenant from their pulpits were howled down and driven from them by their congregations.

Scotland had its own parliament and government, led by provosts, church leaders, academics and clan chiefs. The last included the Calvinist Campbells, Earls of Argyll, and James Graham, Marquess of Montrose. Its church was governed by the General Assembly of the Presbyterian Church in Glasgow, which declared all bishops dismissed and Laud's prayer book 'heathenish, Popish, Jewish and Arminian'. Scotland might offer formal homage to England but in matters of religion it could hardly have expressed its independence more vigorously, not least to its own king. The Scottish Covenant was a first daring taste at least of an institutional British democracy.

The Bishops' Wars

History books describe the British Isles in the 1630s as lurching towards civil war. Most of Europe was in the death throes of the Thirty Years War (1618–48), a dispute rooted in Catholic opposition to the Lutheran Reformation. Though it had religious overtones, England's conflict between Charles and Parliament was essentially political. It was an argument over the nature of popular consent to monarchical rule, a tension that had run intermittently through English politics since Magna Carta (1215). Now an implacable king and an implacable Parliament rendered it insoluble short of war.

That was one civil war. In reality there was a second, known at least in Scotland and Ireland as the War of the Three Kingdoms. It tested to destruction the one-sided treaties and concordats that had bonded England, Scotland and Ireland over the centuries since Edward I. At issue were to be Ireland's repressive Poynings' Law and the plantation and Scotland's rebellious Covenant. As England divided and took to arms, Scotland and Ireland found their loyalties conflicted and their freedoms jeopardised.

Charles's immediate reaction to Scotland's Covenant was reckless. There would be no compromise. With no money voted by his mildly pro-Scottish Parliament, the king in 1639 assembled a ramshackle army and marched north to Berwick. There he confronted a Scottish force led by Alexander Leslie, commander of hardened troops recently serving with the Swedish army in the Thirty Years War. After negotiations in which the Scots refused to concede, the two sides reached stalemate.

The following year Charles tried again, and again failed to raise funds from a Westminster Parliament now strongly sympathetic to the Scots. He demanded that his deputy in Ireland, the Earl of Strafford, send him troops, despite fierce Irish opposition from Ulster Protestants supporting the Presbyterian Covenant. No battle of any consequence ensued, largely because the king's soldiers were not considered fit to fight. By the end of 1640 the so-called Bishops' Wars has dissipated and the Scots were left in control of the north of England, including Newcastle and Durham. Strafford was summoned to London by Parliament, impeached and executed in 1641. Scotland had won and was relatively at peace.

Ireland and plantation

In 1640 Charles in England had ended eleven years of 'the tyranny' by summoning what became the Long Parliament. It was composed largely of a new middle class of gentry, strongly Protestant and opposed to the king's assertion of divine supremacy. This appalled Catholic Ireland. For almost a decade it had been ruled by Strafford and Dublin's oligarchs. Strafford was now gone and the arrival of a Protestant London Parliament was the starting signal for another Irish rebellion, one that was to last from 1641 to 1653.

The O'Neills of Tyrone under Owen Roe O'Neill returned from the flight of the earls with bands of seasoned veterans of the Thirty Years War. O'Neill's opponents were now legion. They embraced the London Parliament, the Protestant 'ascendancy' in Dublin, the plantation communities of the north and a new threat, of Scottish 'Covenanter' soldiers being sent to Ulster by Edinburgh to enforce London's anti-Catholicism. Ireland's sole ambition was to be left alone with its lands intact and its faith Catholic.

The rebels seized much of Ulster, massacring Protestant settlers and driving thousands back to Scotland or to the security of Dublin's Protestant Pale. An atrocity in Portadown saw Catholics drive a hundred settlers off a bridge into the River Bann, to be shot as they struggled in the water. An alleged quarter of Ireland's Protestant population was killed and parts of Ulster were described as 'looking like hell if hell could exist on earth'. Within weeks in 1641 O'Neill, was in control of much of Ireland, though not Dublin. He professed loyalty to King Charles – assuming the king's sympathy for Catholicism – but opposition to the Westminster Parliament.

In 1642 the Scots agreed with London to send an army to Ulster, which set sail and held the north-east in alliance with Ulster Protestant militias. It proceeded no further. In May that year an Irish Catholic Confederacy was formed in Kilkenny that was soon well enough established for Spain, France and the papacy to support it with ambassadors and military aid. The confederacy claimed to rule most of Ireland, if not all. It was the nearest the island was to come to 'home rule' until the twentieth century.

The 1640s thus saw the Bishops' Wars enable the Scots to repossess the religious and political sovereignty for which they had long fought and which they felt they had achieved in the 1328 and 1560 Treaties of Edinburgh. To that extent, they had no further quarrel with England. Meanwhile across the Irish Sea the Irish confederacy, at least in 1642, had achieved Catholic supremacy over much of the island and even seen itself widely recognised internationally. Both nations had won a sort of independence from England. Yet at the very moment when they might have achieved a settlement with an England that was itself about to fight over its constitutional status, the Scots and Irish plunged into internecine religious conflict.

Scotland plays its hand

In 1642 Charles raised the standard of revolt against Parliament and fought the first battle of his Civil War at Edgehill in Warwickshire. The outcome was indecisive and left Parliament in a quandary. It pleaded for aid from the Scots, whose Bishops' Wars army under Leslie was still intact and experienced. The Scots knew they were in a powerful position. They would aid their Puritan brothers in England, but only so long as it was to fight against bishops and the 'popish' worship of the English king. Scottish negotiators in 1643 duly drew up a Solemn League and Covenant with the English Parliament, agreeing that Leslie's army would march south against Charles in return for a reform of the Anglican church on Presbyterian lines. In addition, £31,000 would be paid to Scotland for each month its army was in service. A desperate London Parliament agreed.

In the summer of 1644, 2,000 Scottish soldiers joined Oliver Cromwell's Roundhead force and other regiments outside York. At the Battle of Marston Moor they overwhelmed Charles's Royalists, killing over 4,000. 'God made them as stubble to our swords,' said Cromwell. This early intervention by Scotland was decisive. Defeat would have left the Royalists with the initiative, whereas Cromwell's troops now emerged as the strongest weapon in the Parliamentary armoury.

At home, Scotland was divided. It had begun the war on Parliament's side but a number of Highland clans remained loyal to the Stuart monarch, in particular the MacDonalds. In his cause the latter threw a group of Campbell women over a cliff to their deaths. Then in 1644 James Graham, Marquess of Montrose, switched sides to support the king and seized and sacked Aberdeen. He crossed Scotland to Campbell country and burned the Argyll castle of Inveraray to the ground, with enthusiastic assistance from MacDonalds and Macleans. Montrose's campaign ended in the taking of Glasgow in the spring of 1645, when for a brief period he and the Royalists had most of Scotland at their feet.

To Charles in England this was scant consolation. His last personal stand was at the Battle of Naseby in 1645, after which he fled for refuge to what he thought was a sympathetic Scottish camp at Newark. The Scottish commanders debated his fate, his case being undermined by letters discovered from his wife Henrietta Maria in Paris, begging for military aid from Catholic France. The queen pledged that Charles would ensure in return that England would go 'back to Rome'. The king's plea for Scottish refuge was now denied and the Scots handed him over to Parliament for the enormous sum of £400,000.

The Scottish army returned home to overwhelm Montrose, who fled not to France but to Norway. Three years later, when Charles was scheming his restoration in prison on the Isle of Wight, some Scots did gather in his support. This time it was, bizarrely, in return for Charles agreeing to 'give Presbyterianism a trial' in England. But a Royalist Scottish force under the Duke of Hamilton was swiftly put down by Cromwell, who visited Edinburgh and received a hero's welcome staged for him by Argyll and other Covenanters. The Scots were not always of one mind. In 1649 Parliament despaired of Charles's encouragement of Scottish insurrection. He was duly brought to London and execution, a republic being declared with Parliament as 'the supreme power in this nation'. The word 'nation' was undefined.

Wales's sad Royalists

While the Irish were mostly for Charles, and the Scots were sometimes for him, the Welsh were overwhelmingly so. They had been happy with Laud's prayer book – Laud was formerly Bishop of St David's – and only one of the twenty-seven Welsh MPs in the Long Parliament was strictly a Puritan. Welsh pockets of support for Parliament were confined to the 'English' settlement of Pembroke and the borders round Wrexham. In 1642 the Royalist Earl of Worcester in Raglan even offered refuge to Charles after Naseby and to the young Prince of Wales, the future Charles II. The Venetian ambassador reported that the Welsh were 'beseeching the king to go and live in that corner of the kingdom'.

The principality at one point contributed 10,000 men to Charles's army, and the castle at Harlech was the last Royalist stronghold to hold out in Wales, not surrendering until 1647. A year later a disgruntled Parliamentary force in south Wales rebelled and staged a Royalist uprising of 8,000 troops in Pembroke. It was quickly defeated at the Battle of St Fagans outside Cardiff, reputedly the largest battle ever fought on Welsh soil. Wales was pacified by Cromwell himself in a march to Pembroke.

Royalist Wales now had its officers stripped of their estates. They were transferred to four Parliamentary colonels, all with the name of Jones. Its castles were slighted, with Caerphilly and Raglan showing the scars to this day. Though Wales was firmly Protestant, a commissioner for the propagation of the gospel was sent to introduce strict Puritan worship and 270 conservative Anglican clergy were dismissed from their posts. At the same time seventy English-speaking grammar schools were set up, including some for girls. Cromwell said of Wales that 'God hath kindled a seed there hardly to parallel since ancient times'.

The devastation of Ireland

Ireland's independent Catholic Confederacy remained firmly Royalist and was treated by Parliament with none of the leniency Cromwell had shown towards Wales. It had since 1641 been in formal rebellion against England, though English Parliamentarian forces had re-established control of the Dublin Pale. Ulster Protestants were also in control of most of Ulster. With the death of Charles I, the confederacy was in formal alliance with Charles II, based in France and ready to stage an invasion of England. It was a threat London could not ignore.

In the summer of 1649 Cromwell arrived in Dublin with his general Henry Ireton, a hundred ships and a battle-hardened army. He systematically crushed the increasingly divided confederacy. The town of Drogheda, on refusing to surrender, suffered atrocities and executions. Rebel leaders were exiled as an alternative to execution and their land was confiscated and given to English soldiers. It was the Thirty Years War on Irish soil. The proportion of land now held by Protestants rose from 41 per cent to 78 per cent. Gaelic schools were closed and some 12,000 rebel Irish soldiers were shipped to the West Indies as indentured labourers, in effect slaves. Of some 1.5 million Irish it is estimated a third died during the confederacy, killed, starved or diseased. Cromwell declared Ireland a republic. Its eight years of home rule had come to a bloody end.

Scotland changes its mind, again

Scotland for its part had been regarded as an ally of Parliament, but the Scots deplored Charles's execution and yet again changed sides, welcoming his son, the uncrowned Charles II, back from exile in France. In 1651 Argyll, though a Presbyterian, crowned him king of Scotland in Edinburgh and supplied him with an army to march south in the cause of restoring a Stuart to the throne. Scotland was now at war in support of the same dynasty it had crushed at Marston Moor. It was an extraordinary about-turn.

Cromwell defeated the Scots that July at the Battle of Inverkeithing, where 800 Maclean clansmen died. Undaunted, Charles amassed a new force and marched south to resume the conflict at the Battle of Worcester, where he was again defeated. This time he hid in an oak tree – the 'royal oak' – and fled to France in disguise. Cromwell's commander in Scotland, General George Monck, put Dundee to the sword and threatened to do likewise to all other towns on pain of massive fines. The Scottish monarchy and parliament were disbanded and the coat of arms symbolically hanged on a gallows. A decade of political duplicity had led the Scots nowhere but to renewed subordination to England.

A commonwealth of the British Isles was declared in London in 1649. Cromwell had successively defeated the Welsh, the Irish and the Scots. He had devastated Dublin and ordered all Catholics to leave. The War of the Three Kingdoms might have begun with Ireland and Scotland enjoying a considerable degree of self-rule. They had now forfeited and lost it utterly.

Cromwell introduced what Edward I, Henry VIII and James I had attempted but not achieved, the total political union of the British Isles. He abolished diocesan bishops and the House of Lords and ordained that the Westminster Commons be elected from England, Wales and Scotland, though not Ireland. Censorship was imposed, theatres and most taverns closed, church ritual banned. It was, as Alexander Pope would later say, a reduction to one dead level all mankind. The centralisation was fierce and certain to evoke resentment and opposition. Cromwell's republican dictatorship lasted five years until his death in 1658.

The constitutional future of the British Isles could at this point have taken a number of paths. Europe's 1648 Peace of Westphalia had dealt at length with the relationship of large states and empires to their subordinate nations. Its participants had deliberated on the status of kings and princes and on the role of religious tolerance. The concept of small-state independence was in the air. In the 1640s Ireland and Scotland had produced strong local leadership, in Ireland from the O'Neills and the Catholic Confederacy and in Scotland from the Campbells and the Church Assembly. Both nations could reasonably have seen a federal commonwealth as freedom's opportunity.

Yet at no point did they propose it or did they liaise with each other on alternatives. Indeed, the War of the Three Kingdoms saw each kingdom at odds internally as well as with each other. Irish confederates had fought Scots Covenanters in Ireland. In Scotland, Highlanders had fought Lowlanders. The Edinburgh mob cheered Montrose, Cromwell and Charles II in succession. Only in Wales did the bulk of the population sit tight and await events. Whatever opportunity republicanism might have offered to unity between the nations passed. It was an exhausted England that eventually found a sort of cohesion.

In 1660 General Monck marched his army south. He took soundings and summoned the members of the twenty-year-old, pre-Cromwellian Long Parliament for consultation. Debate was intense but with Monck always in command. With public opinion clearly in favour of restoration, he invited Charles II (r.1660–80) back from the continent to his vacant throne. Charles arrived in London at Blackheath to a guard of honour of Cromwell's Ironside troops. He entered the city to general rejoicing.

There must have been a sense of déjà vu in London as a Stuart monarchy was restored, a Protestant High Church re-established, complete with bishops, and a Westminster Parliament of English and Welsh MPs reassembled. In line with the Declaration of Breda, issued by Charles while exiled in the Netherlands, widespread pardons were granted and tolerance ordained for 'differences of opinion in matter of religion which do not disturb the peace of the kingdom'. None the less, Catholics and extreme Puritans who refused to take Anglican communion were excluded from public offices by a series of Test Acts. These applied in Ireland and Wales, forming a base on which a formidable Nonconformity was added to an entrenched Catholicism. In Scotland adherence to a strict Calvinism was ordained. It was as if England was determined to sow disagreement and dissention, not union.

13

Picking Up Pieces and Papering Over Cracks

An ever-unstable union

Charles II might be proclaimed king of Scotland, and Scottish law and the Kirk were in place, but all was not calm north of the border. The new king was a sincere searcher after peace, but his peace was diplomatic rather than constitutional. A Scottish royal commissioner and privy council were installed in Edinburgh, answerable to London. Then in 1661 came an inflammatory requirement that all Scottish clergy renounce the 1638 National Covenant. Just as Catholics and Protestants remained at each other's throats in Ireland, so did episcopal Protestants feud with Presbyterians in Scotland. This was not peace. Bands of armed Covenanters roamed the countryside, falling on any clergy they considered unsound.

Charles II never revisited Scotland after the Restoration, declaring that 'Presbytery is no religion for gentlemen'. He appointed a raft of Scottish bishops, leading to Presbyterian uprisings in 1666 and 1679. He even appointed his openly Catholic brother and heir James as lord high commissioner in Edinburgh. James's arrival led to a revolt from the new Earl of Argyll in 1685, co-ordinated with an anti-Catholic revolt in south-west England by Charles II's illegitimate eldest son, the Duke of Monmouth. Both were quickly suppressed, Monmouth's ending in the last pitched battle on English soil at Sedgemoor in Somerset.

In Ireland, Royalists had in 1660 tried to steal a march on

England by inviting Charles II come via them on his way to England. Charles wisely declined. But he summoned a new Dublin parliament, mostly composed of supporters of the Anglican Church of Ireland, estimated to represent less than 20 per cent of the Irish population. Pledges of toleration given at Breda were then overridden by a 1662 Irish proclamation outlawing 'all meetings by papists, Presbyterians, Independents and separatists'. Though this was largely ignored, as in Scotland the Dublin parliament remained subordinate to a London royal appointee, a lieutenant in council. Nothing in the Restoration was as emphatically 'restored' as Ireland's Anglican Protestant ascendancy.

Cromwell's Irish expulsions and land expropriations were not reversed. By the end of the seventeenth century, these resulted in Catholic landownership plummeting from 90 per cent before the plantations of the 1600s to just 20 per cent in 1685. The chief beneficiary of this upheaval was Dublin, whose population of expropriated refugees helped make it, at 60,000, the second largest city of the British Isles.

England's government of its domestic empire under the Stuarts became ever more centralised. Edicts poured from Whitehall to the privy councils in Dublin and Edinburgh. When James took the throne as James II (r.1685–8) there was a hiatus. He was a confessed Roman Catholic and his Declaration of Indulgence freed worship for Catholics and certain Nonconformists. This could have been of great importance to Ireland. But in 1688 the birth to James of a (presumed Catholic) son and heir supplanted the succession of James's Protestant daughter Mary. A sustained Catholic monarchy was now likely, reopening every Protestant wound. James was duly toppled that year in the 'Glorious Revolution' of Whig peers in collusion with Mary's husband, the Dutch William of Orange.

A very Irish revolution

The invasion of England by the Dutch in 1688 imported many of the conflicts still blighting Europe after the Thirty Years War. William's marriage to Mary had been intended by him to forestall any alliance between a possibly Catholic England and William's enemy France. The 1688 invasion and coup restored that security but did nothing to resolve relations between England, Scotland and Ireland, bedevilled as they were by the ongoing religious divide that continued to vex Europe.

Ireland still had a mostly Protestant parliament ruling a population that was four-fifths Catholic. Scotland had a Protestant population but with extensive loyalty to the (Catholic) Stuart exiles now gathering in Paris. William thus had good reason to fear encirclement by forces with whom Louis XIV of France might make common cause. In this sense the Dutch leader had merely moved the Netherlands border west into the Irish Sea.

Ireland's lord deputy at the time was the Catholic Earl of Tyrconnell, appointed by James II. Under James, he had admitted Catholics to the Dublin parliament and army, and he now refused to acknowledge William's seizure of the English throne. In March 1689 James sailed for Ireland in French ships and with French troops. The Irish under Tyrconnell rallied to his flag, rekindling the fires of the 1641 civil war. Ireland was again in revolt against the English crown. To William this was precisely his most immediate danger.

On landing in Ireland, James's army marched north to besiege the Protestants in Londonderry, whither thousands of plantation settlers had fled from the surrounding countryside. Here they were kept at bay by a militia known as the Apprentice Boys, to be forever celebrated as heroes of Ulster history. In Dublin, the parliament was in two minds. James was acknowledged as king, but by a parliament eager to rid itself of Poynings' Law and re-establish its confederate independence.

James was intent on invading England, but did not want to lose his previous authority in Ireland in the process.

William responded by himself setting sail for Ireland in June 1690 with a force of 36,000 troops. He and James met at the Battle of the Boyne north of Dublin in a contest typical of seventeenth-century Europe. The two armies were largely composed of mercenaries and the outcome was thus determined in large part by the financial resources of either side. William led a coalition of English, Dutch, Danes and French Huguenots. James led Irish, French, Belgians and Germans. William won the day, and James fled back to France, never to return.

As William returned to London, an Irish civil war resumed between James's Catholic supporters, so-called Jacobites, and William's remaining troops and Irish Protestant irregulars concentrated in the north. Civilians both north and south paid a terrible price until, in 1691, with the Jacobite cause defeated, the Treaty of Limerick sought some kind of reconciliation. It supposedly returned formerly Catholic lands to their owners in return for oaths of obedience. As in the earlier flight of the earls, more than 20,000 Irish soldiers were allowed to leave and take refuge in France. Dubbed the 'Wild Geese', they were to appear as mercenaries in Catholic armies across Europe.

London again found it impossible to honour agreements it reached with the Irish – or the Scots. Limerick's promise of Catholic tolerance and land restitution was a dead letter almost as soon as it was signed. Catholics were still forbidden to build churches and forced to worship in the open air, at what were called 'hedge masses'. Above all, they were banned from buying land. Catholic landholding now fell to just 5 per cent of Ireland. Access to public office of any sort required an oath denying the Catholic doctrine of transubstantiation. Poynings' Law remained in place. The Protestants were in the ascendant. Dublin proceeded to emerge as one of Europe's most elegant eighteenth-century cities.

Scotland: empire into union

No sooner had the Limerick treaty been signed than Scotland too saw how tentative was any hope that Restoration might improve relations with London. In 1689, a year after the coronation in London of William and Mary (*r*.1689–1702), a spontaneous Jacobite uprising took place in favour of James II by professedly Catholic Highlanders. It was suppressed by Presbyterian troops from Edinburgh. In the course of this suppression in 1692, a group of Campbells slaughtered a settlement of their ancestral foes, the MacDonalds, in their huts in Glencoe. The Massacre of Glencoe, though of just thirty or so people, came to symbolise the barbarism of the Highlands and the longevity of the clan fissures. It was later commemorated as such by Sir Walter Scott: 'Each chord should imprecations fling /Till startled Scotland loud should ring/ Revenge for blood and treachery!'

The crude reality was that to eighteenth-century English strategists, Scottish and Irish borders were 'England's back door', and one that seemed always ajar. Across Europe the Counter-Reformation was recovering from the Thirty Years War and pushing forward the boundaries of a Catholic revival. Protestantism still regarded itself as insecure. In Ireland and Scotland Catholics had a monarch in waiting in Paris and knew they could count on support from France and Spain, theoretically drawing on armies much larger than England's. At the height of the 1640s rebellion, Tyrconnell had even pondered offering Ireland as a subject state of France, as Scotland had notionally and briefly been under Mary Queen of Scots.

The English Parliament reacted with a policy of belt and braces. By the Act of Settlement of 1701, it vested in itself the right to determine the succession to the throne. It also declared that the monarch could never be a Catholic. This meant searching the Stuart line back over what proved to be fifty-seven Catholics in line of hereditary succession to find a Protestant to succeed William and then Anne (r.1702–14). The candidate turned out to be a distant relative of Henry VII, the German Electress Sophia of Hanover, followed by her son George.

In addition, the English Parliament reversed its previous opposition to union with Scotland under James I and now voted for it. This time it was the Scottish parliament that was less sure. Insofar as can be judged, Scottish opinion was overwhelmingly hostile to union. The assembled burghs were opposed and there were riots in Edinburgh and Glasgow. The Highlands were strongly against.

There followed a duel of two parliaments, with Scotland reeling from seven years of severe famine and starvation in the 1690s and England threatening the Scots with alien status and trade barriers in the absence of union. English negotiators offered Edinburgh retention of its judicial system and of its Presbyterian version of Protestantism and its Kirk. The key to a deal lay in trade. In 1699 Scotland was shocked by the failure of a Scottish trading colony at Darien in Central America. This was attributed to trade rivalry and even sabotage by English ships accused of denying the colonists aid. Hundreds died and thousands of Scots lost their savings.

Under the union agreement England would pay compensation to the Darien investors – though not the families of the dead – and the Scottish exchequer would receive the sum of £400,000. In addition, existing customs dues between the two countries would be abolished and free trade established. Scotland was still reluctant but a flurry of last-minute bribes to Scottish parliamentarians resulted in them narrowly agreeing to dissolve themselves. They would join Wales in sending MPs to London. The Edinburgh parliament would be disbanded.

The Act of Union was signed in 1707 by a delighted new monarch, Queen Anne, who hoped that 'two nations might become in time one people'. Forty-five Scottish MPs set off for Westminster and Scotland was declared one nation with

England and Wales, to be named Great Britain. Article I of the act stipulated bluntly that the union under a single Parliament should last 'for ever after'. The Lord Privy Seal remarked, 'There's an end of an auld sang.'

Not many Scots sang it with pleasure, aware that the dismantling of Scottish home rule had relied on 'the Darien bribe'. To Scots of most political and religious persuasions it was the nadir of a humiliation dating back to Edward I, the more shocking as Scotland's parliament had corruptly assented to it. One vocal critic, Andrew Fletcher of Saltoun, objected to Scotland becoming 'subservient to the designs of the court of England . . . We have appeared to the rest of the world more like a conquered province than a free independent people.' The poet Robbie Burns (1759–96) later uttered a retrospective lament: 'The English steel we could disdain/ Secure in valour's station;/ But English gold has been our bane –/ Such a parcel of rogues in a nation.' Burns's setting of the song 'Auld Lang's Syne' is said to echo a similar nostalgia, with 'auld acquaintance been forgot, and never brought to mind'.

Angry in a different way were the Irish. The title of Great Britain clearly excluded them, leaving them to all appearances as an offshore colony. Jonathan Swift wrote to his friend Esther Johnson ('Stella'), 'I never will call it *Britain*. Pray don't call it *Britain* . . . pox on the modern phrase, *Great Britain*.' The Irish came to treat the phrase as toxic, and many refuse to use it to this day. They have had their way. Great Britain does not include Ireland – or most certainly did not after the eighteenth century – not even the present Northern Ireland.

The Stuarts' last gasp: the '15 and the '45

Within eight years, continuing Scottish opposition to the Act of Union went critical. Support for James II's Paris-based son James Stuart (1688–1766) was widespread in Scotland, as well as in some Tory circles in London. Had he renounced his Catholicism on Anne's death in 1714, he would almost certainly have gained the throne. He did not do so, and threw in his lot with Scottish anti-unionists.

The Whig government in London was already treating Scottish MPs at Westminster with contempt. They were told that, like Wales, they represented 'now but a county of England'. Daniel Defoe, London's agent in Edinburgh, reported back, 'I never saw a nation so universally wild . . . it seems in a perfect gangrene of the temper.' When he visited the Highlands he was advised to pretend to be a Frenchman. Such a climate fed Jacobite dreams of a glorious Stuart return, if not to the throne of England at least to that of Scotland.

With George I's accession, James Stuart decided in 1715 to sail for Scotland, to raise the clans and invade England, being assured of an uprising in his favour. This expectation was short-lived. The clans split for and against him. The Frasers, Gordons, Sutherlands and Mackays stayed with the Hanoverians, with the Campbells under the Duke of Argyll as their leader. James was supported by the Highland MacGregors, Macleans, MacDonalds and Camerons. The Jacobite cause prospered briefly under the Earl of Mar, but the rebels delayed in Perth and were attacked with customary savagery by the Campbells. As government troops from London began to arrive, desultory skirmishes took place until eventually the rebels abandoned Perth and went home. Spasmodic uprisings occurred in Northumberland and the West Country, but James fled back to France.

London's reaction was fierce and familiar. Its army rounded up hundreds of Jacobites and condemned them to indentured labour in the West Indies. Orders formally to dissolve the clans now came from London. The carrying of arms was banned in Scotland, as was the Gaelic tongue in schools. Roads were built by a new Scottish military commander, General George

Wade, to aid the movement of a new Highland regiment – half composed of Campbells – for 'disarming the Highlanders, hindering rebels and attainting persons for inhabiting that part of the kingdom'. It was later to be called the Black Watch.

This was not sufficient. Thirty years later, in 1745, the curtain rose on the final act of the Stuart tragedy. James Stuart's glamorous son Charles, 'Bonnie Prince Charlie', undeterred by his father's misfortunes and again buoyed by French support, landed in the Hebrides to again raise the flag of revolt. As before, MacDonalds, Macleans and Camerons came out in support. Unlike his father, Charles acted with speed, marching south and entering Edinburgh to an ecstatic crowd, which duly acclaimed him king. Had he halted at that point and rested content with the Scottish crown, Scottish history might have been different. He did not.

The prince sped south, with allies dwindling as he went. He was so confident of Welsh aid that he sent the prominent Royalist Sir Watkin Williams-Wynn a letter pleading, 'I am persuaded that you will not break my expectations'. Sir Watkin thought twice and broke them. It was said of Welsh Royalists that they were 'always ready to raise a glass rather than a sword'.

Charles reached Derby before a panic-stricken London realised that he presented a real danger. George II (r.1727–60) even contemplated flight to his family home in Germany. The English army was made of sterner stuff, and the 5,000 Jacobites soon faced a force of 30,000 men. Charles's officers told him that to reach London would be impossible and, though he pleaded to stand and fight, in December 1745 he returned north.

Here the Jacobites wintered in Inverness, but there was no security. The Duke of Cumberland, his troops armed with modern muskets and artillery, hunted down an army that had little more than claymores. In April 1746, on the field of

Culloden outside Inverness, Cumberland massacred the High-landers, leaving Charles to flee, in the words of the song, 'over the sea to Skye'. He left for that eternal Scottish refuge, France and oblivion.

Cumberland exacted a savage revenge, despite pleas from Scottish moderates for mercy and reconciliation. Under instructions from London to smash the clan system, Cumberland executed, deported or evicted dissident clan chiefs and expropriated their land. Dr Johnson, though no fan of Scotland, commented that 'to govern peaceably by having no subjects is an expedient that argues no great profundity'. Highland culture was to be eradicated, Gaelic, tartans and bagpipes were forbidden. The pipes were declared 'weapons of war'.

14

Towards a New Union

An old empire and a new one

When Queen Anne was crowned in April 1702 it was as 'Queen of England, Scotland, Ireland and France'. This embraced echoes of two English empires, one real, one defunct. A third now beckoned that was to dwarf them both. Two figures towered over the new government of eighteenth-century Britain, Sir Robert Walpole (1676–1745) and William Pitt (1708–78), later Lord Chatham. Neither showed any great interest in Scottish or Irish affairs. Their attitude was summed up in Walpole's motto, 'Let sleeping dogs lie'. But would they sleep?

Both statesmen were drawn into conflicts alive in the rest of Europe as its nations developed imperial ambitions around the globe. Just as Norman and Plantagenet England had fixed its sights on an empire across the Channel to the neglect of its empire at home, so Hanoverian England fixed its sights on an empire across the oceans. In the course of the Seven Years War (1756–63) Britain had held aloof from military action on the European mainland, but it had been ready to snatch advantage elsewhere in the world. By 1759 India, Canada and most of the West Indies had been invaded by British fleets and armies. As Horace Walpole wrote, 'Our bells are worn threadbare with ringing for victories.'

This new empire offered unprecedented openings to the growing populations of Ireland, Scotland and Wales. Most of their inhabitants had previously emigrated for reasons of politics or faith. They now did so to acquire fortunes and status inconceivable at home. The impact of this is hard to exaggerate. Two historians of the diaspora, Neil Davidson and Tom Devine, argue that the Irish and Scots were not so much flag-waving imperialists, rather loyal governors, soldiers, merchants and settlers. For them, the empire was a new meritocracy, breaking down walls of class and wealth that seemed impenetrable at home. Canada became New Scotland and Australia New South Wales, just as a New England was dotted with Hampshires and Suffolks.

A third of British colonial governors were estimated to be Scottish. Half of the British army in India were Irish Catholics. Legend holds that Indians speak with a Welsh accent through serving under Welsh military engineers. The effect back home was by no means altogether benign. For two centuries Ireland, Scotland and to an extent Wales were stripped of their talented young. Nor did the example of empire feed back to the politics of the home front. As the Irish MP John Redmond was to remark in 1893, 'While in the government of the empire, Irishmen have proved themselves equal to the best of Englishmen, Scotchmen or Welshmen . . . the one spot where the Irish could not fully practise their virtues and talents was in the land of their birth and affection.'

Enlightenment comes to Scotland

Scotland, unlike Ireland and Wales, was at least able to capitalise on the empire's pecuniary benefits. The industrial revolution sweeping the north of England swept also into the Scottish Lowlands. Between 1750 and 1800 Scottish commerce trebled while that of England only doubled. The city of Glasgow boomed, particularly its trade with the Americas. The plantations of the slave-driven Caribbean and the Deep South poured sugar, cotton and tobacco onto its quaysides. Half of Britain's 'tobacco barons' were Scottish. A third of Scotland's 2.5 million people were soon living in cities. While they did so in considerable squalor, the squalor was usually an improvement on conditions in the countryside. Scottish life expectancy rose throughout the eighteenth century.

Other forces were also at work. With a cultural and religious tradition distinct from that of England, Scotland's universities and church had been in the forefront of the north European Reformation. They were now in the vanguard of the so-called Enlightenment. Initial impetus came from Francis Hutcheson (1694–1746), born a Presbyterian in Ulster but writing and lecturing on philosophy and ethics in Dublin and Glasgow. To the economic innovations of Adam Smith (1723–90) were added the history and philosophy of David Hume (1711–76) and the mathematics of Adam Ferguson (1723–1816). Art saw the paintings of Allan Ramsay (1713–84) and Henry Raeburn (1756–1823) and the writings of Robbie Burns.

Leading figures of the similar French movement were ready to marvel at the maturity and prosperity of Georgian Britain, and of Scotland in particular. Voltaire revered Britain's political tolerance and Montesquieu the pluralism of its Parliament and legal institutions. To them, the British people had fashioned a constitution that no one called democratic but which enjoyed popular consent sufficient to hold revolution at bay. As for where the intellectual hub of this Britain lay, there seemed no doubt. Voltaire proclaimed in what became a Scottish motto, 'We look to Scotland for all our ideas of civilisation.'

Most lasting symbol of this Scotland was the city of Edinburgh itself. James II as lord high commissioner in Holyrood in the 1680s had first proposed a new town outside the walls of the ancient citadel, but it was not until the 1760s that a true suburb, so named, began to emerge. Terraces of townhouses serviced a new Scottish bourgeoisie, marrying classical grace to northern robustness and eventually outdoing Dublin and rivalling even London in stately decorum. By a miracle, their essence survives to this day. A New Town terrace house makes its London equivalent look like a cottage.

The Scottish Enlightenment was the product of a nation newly confident in its identity and apparently unhandicapped by union with England. The paradox did not pass unnoticed. Hume reflected, 'At a time when we have lost our princes, our Parliament, our independent government . . . and speak a very corrupt dialect of the tongue, is it not strange that in these circumstances we should really be the people most distinguished for literature in Europe?' This was a political paradox. Here was a Scotland clearly benefiting from the wider horizons, commercial and intellectual, offered by union with England, and with it a broader outlook on the world in general. As Hume implied, what need had it of self-government?

The Celtic revival

The Scottish Enlightenment was a phenomenon of European scope. Its impact closer to home on the identity and ideas of the Scots, Irish or Welsh, on their history and language, was less evident. But it undoubtedly coincided with a surge of interest in the past, and in the putative origins of the emerging nations of the British Isles. Isolated scholars such as Scotland's George Buchanan and Wales's Edward Lhuyd had joined with the Breton Paul-Yves Pezron in deciphering the similarities between the various Celtic tongues. These had long been treated as the incomprehensible mumblings of prehistoric tribes. It had been seen as the task of the new learning to help the poor escape linguistic imprisonment into the light of English.

As the eighteenth century progressed, what Lhuyd had classified as the Celtic languages began to attract interest in their own right. They took flight from history and myth into the realms of antiquarianism, literature and even music. In

Wales in the 1730s, three Morris brothers in Anglesey sought a self-conscious Welsh 'renaissance' through promoting 'Welsh scholarship and knowledge' and publishing almanacs of Welsh writing and song.

The most articulate concentration of Welsh speakers was in expatriate London. In 1715 the London Welsh formed the Honourable and Loyal Society of Antient Britons. The word loyal was to stress its deference to the Hanoverian crown – unlike certain rebellious Scots. True to Welsh form, it in 1751 split into the Honourable Society of Cymmrodorion and the more popular Gwyneddigion Society, committed to Welsh-speaking and Welsh-singing, particularly among Gwynedd expatriates.

This activity stimulated a burst of interest in Welsh education, notably the remarkable 'circulating schools' of Carmarthen's Griffith Jones. A shepherd turned Anglican clergyman, Jones in 1734 invented a mobile school that would settle for three months in a community, usually in winter or when farms were quiet, and invite children and their parents to learn reading and writing in Welsh. The teachers would then move on. Jones could be operating three dozen schools at a time.

The teaching method was full-time and intensive, immersing pupils, mostly through the Bible and psalter, in their written and spoken language. The method was successful. By the time of Jones's death it was estimated that almost 3,500 Welsh schools had been held and 250,000 children and adults taught to read and write. The result was that Wales was one of the few European countries at the time with a literate adult majority. The intensive teaching method appears to have been far more efficient than today's low-intensity schooling, aimed at keeping children occupied and teachers employed over years of formalised lessons. It lives on in high-speed commercial language courses.

The challenge faced by this burst of chiefly antiquarian

revivalism was whether it was specifically Welsh, Scottish and perhaps Irish, or was in any sense a new 'Celticism'. It also suffered from a hazy borderland between scholarship and the wilder shores of fantasy and invention. The Irish-speaking philosopher John Toland (1670–1722) envisaged a Celtic existence rooted in pre-Christian paganism. He founded an Ancient Druid Order that met on London's Primrose Hill in 1717, with no shred of archaeological evidence. A clergyman, William Stukeley (1687–1765), took up the call and appointed himself an archdruid, claiming Stonehenge as Druidism's temple on a theory advanced by the antiquarian John Aubrey. No amount of scepticism has allowed the theory to die.

London's Welsh were briefly captivated by a stonemason turned antiquarian, Edward Williams, who called himself Iolo Morganwg (1747–1826). Williams collected (or wrote) old Welsh writings and songs, linking them with a putative Welsh prehistory. He founded a group of literati called the Gorsedd, or throne, and held its first ceremony in 1792, also on Primrose Hill. The resulting fantasy of Druids, bards, legends and Welsh verse, much of it invented by Morganwg, found an eager market among London's Welsh exiles. An attempt to bring the Gorsedd to Wales was baulked by the authorities for its supposedly revolutionary potential.

Scotland was not left out of this movement for long. James Macpherson (1736–96) was a Scottish collector, politician and, as it turned out, fraudster. He claimed to have discovered and translated an epic saga by a third-century Scots-Irish bard named Ossian on the subject of his father, Fingal. Ossian duly became a publishing sensation across Europe and did more than anything to sow the seeds of a so-called Celtic revival, otherwise known as 'Celtomania'. The American founding father Thomas Jefferson declared Ossian 'the greatest poet that has ever existed'. Voltaire wrote a parody of his verse. Beethoven wrote music for twenty-five Scottish songs in Ossian's honour, and Mendelssohn composed his 'Fingal's Cave' overture. Macpherson's verses were soon exposed as fabrication. Their Gaelic was dire – indeed a back translation of Macpherson's own verse – and they were panned by Dr Johnson. This in no way diminished their appeal.

Even Napoleon Bonaparte was soon seeing himself as a ruler in a Celtic line of descent, convinced that 'the French were a nation of empire-building Celts'. He went on to found the Académie Celtique (now renamed Société des Antiquaires de France) in Paris in 1804, dedicated to a glorious French past. In Germany, too, a new national self-consciousness was eager to find branches in the Celtic tree. All Europe seemed delighted to have at last discovered a pre-classical history of its own.

This was particularly relevant to the nations of the British Isles. Celtomania offered the Welsh, Scots and Irish an identity, whether collective or specific to each, that could be set against that of England, so long their oppressor and custodian of their history. It was good news.

Part Three

The Seeds of Dissolution

15

A Kingdom Struggling to Unite

Enter America and France

The British Parliament's Declaratory Act of 1766 stated baldly that its colonies in America were, like all its possessions, 'subordinate unto and dependent upon the imperial crown and Parliament of Great Britain'. That Parliament's authority, rooted in military might, allowed it 'to make laws and statutes of sufficient force and validity to bind the colonies and people of America'. Despite that affirmation of supremacy, the Americas were considered the pride, even the jewel, of Britain's empire, the embodiment of good achievement.

This was particularly true of New England. Its mostly expatriate citizens enjoyed widespread favour among London politicians, who described them as 'being our own people, our brethren'. One of them, the Englishman Thomas Pownall (1722–1805), was governor of first New Jersey and then Massachusetts Bay before returning to become a British MP. He campaigned for American representation in the Westminster Parliament, advocating that the empire become 'a grand maritime domain' under one legislative authority. The British government did not agree. The American colonists gained no presence at Westminster and, while they enjoyed virtual self-government, this did not extend to foreign affairs, trade or taxation.

When, in 1773, London introduced complex new rules and duties for tea, the Massachusetts colony promptly rebelled. In this it had considerable support in Britain, the Irish Tory

Edmund Burke warning the government of George III (*r.*1760–1820) to 'leave the Americans as they anciently stood . . . to tax themselves. If you impose on them the unlimited and illimitable nature of supreme sovereignty, you will teach them by these means to call that sovereignty into question.' He asked in a query redolent of his native Ireland, 'If freedom and [British] sovereignty cannot be reconciled, which will they take?'

The government seemed at a loss how to react. In America, where orders from London took weeks to arrive, there was no Parliament or federal forum in which to debate policy or treat with the rebel leaders. A tax protest and a guerrilla uprising escalated into a war of independence. Over eight years, error followed disaster until the Americans, crucially assisted by the French, defeated a British army at Yorktown in 1781. George III was baffled and mortified. What was termed the 'first British empire' in North America was no sooner assembled than it began to disintegrate.

The blow to Britain's pride was severe, but when in 1785 George III greeted John Adams as the first American ambassador to London, he welcomed him as 'of the same language, a similar religion, and kindred blood' as England. A special relationship was formed, aided by a shared lexicon and culture. A similar if briefer welcome accompanied the French Revolution in 1789. Everywhere a new radicalism entered political discourse. The prime minister, William Pitt the Younger (1759–1806), declared that the revolution in France marked a 'new chapter of peace'.

Neither revolution was read by London as suggesting any need to change policy towards Scotland or Ireland. Instead, the authorities sought to suppress any sign of revolutionary fervour, in particular towards the new French regime. By 1793 Pitt's government was proclaiming that any revolutionary opinion, even the advocacy of 'political reform', was an offence against public safety.

The lesson strikes home

One place where events in France were watched with keen attention was on the streets of Ireland. London's disregard of the 1691 Treaty of Limerick were coming home to roost. There had been no promised advance in Catholic civil rights. There had been no extension of the franchise to Catholics or access to public jobs or land-holding. The Irish parliament, despite being packed with Protestants, remained shackled by Poynings' Law. Its every decision was subject to a London veto.

Absentee English landownership had by now extended to virtually the whole of Ireland's productive farmland. Catholic tenants were required to pay rents to English landlords and tithes to Anglican churches. The unfairness was ingrained and toxic. An additional source of Irish tension in England was the uncontrolled migration into England of landless Irish labourers. Squatter encampments sprang up wherever a canal needed to be built or a London estate extended. The infrastructure of Britain's industrial revolution and of London's bourgeoning middle class was largely constructed on Irish labour.

The result was rising anti-immigrant resentment. A modest parliamentary measure, the Papists Act of 1778 easing penal restrictions on Catholic employment in England and Ireland, was met, on its passing in 1780, with street demonstrations not seen in London since the Civil War. The so-called Gordon Riots attacked Catholic houses and churches with a violence exacerbated by the incompetence of London's hopelessly amateur constabulary. When armed soldiers were summoned as a last resort, they killed some 300 rioters.

The Gordon Riots galvanised politics in Ireland at the very moment in the 1780s when London was losing control of America. A Patriot Movement was formed in which were joined not just Catholics but Protestants and Dublin's Anglo-Irish community, all collectively exasperated at London's draconian authority over their country. A senior MP in Dublin's parliament, Henry Grattan (1746–1820), warned London to repeal Poynings' Law and install home rule, or face another rebellion on the scale of 1641.

In 1782 the warning struck home and Pitt's government conceded reform. A new act stated baldly that the 'right claimed by the people of Ireland to be bound only by laws enacted by His Majesty and the parliament of that kingdom [Ireland] . . . is hereby declared to be established and ascertained for ever, and shall, at no time hereafter, be questioned or questionable'. Poynings was repealed. The assertion of home rule seemed explicit and final. London had heard the message of America.

Although the Dublin executive was still appointed by London, the new 'Grattan's Parliament' proved to be Ireland's last chance of an orderly progress to self-government. In 1792–3, under Grattan's leadership, it enacted laws extending the role that Catholics could play in Ireland's political and economic life. In this it was supported by the viceroy, Lord Fitzwilliam. But London became increasingly hostile to this emancipation, aware of the strong opposition to it of the implacably anti-Catholic George III, who retained the royal prerogative to veto it and indicated he would use it. He was acting, so he said, 'as guardian of the Church of England'. The law could not pass.

This act of royal defiance by a monarch whose decisions had just lost America left Grattan with no option but to resign, warning London that Ireland was on the brink of rebellion. Irish legislative independence was clearly not 'for ever' and 'unquestionable', as Pitt had pledged, but strangled at birth in the name of religion.

The Irish rebellion of 1798

Ireland erupted. In 1796 a young Irish radical of Protestant parentage, Theobald Wolfe Tone (1763–98), rose to prominence as co-founder of a radical party known as the Society of United

Irishmen. The society was actually founded in Belfast by Protestants angered, like the Catholics, by London's baulking of home rule. Many Irish Protestants were Presbyterians and thus outside the 'ascendancy' of the Church of Ireland. They joined their Catholic countrymen in swearing 'never to desist in our efforts until we have subverted the authority of England over our country and asserted our independence'.

Tone travelled to America, where George Washington had declared in 1788, 'Patriots of Ireland, your cause is identical to mine.' But he suffered an unsympathetic reception from Americans who seemed content to leave Britain to its fate. In Paris, Tone's welcome was fulsome. The Bourbons might be gone, but Paris still offered comfort to anyone with a grievance against London, be they Welsh princes, Stuart pretenders or Catholic revolutionaries. The Paris Directorate was happy to offer Tone practical support, initially with enthusiasm.

In December 1796 a French force of forty-three ships and nearly 14,000 men was sent to the west coast of Ireland, where they were assured of an imminent Irish uprising. As so often with overseas invasions, the weather was the British Isles' best defender. The sea was so rough that, to Tone's dismay, the army could not land and decided to return home. French support now waned. A bizarre French landing in Pembroke occurred in early 1797, hoping to stir a Welsh uprising and a march on Bristol. A rabble of 1,200 men landed near Fishguard, ran drunkenly amok and were rounded up by the local militia. One group was arrested with a pitchfork by a woman, Jemima Nicholas, who was duly celebrated as the 'Pembrokeshire heroine'.

Britain at the time was formally at war with France, and for the Irish to have openly welcomed French troops onto British territory was intolerable. It recalled the Tudors' reaction to Scottish flirtation with the same foe. However, by 1798 the British authorities in Dublin faced a rebellion by a reputed 280,000 Irishmen under arms, embracing Catholics and northern Presbyterians. British soldiers on the ground were operating under de facto wartime powers, and the result was extremes of violence against the Irish and their forces.

The war dragged on. Lesser French raids in 1798 were partly successful. Wexford and Wicklow were at one point lost to government control and Wexford was briefly declared a republic. In the course of one naval encounter Tone was arrested and imprisoned, as a result of which he committed suicide. An able and articulate man, he joined the ranks of Irish heroes cheated of any chance to put his talents to his country's service.

By the end of the year the rebellion had petered out. The rebels were subject to mass executions, with estimates ranging from 10,000 to 50,000 dead. The historian Roy Foster described it as 'the most concentrated outbreak of violence in recorded Irish history'. A tree in Wicklow to which a group of prisoners had been tied for shooting was so full of lead no saw could bring it down.

A most unequal marriage

The 1798 Irish rebellion was significant in embracing almost all Ireland's communities, Catholics and Nonconformist Protestants, Belfast merchants and Dublin professionals, even landowners and gentry. This was no Catholic confederacy but an all-Ireland independence movement. For its part, London had learned some lessons from the American secession, but they applied to its new empire and not its old one. The India Act of 1784 and the Canada Act of 1791 were both designed to grant a measure of local devolution under imperial authority. There was no such devolution to Dublin, even to its Protestant ascendancy.

Instead, London decided to take Ireland down the same path to enforced matrimony as it had taken Wales in 1536 and Scotland in 1707. It was merged politically and legislatively with England. The Dublin parliament, in one of its last acts, voted in 1799 against a union bill sent from London. It changed its mind a year later, as had Scotland's in 1707, in a flurry of bribed votes. A sick Grattan staggered into the chamber and gave a seated but storming two-hour speech in opposition. He declared his 'fidelity to the fortunes of my country, faithful to her freedom, faithful to her fall'.

The Dublin parliament now ceased to exist and a hundred pro-union Irish MPs, two-thirds of them from small Anglo-Irish boroughs, took ship for London and swore loyalty to the crown. A lord lieutenant continued to govern Ireland from Dublin Castle, but unaccountable to any assembly. The Anglican Church of Ireland was merged with the Church of England and an archbishop and three bishops came to sit in the House of Lords.

The name of the new union that came into being in 1801 was the United Kingdom of Great Britain and Ireland. When the question of the title of the monarch arose, it was provocatively proposed that George III be named as Emperor of the British Isles. This he declined, but James I's Union Jack was squeezed to include a new cross of St Patrick. Wales was again omitted as a 'home nation'. The flag was imperial propaganda, bequeathing to the United Kingdom one of the most bizarre banners in the world. People were to ask, did it represent one nation, three or even four?

To London, the crushing of Grattan's Parliament was necessitated by a wartime emergency. Like most such emergency measures it outlasted its cause. The United Kingdom that came into being on 1 January 1801 was in effect the restoration of Cromwell's Commonwealth. There would be no Irish national assembly, no local autonomy beyond the county magistracy and no home rule. Laws concerning Ireland were to be passed in London. To the British government this presented no ideological problem. The nations of the old English empire all shared one monarch and were present in one parliament. As under the Normans, unity would be achieved not by confederal institutions but by political assimilation.

For most of the eighteenth century Scotland and Wales had begun to acclimatise themselves to this centralised form of union. Optimists now hoped that, in the afterglow of the Hanoverian 'golden age', the British Isles could indeed fuse four peoples into one. The concept of Britishness was already widening to embrace an overseas empire – in which Scots, Irish and Welsh were playing an equal role. Surely the past grievances and imbalances of power implied by an English empire could pass into history.

An inauspicious birth

It was not to be. As Linda Colley has pointed out, imperialism acquires an authoritarian voice largely through the mechanisms of its formation, those of violence. Great Britain might be tolerable to the Scots, for many of whom the British empire had become a source of pride. They could see the English as in some degree partners rather than rulers. The Irish had never seen themselves in those terms. As Colley put it, Ireland saw 'Great Britain as an invented nation, superimposed onto much older alignments and loyalties . . . and forged above all by war.' Back in time, Hibernia had been independent of Roman Britain. The Gaelic tongue had little in common with Brythonic. Ireland had been conquered by Britain and ruled as a conquered people. So much was fact.

In particular, George III was still appalled that a part of his domain should be so emphatically Catholic. In 1793, the few Catholic property-owners even won the vote. The king was insistent that his Church of England 'govern' in Ireland as did his parliament and he was determined to ensure that the new United Kingdom conformed to that insistence. Under the 1800 union agreement, Catholics would be allowed to sit in Parliament and hold public offices. This concession had been agreed by Pitt but it was blocked by the king, now on the brink of mental breakdown. So blatant was this reneging that in 1801 Pitt felt obliged to resign, though he later returned.

Ireland was yet again enraged. A new generation of Irish politicians stepped forward to take up the mantle of Tone and Grattan. In 1823 Daniel O'Connell (1775–1847) founded the Catholic Association and five years later won a well-financed by-election to Westminster in County Clare. His victory, the first for a Catholic in over a century, was so emphatic that the House of Commons in London dared not force on him the customary oath of loyalty.

The following year, in 1829, with George III dead, a breakthrough in Catholic emancipation was achieved in another Catholic Relief Act. This admitted Catholic householders to the franchise and to jobs in the law and civil service. Faced with the certainty of a resumed Irish rebellion, even the High Tory prime minister Lord Wellington saw that he had to push the bill through Parliament. He still had to survive a mock duel on Battersea Fields with a fanatical anti-Catholic peer.

In Ireland O'Connell was now viewed as 'the Liberator', though a furious George IV called him 'King of Ireland' while he himself was merely 'Dean of Windsor'. At the next, 'Reform Bill' election of 1832 a third of Irish votes went to candidates demanding the repeal of the 1801 union. By 1843 Ireland was again at fever pitch with O'Connell making a rousing speech on the ancient Hill of Tara to a crowd estimated at 750,000. His voice must have required an army of 'barkers' to be repeated across the hillside. He demanded land ownership reform, an end to Anglican tithes and full home rule for Ireland within the United Kingdom.

O'Connell now ran into headwinds of controversy. He insisted on non-violent campaigning and thus split his own supporters between moderates and militants. He also added that Irish identity 'lay in religion' and that Ulster's Protestants were 'northern holders of foreign heresies'. This ensured him the hostility of much of Ulster as the lingering divide between Ireland's north and south became a chasm. A Belfast newspaper even opined, presciently, that the north might one day need partition and 'its own distinct kingdom'.

The 1841 census was dramatic. Ireland's population had been 4 million in 1800 and had now more than doubled to 8.5 million. This was more than half England's 16.5 million. For England's nervous Anglicans, Catholic emancipation was now not an issue only of religion but also of demography. With Scotland at 2.6 million and Wales at 1.1 million, almost two-fifths of the population of the British Isles were not English. At this rate of growth, it was conceivable that one day Irish, Welsh and Scottish voters might be the tail wagging the British bulldog. This was not how empires were supposed to turn out.

The great famine

Fate now offered the grimmest of correctives. The Irish famine that broke out in 1845 resulted from a blight hitting Ireland's staple source of calories and protein, the potato, an easy-to-grow all-purpose foodstuff. A virtual potato monoculture over much of the west of Ireland left no alternative source of food. There were now no seed potatoes for the following year's crop and there was no cash spare for food imports. To maintain the Irish trading economy, the London government refused even to ban Irish grain exports, which continued from Dublin throughout the five years of famine.

The consequence was that by 1850 over a million Irish had died of starvation or related causes. Another million piled into ships to reach safety in Britain and America. In just half a decade, the population fell from 8.5 million to 6.5 million and continued down to 5 million. Unknown numbers became vagrant across Ireland, their bodies lying by the road. The population of the poorest western province of Connacht reportedly plummeted from 1.4 million to 400,000. Emigration meant that by 1851 a quarter of the population of Liverpool was Irish and much the same proportion of Glasgow. For a developed and supposedly united European kingdom already living amid the fruits of an industrial revolution, this seemed an inexplicable disaster.

British governments – whether under the progressive Tory Robert Peel or the Whig Lord Russell – were adamant that they had no obligation to change policy. They believed Ireland's food should rely on the market's laws of demand and supply. Only after two years, in 1847, was poor law relief introduced, but since this was financed by local taxation on absentee landlords, the impact was patchy. Landlords could avoid the burden of new taxes through evictions, and many paid for their tenants' passage to America. One prominent landowner, Britain's foreign secretary Lord Palmerston, reportedly evicted no fewer than 2,000 tenants from his Irish estates.

Potato blight afflicted much of Europe, including Scotland, but only in western Ireland did the population's total reliance on the vegetable render it disastrous. London officials in Dublin were closer to the front. One of them, Lord Clarendon, wrote to Russell, 'I don't think there is another legislature in Europe that would disregard such suffering as now exists in the west of Ireland, or coldly persist in a policy of extermination.' He was ignored. London was finding £20 million to compensate British plantation-owners for the abolition of slavery. Irish relief eventually ran to £7 million.

The famine demonstrated an uncomfortable reality, that the people of Ireland were seen by many in Victorian England as a separate tribe, descendants of those cleared from England by the civilising Anglo-Saxons. The British official charged with organising famine relief, first in Ireland and then in Scotland, was Sir Charles Trevelyan (1807–86). Before moving on to become a noted civil service reformer, he believed the famine should be left to the market to correct. He declared, 'The judgment of God sent the calamity to teach the Irish a lesson . . . as a mendicant community.' Trevelyan saw part of his task as to rid the British Isles of the Catholic Irish, preferably by sending them across the Atlantic. They should be replaced by Germans, 'an orderly, moral, industrious, frugal people, less foreign to us than the Irish or Scotch Celt'. It was a rare use of the word Celt.

The famine reduced most of Ireland to numb exhaustion, a struggle for survival by communities made worse by the emigration of their able-bodied males. Forty per cent of men and women born in Ireland over the mid-nineteenth century were by 1890 living abroad, mostly in America, though it should be said that Italy and Spain experienced similar emigrations across the Atlantic. Half of America's forty-five presidents were to be of Irish extraction, fourteen of them Scots-Irish from Ulster. Back in Ireland the post-famine era was called the Great Silence.

16

A Scotland Transformed

The Highland clearances

While this agony unfolded across Ireland, a pain of a different sort was experienced by Scotland. The disbanding of the Scottish clans after 1745 had been accelerated by an agricultural revolution already well under way in England and much of Europe. Crop and livestock specialisation had transformed a predominantly subsistence localised economy into one of land enclosure and monetary exchange. Common land was privatised and uplands devoted largely to sheep.

Scotland's glens had long been populated by settlements of smallholders, subtenants of so-called 'tacksmen', who were agents of clan chiefs or absentee landlords. These glens were now more profitable for sheep and were duly cleared of crop farmers. In England such clearances and enclosures had taken place over generations, with farm workers migrating into industrial towns and cities. In Scotland the revolution was sudden. Whole communities were evicted, mostly into coastal settlements, where they were expected to find work in fishing and kelp gathering. Here some landlords found them 'crofts', or plots of adjacent land, others financed their emigration.

Economics now disbanded the Highland clans more effectively than any government edict after the '45 uprising. In the second half of the eighteenth century, some two-thirds of Highland estates were sold to outsiders, often by clan chiefs claiming ancestral ownership. More conscientious owners made some effort to rehouse their people in crofts, while many paid for passages on migrant ships to North America. The Chinese opium tycoon Sir James Matheson, son of a Sutherland tacksman, bought the entire Isle of Lewis in 1844 for half a million pounds and transported 2,300 of its inhabitants to Canada. It was estimated that the province of Nova Scotia received 50,000 Highlanders in the early nineteenth century and remained Gaelic-speaking for three generations.

Protests were fragmentary but sometimes fierce. Between 1807 and 1821 the largest landowner, the Countess of Sutherland in north-west Scotland, cleared thousands of tenants into what she intended to be model coastal villages. While the family's declared intentions were constructive, their execution was less so. The local agent, Patrick Sellar, called the victims 'primitives and aborigines', and the name of Sutherland was associated with the worst abuses. Dubbed 'the Devastation of Sutherland', it led to demonstrations and death threats outside the family's London mansion.

The clearances stripped Highland Scotland of its human geography. A third of the population left the uplands in half a century, moving either to coastal settlements or to America. Few headed for the booming Lowlands industries, illustrating the depth of Scotland's internal divide. Gaelic-speaking plummeted, since resettlement mostly required a facility in English.

One experience Scotland did not share with Ireland was starvation from the potato famine. This was in large part because of a continued supply of oats. When famine hit in 1846, churches and other charities raised funds for local relief. In Edinburgh, official destitution boards were set up to record those in need of help, with some 250,000 names listed as being at risk, a fraction of those suffering in Ireland. There was hunger and resulting disease but little actual starvation. None the less, parallels were drawn. The Scottish historian Tom Devine estimated that 90 per cent of Scotland was still owned in mid-century by 1,500 mostly absentee families, a proportion similar to Ireland. Many were Lowlanders. There was the same lack of security of tenure, though in Scotland smallholders were allowed to own land.

Apologists for the clearances pointed out that they were an economic necessity and that most Highlanders went sadly but peacefully to their new homes. Emigration was long a fact of life in Ireland and Scotland, as it was in Scandinavia and Italy. Even the Lowlander Robbie Burns was so desperate for work that at one point he applied for a job on a Caribbean slave plantation. When Dr Johnson remarked that 'the noblest prospect which a Scotsman ever sees is the high road that leads him to England', he might have extended that destination to the world. But nothing in Scotland generated a political response, a yearning for self-rule, comparable to the famine in Ireland.

A Scottish romance

Scotland's eighteenth-century Enlightenment had, by the time of the Regency, turned Edinburgh into a city of European celebrity. It was now enhanced by a cultural rebranding through the efforts of its most famous citizen, Sir Walter Scott (1771–1832). As a popular novelist and champion of the Romantic movement, the young Scott had opposed union with England, but that was past. His writings had alerted him to the dramatic potential of a revived Scottish history, notably of the Highlands as dubiously exploited by James Macpherson in the 1780s. Even as the Highlanders were being driven from their homes, Scott prepared for them a glamorous renaissance. He declared in 1814 that no European nation in the past half century 'has undergone so complete a change as this kingdom of Scotland'. He went so far as to warn England that 'if you un-Scotch us you will find us damned mischievous Englishmen'.

The rock on which Scott built his new Scotland was the

Highlands. He transformed what had long been regarded as primitive and squalid backcountry into a land of exotic excitement. In 1820 he was a founding member of the Celtic Society of Scotland, using an epithet almost never applied to the Scots. He did not indicate it was an epithet to be in any way shared with Ireland or Wales. Two years later the new British monarch George IV (r.1820–30) signalled Scotland's elevated status by declaring his intention to be the first monarch to set foot there for 171 years. Scott was to be his master of ceremonies, with the Celtic Society staging a rolling pageant of Scotland's history and fashion.

Most conspicuous was Scott's decision to make the star of that pageant none other than the recently condemned Highland clans and their banned kilts and tartans. The unmentionable became, as if overnight, the fount of Scottish glory. The tartan was a patterned fabric – tribally non-specific – that had vanished along with the kilt after the Disclothing Act that was passed following the '45 uprising. The ban had been lifted in 1782. Though tartans and kilts were not Lowland garments, Scott ordered the Edinburgh crowds to greet King George's procession 'all plaided and plumed'. Clans were rediscovered and celebrated as the foundation peoples of the Scottish nation. To Norman Davies it was 'one of the greatest publicity stunts in history' and brilliantly successful. Over the next ten years 900 people would attend the Celtic Society's annual Celtic Ball, with kilts and tartans compulsory for men and women. In 1873 the society was accorded the epithet 'Royal'.

Scott was accused of 'Celtified pageantry'. It would today be called Disneyfication. But after a millennium of neglect a northern people calling themselves Gaels were in the spotlight. A territory formerly regarded as hostile and with a population devastated by clearances became the object of fascination and study. The paintings of Alexander Nasmyth (1758–1840) and Edwin Landseer (1802–73) brought the Highlands into English drawing rooms. Landseer's majestic stag, the *Monarch of the Glen* (1851), was the most noted of Scottish paintings, almost a national emblem. The artist was not averse to acknowledging current history with his bleak *Rent-Day in the Wilderness* (1868).

The enthusiasm for Scotland shown by George IV was redoubled by Queen Victoria (*r.*1837–1901). She and her husband Albert first went north in 1842 and spent a week touring the country, publicly lauding its charms. They leased Balmoral Castle (sight unseen) in 1848 and purchased it four years later, greatly extending it to accommodate their retinue. At the gateway to the Highlands, Balmoral supplanted Edinburgh's Holyrood Palace as effectively the second seat of the British monarchy. The men of the royal family wore kilts when in residence, and the formerly illegal Stuart tartan was deftly relaunched (and respelled) as the Royal Stewart. Victoria wrote in her diary of the 'romance of wild loveliness . . . beloved Scotland, the proudest, finest country in the world'. Her tartaned Albert declared it '*so gemütlich*'.

Scotland was now presenting itself as a supposedly Celtic brand under the sponsorship of a Saxon monarch. Royal patronage made owning a Highland estate a status symbol of English aristocracy. Dukes, marquesses and earls patrolled the recently emptied glens, guns under their arms. The Bloomsbury Group's Lytton Strachey scornfully remarked that German industry in the nineteenth century overtook British because German tycoons invested in factories while the English built hunting lodges. Tourism boomed. Dr Johnson's grim Highland visits of the 1770s mutated into a Caledonian grand tour. George Earl's painting *Coming South: Perth Station*, showed a platform crowded with wealthy visitors returning from a Highland break.

What is a Celtic revival?

The one facet of Celticism that Scott did not summon to his cause was Gaelic. It was never the tongue of the Lowlands, which had now long been an English dialect known as Scots English. When eighteenth-century Edinburgh had dubbed itself 'the Athens of the North', linguists had described its Scots English as 'Attic' and provincial north-east Scottish as 'Doric', both in reference to the regions of ancient Greece. These dialects are traceable back to Old English, Scandinavian and other Germanic roots. They have no link with Gaelic.

When Burns turned his nationalism to verse he sought to do so in this Lowlands vernacular, which he termed Lallans, a tongue that he wished to be written and sung with pride. True Scots 'took nae pains their speech to balance/ Or rules to gie/ But spak their thoughts in plain braid Lallans/ Like you or me'. Ulster was later also delighted to find in Burns's language an echo of their own Ulster Scots dialect, since christened Ullans. I am told that some Aberdeen carol concerts are conducted in Doric, Lallans, Latin and Greek.

Language thus reflected a distinction that most Scots still recognised between the Gaelic-speaking Highlands and Islands and the Lowlands of the east and south. Sir Charles Trevelyan, who had moved on from the Irish famine to the Scottish one, detected a difference even among the northerners. The North Sea coast, non-Gaelic speaking, had been peopled 'by the Danish or Norwegian race', whom he described as harder working and thus less afflicted by famine, whereas the Gaelic-speakers facing the Atlantic were no different from the Irish.

The prominence given to such distinctions fed the Victorian fashion for ethnic stereotyping. The playwright George Bernard Shaw in his *John Bull's Other Island* depicts a fellow Irish expatriate deriding his compatriots back home. An Irishman's imagination, he says, 'never lets him alone, never convinces him, never satisfies him; but it makes him that he can't face reality nor deal with it, nor handle it, nor conquer it: he can only sneer at them that do. It saves him from working.' Others extended such generalisation to the Welsh and Scots. The poet Matthew Arnold (1822–88) was one of many who distinguished the newly defined 'Celts' from Anglo-Saxons. After visiting a Welsh eisteddfod in Aberdare in 1861 he was 'filled with admiration at the enthusiasm awakening in your whole people'. He duly characterised 'the Celts' as a people of 'sentimentality, poetry and romance . . . always ready to react against the despotism of facts' – a splendidly loaded remark.

Some responded by acting up to the music-hall caricature. In Scotland the Highlander was presented as a noble savage on a wild mountain, tartan-kilted and with claymore in hand, apparently waiting to smite the English. The Welshman was the hairy last Bard of John Martin's magnificent painting of that title (1817), chanting above a precipice before hurling himself to his death before Edward I's army. The Irishman was a mischievous, green-hatted leprechaun, musical, poetical, prancing and chuckling. He was the cheery Irish busker I watched swaying down a London Tube train with his fiddle. An enchanted American sitting opposite caught my eye and remarked, 'Oh I do love your Celts.'

This depiction was of a people of the British Isles supposedly unsuited to business and public affairs. To Arnold they were lacking 'the skilful and resolute appliance of means to ends . . . and the right temperament to form their own organised political entity'. All were to be contrasted with the Anglo-Saxon, who, in an age of Hanoverian and Saxe-Coburg dynasts, were lauded as 'a disciplined and steadily obedient people, retaining an inalienable part of freedom and self-dependence'.

Such caricature perhaps explains why so many Scots in the nineteenth century were reluctant to identify themselves with the word Celtic, while the concept of union with England was bedding down. Edinburgh's New Town was growing ever more extensive, while Glasgow's industrial prosperity gave it the title of 'second city of the empire'. The latter's wealth expanded from commerce to manufacturing, notably of ships and clothing, drawing in so many Irish that a third of Glasgow's population claimed to be Catholic. In 1887 a football club was founded in east Glasgow to serve this community, taking the name Celtic, pronounced with a soft initial 'C'. No one would dare call fans of Rangers, their rival team, Celts.

Scotland's aristocracy continued to attended English private schools and universities and spoke with English accents even as they asserted their Scottishness. Regiments, railways, hotels and even postal addresses were renamed 'North British'. Edinburgh's grandest hotel was still the North British until renamed the Balmoral in 1991. The attempted Irish equivalent of 'West Britain', unsurprisingly, did not catch on. The Scots were as Scottish as the Irish were Irish, but the identity was carried with a confidence that did not seem to require political expression.

17

Do You Speak Celt?

A stronger Welsh in a stronger Wales

Wales in the eighteenth and nineteenth centuries experienced few of the political and economic traumas of Ireland and Highland Scotland. The reason is that Wales was in the process of becoming one of the most prosperous regions of Britain, with the added security of economic diversity. Its uplands had long favoured the rearing of sheep that could be easily driven to English markets, while the well-watered valleys of the south and the border country were ideal for cattle. Wales was a long-standing source of England's wool fleeces and dairy products. Hardly an English high street lacked a Welsh dairy well into the twentieth century.

This prosperity was enhanced by minerals, with reserves successively of gold, copper, tin and iron ore. Then from the 1800s Wales delivered the world's finest coal and roofing slate. A walk almost anywhere in Wales today reveals the remains of this prosperity, of mine workings, quarries, rail tracks, warehouses and cloth mills, even in the most inaccessible places. The old Merioneth capital of Dolgellau boasted, apart from farming, a booming glove-making industry, slate quarrying and 500 people employed in local gold mines. The nearby coastal village of Aberdyfi not only farmed its land and fished its sea but also mined copper and slate and boasted clothing mills on its streams and shipbuilding on the foreshore. By the early twentieth century the village had six places of worship and three schools.

This prosperity produced its own stresses. The Napoleonic Wars sent demand for iron soaring and the Merthyr valley was its cradle, with plentiful adjacent coal, timber and water power. Only transport was lacking, with fifty-two locks needed for the canal to Cardiff. Wages rose to match. John Davies has a Merthyr worker 'earning three times as much as the shilling a day received by a farm servant . . . and even a labourer owned a watch'. This in turn bred a 'valleys' personality, Welsh-speaking, chapel-going and with a turbulent relationship with employers in the isolated communities.

Thus Merthyr became a focus of a militant uprising in 1831 when an economic downturn led to wages being cut at the Cyfarthfa Ironworks. Highland troops were sent to suppress the riots and some twenty people were killed. An innocent supposed leader was hanged. The south Welsh were prominent in joining the English Chartists in demanding a wider franchise, culminating in a riot in Newport in 1839. Other disturbances were against new road tolls and related agricultural poverty, termed 'Rebecca' riots after the participants being disguised as women. But unlike similar protests in Ireland, such militancy was not peculiarly Welsh and was unrelated to the issue of nationalism or self-government.

Emigration certainly occurred, but nothing like on the same scale as in Scotland or Ireland. Early Welsh settlements in the Americas tended to be of religious sects, as in Wisconsin, Pennsylvania and Patagonia in Argentina. The Wisconsin constitution was even published in Welsh. Some 25,000 American Mormons claim Welsh ancestors from this period. The famous Mormon Tabernacle Choir was reputedly a Welsh inspiration.

Wales displayed few of the aristocratic palaces and great estates of adjacent England, rather a plethora of Georgian and Victorian gentry houses on the more modest scale of Hafod and Nanteos outside Aberystwyth. The tragic demolition of so many of them in the 1950s and 60s was recorded by the historian Thomas Lloyd. On the other hand, villages and market towns such as Ruthin, Meifod, Montgomery and Carmarthen display streets lined with handsome terraces and double-fronted houses, far more spacious than their equivalents in the Irish or Scottish countryside.

The result was that a Wales whose proximity to the English cities of Bristol, Birmingham and Liverpool might have made it vulnerable to English cultural assimilation remained socially stable. A merchant and professional class did not desert its roots for the outside world. The twentieth-century Welsh economist Brinley Thomas was unequivocal: 'It was the ability of industrial Wales to offer a livelihood to a substantial population which provided the basis for a mass culture to flourish in the Welsh language.' Between 1851 and 1921 – a period of steep agricultural decline across the rest of Britain – the rural population of Wales shrank only from 170,000 to 114,000. The actual number of individual farms stayed remarkably steady at around 40,000.

Religion also served as a communal glue. A lethargic Anglican church was galvanised – or circumvented – by a generation of celebrity preachers such as William Williams, Daniel Rowland and Howell Harris. Thousands came to hear them, often preaching on hillsides in the open air. The Welsh language had a fervour that appealed to all classes of men and women. The singsong *hwyl* of the sermons offered a foretaste of American hot-gospellers.

In 1811 one clergyman, Thomas Charles, broke with the Anglican church and brought tens of thousands of followers over to Methodism. With them came families, Bible classes, Sunday schools, legacies and donations. Nonconformity also fragmented into a plethora of sects, Baptist, Presbyterian, Calvinist, Wesleyan and Congregationalist. Welsh Dissent was not in itself politically radical. Davies points out that Griffith Jones's schools, described in Chapter 14, were hotspots of conservatism. To Jones, teaching the Welsh to read and write their native language should create 'a barrier to prevent the Welsh from adopting dangerous ideas and loose practices', by implication from the English. Faith and the Welsh language would bind young people to their communities and to the land. The Anglican church in Wales would always be seen, as it was in Ireland, as an alien English import.

The response of the English government was not as hostile to Dissent in Wales as it was to Catholicism in Ireland, but it was still opposed. In 1844 a commission was set up under three English scholars to study the state of Welsh education. Its evidence came largely from Anglican clergymen alarmed at the spread of Welsh language teaching and of Methodism. The commission produced three so-called Blue Books, controversial even in their day for deploring Welsh as 'a manifold barrier to the moral progress and commercial prosperity of the people'. It issued the bizarre warning that Nonconformist worship had led to 'Welsh women being almost universally unchaste'.

Such inept language evoked outrage. Reform stalled, and it was not until the 1870s that a series of Welsh education bills initiated a programme of non-denominational national schools and colleges. These were championed by a skilled Welsh civil servant in London, Sir Hugh Owen (1804–81). The establishment of compulsory education in England and Wales in 1870 was followed in 1889 by the devolution of schooling in Wales to local county education committees, out of the hands of the English.

The medium of the teaching remained controversial. In Ireland Daniel O'Connell was outspoken. He saw the Irish language as a bondage 'imposed on mankind as a curse at the building of Babel'. To him the Irish language shackled his people to their poverty. While it had 'many recollections that twine the hearts of Irishmen . . . I am sufficiently utilitarian not to regret its gradual abandonment'. To O'Connell a refusal to teach and learn English was 'linguistic suicide'.

Likewise in Wales, the prerequisite for children to advance in life, given that they spoke Welsh at home, was to learn English. The objective was seen as not the suppression of Welsh but the achievement of bilingualism. Welsh language and history were taught in the new grammar schools. To have denied any British children access to English in the nineteenth century would have been widely regarded as regressive and handicapping. As it was, by the end of that century the majority of Welsh children emerged from school bilingual and rated among the best taught in Britain.

This issue was hampered by the bizarre reputation of the 'Welsh not'. This was a punishment token to be worn by children heard speaking Welsh in school, to be passed on to the next child caught doing so. Whoever was holding the 'not' at the end of the day would be punished. Such a facile discipline administered by children on each other was actually common in many school systems. Cases are recorded in Japan, Russia and Canada. Robb describes French Breton children made to carry a *symbole* if heard speaking Breton. The day's final holder had to clean the toilets. This practice was said to date from the *signum* used to make medieval seminarians in Paris speak Latin.

A greater threat to Welsh cultural distinctiveness came from a different quarter, the surge in Glamorgan's mineral wealth. Drawn by tinplate and copper mined in eighteenth-century Swansea, and by the ironworks of Merthyr Tydfil, workers poured into the south Welsh valleys. Initially the inflow was largely Welsh. Merthyr grew to be Wales's most populous town in 1860. It was said to be 90 per cent Welsh-speaking, and with no fewer than eighty-four churches and chapels. As the boom in coking coal developed later in the century, migration was reinforced by incomers from the Midlands and further afield.

The sheer scale of this immigration led to Welsh-speaking plummeting, such that by the end of the century, the census showed 50 per cent of residents no longer speaking Welsh, albeit these were overwhelmingly in Glamorgan. Outside that county most Welsh people still spoke the language, at a time when fewer than 10 per cent of Irish or Scots were speaking Gaelic. In 1899 there were 136 magazine and newspaper titles printed in Welsh. There were virtually none in Irish, until the Gaelic League's *An Claidheamh Soluis* begun that year.

The return of Celtomania

In the mid-nineteenth century the Georgian craze for Celticism returned in a more scholarly vein. It was carried forward by a formidable German linguist, Johann Kaspar Zeuss, whose *Grammatica Celtica* appeared in 1853, its influence restricted by it being written in Latin. Zeuss broke new ground by embedding the Celtic languages firmly in the newly identified Indo-European tradition. This was enhanced by the discovery in 1846–57 of the Hallstatt and La Tène settlements, tentatively linked to classical references to peoples of pre-Roman Europe. At a time when Prusso-German nationalism was emerging on the European stage, such exotic antecedents acquired a validity of their own. Any discovery that might be pre-classical fed an appetite for all things to which the term 'Celtic' might be applied.

This took particular root in what is still termed Celtic art. Its crosses, spirals, knots and curlicues were found in archaeological sites across Europe, lending a coherence to Bronze and Iron Age artefacts. They entered the Victorian revivalist pattern books alongside neo-Gothic and Art Nouveau. The category was later associated with such masterpieces as the Irish *Book of Kells* and the *Lindisfarne Gospels* – sometimes classified as 'insular Celtic'.

As for Celtic speech, it at least had the evidence of living languages to work on, but these showed little collaboration. The London Welsh who gathered round Morganwg's

Gorsedd and the Cymmrodorion had no contact with Scotland's Royal Celtic Society. Scotland's first professor of Celtic studies, Donald MacKinnon, was not appointed at Edinburgh until 1882. There were closer ties between Wales and Ireland, and indeed between Wales and Brittany. But when in 1876 a Society for the Preservation of the Irish Language was formed in Dublin, it was to the Welsh speakers of Wales rather than the closer related Gaelic speakers of Scotland that it looked for inspiration.

The revival of Welsh eisteddfods in 1861 gave a number of Irish enthusiasts a spur to try their own, but not until 1897 was the first equivalent Feis Ceoil (music festival), held in Dublin. Its secretary, Edith Oldham, nervously remarked that the event was 'a Dublin cathedral' compared to the Welsh eisteddfod's St Peter's in Rome. None the less, the assiduous Celtic scholar Caoimhín De Barra counted just 143 uses of the word 'Celtic' in Irish newspapers in 1820, but by 1890 this had surged to 4,702. The growth in Welsh mentions was almost identical. For the most part the adjective was still used in reference to language and not in any other context.

This posed a new challenge to emerging pan-Celticists. They were custodians of a group of languages – and supposedly peoples – thought to be extensive in western Europe before Roman times and still existing. But what really was their relationship with each other? Trevelyan's remarks during the Irish potato famine were now echoed by a Frenchman, Ernest Renan, who in 1854 claimed there to be racial distinctions between Celts and other Europeans. He was intrigued by new anthropological theories involving hair colour, height and skull shape. When passing from England into 'Celtic country', Renan claimed to detect a change 'like entering on the subterranean strata of another world, the impression given us by Dante when he leads us from one circle of his Inferno to another'.

Such fantasies were seized on by enthusiasts for the

late-nineteenth-century resurgence of national purity. In 1864 a French scholar, Charles de Gaulle (or Celt, uncle of the subsequent president), went further and called for a Celtic Union and a new Celtic language. He sought a pidgin that would unite the Celts under one mutually comprehensible tongue, a sort of Celtic Esperanto. De Gaulle summoned a pan-Celtic congress to Brittany in 1867, though only Bretons and Welsh turned up.

In 1888 a Pan-Celtic Society was formed in Dublin, a largely literary gathering that lasted just three years before disbanding. It was succeeded by a pan-Celtic 'movement' and then an 'association' backed by two Irish romantics, Edmund Fournier and Lord Castletown. Fournier was a true eccentric, a scientist interested in electromagnetics, parapsychology, spiritualism and psychical research. Castletown was a soldier in the British army and an ardent imperialist. This led to the usual tensions of minority group politics. There were arguments over how far to ape Welsh practice, whether to admit Cornish, whether to have bardic rites or whether to support or oppose the British empire. And what should they speak? The answer was English.

The first fully Pan-Celtic Congress was held in Dublin in 1901. Papers were read (in English) and a parade was held through the streets. The boundary between antiquarianism, scholarship and mysticism was a fine one. There were local costumes, pipes, choirs and much ridicule of the Welsh Druidical robes. A study of ancient Breton history had reported in 1881 that it had been unable to find any trace of a bard or a Druid. Delegates were disappointed at the Irish failing to wear Celtic costume – despite some confusion over Dublin's mayoral robes.

Mundane debates were held over proposals for a steamer service between Ireland and other Celtic lands, and for heather as the proper flower for a Celtic 'face'. Should there be further congresses, a Celtic Olympiad and even perhaps a nation called Celtia? Two more congresses were held, in Caernarvon in 1904 and Edinburgh in 1907, both popular as street events and as displays of pageantry. The Welsh were numerically the stars of these demonstrations.

The congresses ground to a halt with Fournier's retirement in 1908 and with the lack of an able organiser to succeed him. The eventual admission of Cornwall as a 'sixth nation' along with the Isle of Man distressed more serious members, to whom pan-Celticism was getting more like a fancy-dress show. To others, Celtic bonding seemed elitist and artificial, a view reflected in the term 'inter-Celtic' for 'pan-Celtic'. The predictable split came in 1961 with the founding of a rival Celtic League. These were, in truth, not 'one people' speaking one language, unless it was English. The tart conclusion of one observer was that 'Celts are primarily about millinery'.

These efforts to unite the supposedly Celtic-speaking peoples of Europe suggested that they were no more united in the present than in the past. The concept of Celticism was, as Tolkien later said, no more than a name into which you dump anything you wanted. While there was a respectable academic study of a group of similar languages and of the peoples who spoke them, any perceived unity was a chimera. Its absurdity became the more patent when discussion turned to imagining a land of Celtia. Should it be a resplendent Ruritania or a communist paradise? Likewise, Lord Castletown demanded that true Celts should start the day by singing 'God Save the Queen' while Fournier wanted to establish communion with Celts in the afterlife. The most brutal reality was that, before the First World War, every congress had an elephant in the room. It was that of Ireland's political aspiration.

How Celtic is a Gael?

Ireland's ambition was straightforward. It was to achieve independence of England. So keen were the Irish to distance themselves from antiquarian fantasy that they narrowed Celt down to Gael. Though cognate with Celt, the term excluded the Brythonic-speaking Welsh, whom the Irish regarded as feebly subservient to the English. The word Gaelic also referred to the Highland tongue, but a difference was maintained by that being voiced as 'gallic', against the Irish 'gaylic'. After Irish independence, any confusion was resolved by calling the Irish version just 'Irish'.

A separate nationalist Gaelic League was formed in Dublin in 1893, its central purpose being to preserve and promote the Irish language banned from British government schools. Its first president, Douglas Hyde, was a Protestant nationalist who attracted a range of adherents, including briefly the grand master of Ulster's Orange Order lodge. The league's objective was 'to prevent the assimilation of the Irish nation by the English nation'. Its purpose could hardly be more explicitly anti-English, viewing 'the Irish language as a political weapon of the first importance against English encroachment'.

Rather than fuse with the pan-Celticists, the Gaelic League was ever more a nursery for a new generation of Irish republican politicians and soldiers. It saw Irish language as the defining badge of nationalism. It dismissed pan-Celticism's Castletown and Fournier as 'Protestants playing at pagans'. They should cease their obsession with the past and deal with the present, the ongoing struggle against the English. A crisis occurred at one pan-Celtic meeting when a Welsh archdruid called on Almighty God to bless the cause of the British army 'against the falsehood, iniquity and error' of the Boers in South Africa. He unsheathed his sword and called on all present to touch it. The Boers enjoyed wide support in Ireland.

Where the Celtic revival did strike home was among Irish intellectuals, deepest in the Irish expatriate diaspora in London. Its leading figures, such as George Bernard Shaw, Oscar Wilde, James Joyce, John Millington Synge and W. B. Yeats, were to adorn Britain's culture as much as Ireland's. Yeats might consort with the literati of Bloomsbury and Bedford Park, but it was the land that he had deserted that seemed to grip his imagination. His poem 'The Lake Isle of Innisfree' evoked the supposed purity of Ireland's far west. His heart told him he should 'arise now, and go to Innisfree, / And a small cabin build there, of clay and wattles made . . . the deep heart's core'.

When in the 1890s a Celtic Mystical Order was formed, it led Yeats and his colleagues back at least in spirit to the western Aran Islands and the enshrined soul of Celticism. Here were 'lands tortured by the sea, scourged by the sea wind. A myriad lochs, fjords, inlets, passages serrate its broken frontiers.' Yet they were kept firmly at a distance. When Yeats and his fellow poet T. W. Rolleston joined with the Anglo-Welsh publisher Ernest Rhys in founding the Rhymers' Club to advance the cause of Celtic poetry, they did so in the Cheshire Cheese pub in London's Fleet Street. As Rhys wrote in a confessional note, 'Wales England wed; so I was bred. 'Twas merry London gave me breath.' Even Yeats admitted that 'everything I love has come to me through English'.

It might seem a tenuous Celtic affectation that so bonded in London, but the influence of Yeats's romanticism over Ireland's Gaelic revival is hard to exaggerate. It was on a par with Walter Scott's earlier reinvigoration of Scottishness. Yeats dreamed of an Irishness that would 'unite the radical truths of Christianity to those of a more ancient world'. He encouraged the young John Millington Synge to leave Paris and live in the Aran Islands, the 'last fortress of the Celt', and to do so 'as if you were one of the people themselves'. Poor Synge felt he had no option but to obey. The western shore duly took on the qualities of a Celtic Mount Olympus, a geographical muse for any writer wishing to see what Synge called 'the most primitive society left in Europe . . . where it is only in wild jests and laughter that they can express their loneliness and desolation'. That did not stop him carefully satirising it in *The Playboy of the Western World*.

This was surely an ersatz Celtic identity. Like that of Walter Scott, it retraced a nation's evolution from an ancient folk culture to a supposed moral core. As Foster puts it, 'the barefoot children, turf fires and unrelieved diets of the west were romantically approved by the Gaelicist intelligentsia – who felt accordingly let down by the Connacht people's propensity to emigrate.' But then almost every narrator of the Celtic past was an émigré. The nature of Celticism was a detachment from the front line, an existence fabricated in the minds of antiquarians and academics and experienced most fiercely in absentia.

Much the same applied to the role of religion. Conventional Irish history tends to root its troubles in the Catholic/Protestant divide. This divide was undeniable, but it was not unique to Ireland. It tended to reflect deeper divisions both within Ireland's past and in attitudes to English rule. In the nineteenth century the Catholic church was conservative and mostly supported the unionist status quo. Most of Ireland's prominent nationalists, from Tone, Grattan and the MP Charles Stewart Parnell, to Yeats and the woman who would become the Dáil's first female TD, Constance Markievicz, were not Catholic. If Irish Catholics were anti-English it was because English policy was so anti-Catholic. Irish religious fundamentalism vanished, eventually, with independence, prosperity and sexual scandal.

The reality was that, as the nineteenth century progressed and democratic forces emerged within England, London's policy towards Ireland became untenable. This had nothing to do with Celticism. Caoimhín De Barra is unequivocal. Ireland at the time faced an existential crisis demanding a 'single-minded insistence on the separate and distinctive nature of Irish nationality'. Celtic identity's utility was 'to distinguish [the Irish] from Anglo-Saxon England, not to acknowledge their connection with the rest of Britain'. The issue was Irish home rule. This had nothing to do with Celts.

18

A Terrible Beauty is Born

The rise and fall of Parnell

If Ireland shared an identity with anywhere it was not with its supposed Celtic cousins on the western fringe of Britain, it was with oppressed nations across Europe and their aspiration for freedom from alien domination. When revolutions erupted in France, Italy and Germany in 1830 and again in 1848, British governments realised belatedly that political reform could not be postponed. The 1832 Reform Act began a process of change in Britain's industrial conditions, local government, poor law, tariffs and trade. Peel's Tories were, at least for a while, a self-consciously reformist party, while the Whigs converted to Gladstonian Liberalism. Parliament at Westminster was where the argument took place, on how far and how fast reform should occur. It was Parliament that kept British revolution at bay.

Except in Ireland. Here the chasm that gradualist 1830s-style reform had to bridge was simply too wide, the sense of grievance too deep. After the 1840s and the famine, Ireland's clamour for land reform fused with that for home rule. The hundred Irish MPs who came to London after union in 1801 had mostly been in London's thrall. Yet by the 1870s more than half of them, Protestants as well as Catholics, were committed to home rule. This commitment had no institutional forum for its expression and debate. The Parliament at Westminster was too distant and too negligent.

This left direct action as the only option. Irish reformism was now expressed in 'wars' – tithe wars, land wars, wars over home rule and wars over whether wars should be hot or cold. The Fenian Irish Republican Brotherhood was formed in 1858 and was for hot. It was committed to making Ireland an 'independent democratic republic', explicitly inheriting the mantle of the 1798 rebellion. Irish blood was yet again up. At the same time there emerged on the Irish scene a figure of charisma, intelligence and pragmatism, Charles Stewart Parnell (1846–91). He was of Anglo-Irish Protestant background, born in Wicklow to a prominent landowning father and an American mother. Educated in England, he made his way to Magdalene College Cambridge and travelled to America, returning to devote himself to his family estates and rising to become county sheriff of Wicklow.

Parnell was attracted to the moderate Home Rule League founded in 1873 by an Ulster journalist turned politician, Isaac Butt (1813–79). Two years later he was elected Westminster MP for Meath as one of Butt's sixty-strong Irish Parliamentary Party (IPP). The group was a new force in British politics, explicitly committed to home rule. After Scottish union in 1707, Scottish MPs had assimilated into English political life as loyal members of the Liberal Party. Irish unionism saw no such assimilation. The IPP brought to Westminster a hundred MPs – a bloc large enough, if so minded, to disrupt business and upset the bipartisan parliamentary equilibrium. They might sympathise with liberalism but they were primarily Irish.

London responded to the new Irish challenge with gestures of mild reform. The Liberal government in 1869 conceded the disestablishment of the Anglican Church of Ireland and the ending of Irish tithes. This was followed in 1870 by the Landlord and Tenant (Ireland) Act, protecting tenants and allowing them in certain circumstances to own their farms. Such reform merely encouraged demands for more, raising the issues of absentee land ownership and anti-Catholic discrimination, which lay as ticking bombs on the parliamentary table.

In 1880 the Liberal leader William Gladstone returned to power and Parnell took over as leader of the IPP. This was Ireland's moment. Parnell now headed a disciplined parliamentary force whose sole aim was to advance Irish home rule within the United Kingdom. He was the first parliamentary leader to deploy whipping, filibustering and tactical 'hung parliament' deals. His initial battle was to advance the right to buy land. Gladstone accepted both the justice of the Irish cause and his need for Irish votes in Parliament. He also fell under Parnell's personal spell, finding him 'the most remarkable man I ever met . . . an intellectual phenomenon'. The Commons passed a series of land acts – there were eventually six – enabling rents to be regulated and providing loans for farm purchase.

In 1884 the further expansion of the UK franchise more than doubled the size of the Irish electorate and Parnell now turned his attention to full home rule. Gladstone understood that there was no way the Irish electorate would vote for anything less and was convinced it had somehow to be conceded. He and Parnell went into virtual coalition on the issue. Various options for self-rule had long been mooted. They ranged from total government separation to forms of federation and devolution of 'domestic affairs'. There was talk of a 'Norwegian option', where an autonomous state merely offered 'homage' to the Swedish crown. Few Irish were truly republican and few wanted to break all links with the British monarchy or kingdom. They just wanted to govern themselves.

It was to no avail. In April 1886 an ageing Gladstone made what was widely regarded as his greatest ever speech, over three and a half hours in favour of his Irish bill. He warned that if some such autonomy was not granted it would eventually be seized and Britain 'humiliated'. It was to no avail. In the event ninety-three Liberal Unionists voted against their leader and home rule was lost. Parnell's domestic popularity began to recede, his political downfall completed by a personal divorce scandal. This led to his health deteriorating and an early death in 1891.

Parnell had been the uncrowned king of Irish nationalism. His ambition was to bring self-government to his nation. He wished to do so without bloodshed and to put in place a constitutional relationship that would bring peace between the eastern and western 'sides' of the British Isles. That he failed, even after securing the support of England's dominant statesman, tells to the potency of English imperialism. To conservative London opinion, England's domestic union had to be indissoluble. That was the essence of the United Kingdom.

Like many enthusiasts for home rule, Parnell never fully articulated its implications or its details. To be sure, Irishmen – if not yet women – should decide for themselves the laws by which they should be governed. Whether this should be a reinstated Grattan's Parliament or varying degrees of sovereignty under a crown 'dominion' was left open. The longer debate continued, the more home rule became less a fixed goal than a staging post; the longer it was postponed, the more its champions were driven to the extreme of full independence. As both Grattan and Gladstone had said, the warnings were plain.

There was also a cuckoo in the Irish nest, the Protestants of Ulster, descendants of plantation. A degree of home rule they might have favoured, but they left no doubt they would fight Catholic supremacy in Dublin. The inner weakness of home rule was thus the inverse of its strength. Its lack of definition was an opportunity for some, but a source of division for others. Either way, the failure of home rule in 1886 reopened the well-worn and bloodstained path to yet another civil conflict on the British Isles. London's custodianship of its oldest empire was deaf and blind.

Killing home rule with 'kindness'

Policy on Ireland was now being formed at a climactic in British imperial power. Britain was globally dominant, its sovereignty unequalled and for the most part unchallenged. That it might be at risk was therefore unimaginable. There were plenty of voices warning of overreach, as from India, the Sudan and South Africa. An influential liberal, the Cambridge historian Sir John Seeley, wrote in *The Expansion of England* (1883) of the 'barbarism' of claiming that 'one community should be treated as the property of another . . . whether by conquest or otherwise'. There was no 'vast superiority of the English race'. Yet while Seeley intriguingly applied this warning to England's 'internal and external empires', his concern was exclusively with the latter. The internal empire was taken as secure.

Seeley's recognition of two English empires was rare. British authority was alert to constitutional diversity, if only because it was now ruling a multitude of peoples living inevitably under a variety of regimes. France's smaller empire was fashioned into a greater France, its overseas territories as *départements* of a central state and represented in the Paris assembly. For Britain one size could not possibly fit all.

Seeley's advocacy of diversity was realised on the ground by Lord Lugard (1858–1945), governor of Hong Kong and then Nigeria. He enunciated a concept of indirect rule fashioned to forms of native government already existing in individual colonies. Lugard was experienced in imperial administration and understood that Britain's army and civil service could not hold territories from which, at the end of the nineteenth century, it was deriving little if any profit at enormous cost. A believer in the civilising virtues of empire, he understood that they could work only if administered through indigenous rulers and power structures. Hence the empire's network of dominions, princely states and protectorates.

Although Burke and others had long advocated learning

Irish lessons from the loss of America, there were no lessons learned from Lugard's concept of indirect rule. With the fall of Parnell, London's Irish policy reverted to type. For Tories and Liberal Unionists, 'losing Ireland' would merely set a bad example for the empire elsewhere. The Liberal Unionist Joseph Chamberlain questioned why 'five million Irishmen have any greater right to govern themselves without regard to the rest of the United Kingdom than the five million inhabitants of the Metropolis'. It was classic imperial blindness.

In retrospect the United Kingdom Parliament during the Irish home rule crisis of the 1880s did come within shouting distance of attaining a federal constitution. Gladstone did not give up. As he aged, Ireland became an obsession that was said to consume half his waking hours. He returned briefly to power in 1892 and presented another home rule bill to Parliament. This time Liberal and Irish votes saw him through the Commons, but he was overruled by the Tories in the then hereditary House of Lords. Gladstone left office a year later and it was for the Tories under Lord Salisbury to lead Ireland into the new century.

Salisbury was not deaf to Irish demands. Two decades of land reform had proved insufficient to shift much ownership from English to Irish hands for the simple reason that few Irish farmers could afford to buy their freeholds. Further legislation was now enacted to allow the Dublin government to subsidise the purchase. This de facto land nationalisation was radical and remarkably successful. Big estates were broken up. Absentee landlordism collapsed. The government even built new cottages on acres allotted to landless labourers, a version of state crofting. In this manner, 310,000 Irish tenants bought their farms and more were rehoused, dotting the Irish countryside with identical cottages.

Almost half of all farms changed hands in a generation and Irish landownership went from under 10 per cent of farmers in the 1870 to an extraordinary 97 per cent by the 1920s. Within half a century of the famine, Ireland had been compensated with probably the most progressive land policy in Europe. As if in belated recognition that Scotland was being left out, London in 1886 passed a Crofters Act granting crofters similar rights to the Irish. This included security of tenure and fair rent arbitration, though it did not extend to subsidised purchase.

The Irish were now free of Anglican tithes, free of absentee landlordism and free to exercise the same franchise as the English. Foster concludes that 'by the turn of the twentieth century, English oppression manifested itself in ways that were historical and cultural rather than economic or political. Reforms in land tenure, taxation and local government had transformed Irish society, and a solid rural bourgeoisie was in place.' The Tories were said to have 'killed home rule with kindness'.

Irish reform was a classic of virtue postponed until too late. Had it been enacted under Grattan's Parliament in the 1790s or at the time of Parnell in the 1880s, Ireland would almost certainly have found its way to a peaceful federal concordat with England. As it was, by the turn of the century one rebel diarist, Liam de Róiste, spoke for many in writing that he had had enough. He did not care if Ireland was a monarchy, republic or socialist state, 'so long as it is freed from British rule'. Full independence and even republicanism now gained widespread appeal. Like partition movements everywhere, the cause of 'freedom' took on an emotional momentum that no warnings of economic doom and no offer of compromise from London could stem.

Easter 1916: the long goodbye

In the 1910 general election Herbert Asquith's Liberals came to power reliant on the Irish Parliamentary Party, and therefore unable to avoid a third home rule bill. This was initially vetoed by the House of Lords, but for once England's domestic politics came to Ireland's aid. The Lords had also blocked chancellor David Lloyd George's 'people's budget', a clearly intolerable veto on democracy. Such a veto had to be ended, and it was by the Parliament Act of 1911. Irish home rule was finally enacted in 1914. At last, and with the agreement of Parliament, Ireland had what it had so long desired, the right to govern its own people, albeit under the protective umbrella of the British crown.

A new disaster now struck. Implementation was postponed by the outbreak of the Great War and by fierce opposition from Ulster's Protestants, adamant that they would not be ruled by southern Catholics. In an echo of the Scots in 1643, a quarter of a million Ulster Protestants in 1912 signed a 'solemn league and covenant', this one declaring home rule by Dublin 'subversive of our civil and religious freedom, destructive of our citizenship and perilous to the unity of the Empire'. This was the same Ulster community that in 1791 had helped found the Society of United Irishmen against the collapse of Grattan's home rule.

Ulster Protestantism now pledged itself 'to use all means necessary' to forestall rule from Dublin. An Ulster Volunteer Force was formed to that end. A year later officers at a British army base at the Curragh in the south mutinied and said they would not fight against Ulster if ordered to do so. Meanwhile, the postponement of home rule put the Sinn Féin League and more shadowy Fenian bodies such as the Irish Republican Brotherhood (IRB) on the warpath. They did not trust Britain. Just as Wolfe Tone in 1798 had turned to Britain's enemies in France for assistance, so the IRB turned to its new adversary, Germany. A prominent former British diplomat allied to Sinn Féin, Roger Casement (1864–1916), held talks with the Germans and secured a promise of weapons. The republicans formed the Irish Volunteers to confront the Ulster Volunteers.

The outcome was a chaotic Dublin uprising at Easter 1916. Its leadership was divided and the German arms failed to arrive. Some 1,200 volunteers led by a fervent nationalist, Patrick Pearse, seized buildings in the city centre including the General Post Office, and for five days Pearse declared an Irish republic. However, the rebels failed to capture the government offices in Dublin Castle, the railway station or the port, and were soon overrun by newly arrived British reinforcements. Almost 500 people died, the majority being civilians caught in crossfire. The centre of Dublin was shelled and numerous buildings reduced to rubble, after which the republicans surrendered unconditionally. Sixteen of their leaders including Pearse were executed while 1,800 were imprisoned in England.

The rising had taken most Irish by surprise and did not initially enjoy wide support. The leader of the Irish MPs at Westminster, John Redmond, acknowledged the government's right to suppress it. But the executions, after two weeks of secret and procedurally irregular trials, generated an upsurge of anti-army and anti-British feeling. Criticism was raised even at Westminster, including from Asquith himself and from Ulster's champion, Edward Carson. The executions, the damage to Dublin and revelations of British atrocities against demonstrators undermined the government's cause. Yeats's poem 'Easter 1916' reflected an ambivalence towards the martyrs but ultimate support for their cause. He wrote, 'We know their dream; enough/ To know they dreamed and are dead'. These men 'Wherever green is worn,/ Are changed, changed utterly:/ A terrible beauty is born.'

With home rule already on the statute book, any hope of Britain retaining sovereignty over Ireland evaporated. The militant wing of Irish republicanism under Sinn Féin grew overnight from an extremist republican club to a mass party. There was no Irish plebiscite on a new constitution, on the monarchy or on any federal version of home rule. There was initially not even a negotiation. Instead Lloyd George, Asquith's successor as prime minister, lit a fuse of rage by announcing in early 1918, with the war still on, that conscription into the British army would include Ireland – then on the brink of independence.

The ballot box now took up the cry of 'England, be gone'. At the post-armistice 1918 'khaki' election to the UK Parliament, Ireland saw Sinn Féin win seventy-three of Ireland's 105 Westminster seats. The following month, in January 1919, these MPs met not in Westminster but in Dublin. There they declared themselves the Dáil Éireann, the parliament of a newly independent Ireland. Reporters were baffled when hardliners conducted much of the proceedings in Irish, resulting in nine-tenths of the assembly sitting in silence. A few hesitantly conversed in French. Eamon de Valera (1882–1975), a fighter in the 1916 uprising and an Irish language activist, became chief executive. The Dáil sent delegates to the Versailles peace conference, though only Lenin welcomed them.

The response of the British government to events in the Dáil was inexplicable. It had already conceded home rule and needed only to negotiate its introduction. Instead, it declared the Dáil illegal and sparked an immediate return to armed conflict. A new Irish Republican Army under the leadership of Michael Collins (1890–1922) mounted guerrilla attacks on British police, troops and installations and on Protestant targets in the north. The British government reacted with barely controlled violence. It deployed special police auxiliaries, mostly former soldiers from the trenches, known as Black and Tans from the colour of their uniforms.

The final Anglo-Irish war of independence (1919–22) imitated its predecessors. It saw summary executions, civilian punishment killings and the burning of the city centre of Cork. In one incident unionists drove an armoured car to a Gaelic football match and opened fire with a machine gun, killing a player and spectators. It was as if, in saying farewell to its Irish colony, London decided to reprise five centuries of repression.

Peace through partition

Only after a temporary ceasefire in mid-1921 did Lloyd George and de Valera finally meet in London. It was said that the latter formally addressed Lloyd George in Irish in the absence of an interpreter. Lloyd George duly replied to him in Welsh, conversing with his secretary Tom Jones and leaving de Valera baffled in turn. We thus glimpse the spectacle of the elected leaders of the two principal peoples of the British Isles, each addressing the other in a Celtic language which he could not understand. It is a vignette of the disintegration of the first English empire.

In December 1921 de Valera sent Collins to broker an independence treaty with Lloyd George. The treaty meant that Collins had to face down the more fanatical anti-treaty republicans by pleading what he called 'the duress of facts . . . the freedom to achieve freedom'. Most difficult was how to handle the seemingly insoluble problem of Ulster. To appease unionist opinion, six of Ulster's nine counties were eventually granted 'temporary' secession from the new state, representing roughly a third of Ireland's population. The border was to be fixed by a special commission.

Partition infuriated hard-line nationalists in the south, determined on becoming a republic, but by now the realpolitik was unarguable. A divided Ireland was the only way for all parties to accept a new treaty. The alternative was another Irish civil war. Collins declared himself 'absolutely against coercion: if Ulster is going to join us, it must be voluntary'. He also saw that Ulster in its present state could easily deny his new Ireland its stability. The north was Britain's creation and it should remain Britain's problem. He was right.

The following year, 1922, the so-called Irish Free State came into being, technically loyal to the crown and the Commonwealth and with an (Irish) governor-general in Dublin Castle. Britain had by then committed some 57,000 soldiers to a final struggle to retain control over its disintegrating corner of empire. The army staggered back to England, leaving Ireland to embark on what looked like a perilous and impecunious path to freedom.

Partition proved anything but temporary. The commission, intended to embrace all local Protestant communities, took years to reach a decision. The north's leadership under the implacable James Craig and supported by Carson and other unionists in London, was eager for Ulster to enjoy its own instant home rule. Even before peace in the south was finally agreed, 1921 saw the opening of a new Belfast parliament by George V personally. It was to be housed in a pompous 1930s classical palace on the hill of Stormont in a Belfast suburb. Unionist MPs at Westminster might declare Irish independence as leaving 'the British Empire doomed', but a portion of its oldest colony was left clinging to the raft, blessed with precisely the sort of provincial parliament London had for over a century denied to Ireland as a whole.

19

The Union Left Behind

The loss of Ireland to the United Kingdom was brushed aside by British public opinion, much as had been the loss of America a century and a half before. It was as if the issue had become boring. The question of Irish home rule had so towered over politics for decades that once it was answered the debate seemed over. *Hamlet* had lost its prince.

Home rule now went into decline, or at least was confined to addicts. During the surge in interest in the late 1800s, a Scottish Home Rule Association had been founded in 1886 by two future leaders of the Labour movement, Ramsay MacDonald and Keir Hardie. Its declared purpose was to 'secure a Scottish legislature for purely Scottish matters, maintain Scotland's position within the Imperial Parliament and foster national sentiment'. To MacDonald, 'the Anglification of Scotland has been proceeding apace, to the damage of its education, its music, its literature, its genius . . . uprooted from its past'. These fine words saw little action.

The same largely applied in Wales. Twenty-nine of its thirty-three Welsh MPs, formally Liberals, did form a Welsh sub-party within the parliamentary Liberal Party. They had an articulate leader in Tom Ellis and included among their number a youthful Caernarvon MP, David Lloyd George. Ellis was strident in supporting the Irish cause. 'The interests of Irishmen, Welshmen and Crofters [sic] are almost identical,' he said. 'Their past history is very similar and their present oppressors are the same.' There was no sign of the Irish returning the compliment. One commenter complimented the Welsh for 'rejecting political agitation and the grossest lawlessness'. But he pointed out that, when the Irish would summon a militant home rule rally, 'in Wales they hold an eisteddfod'.

In 1881 Gladstone did concede the Welsh a much-demanded ban on Sunday drinking, and in 1883 Wales was granted universities in Cardiff, Bangor and later Aberystwyth. Three years later a Welsh Land League promoted tenancy enfranchisement on the Irish model. At the same time, a band of London Welsh formed a proto-nationalist group named Cymru Fydd (Young Wales), with home rule as its goal. Like Morganwg's Gorsedd, its roots were expatriate and shallow.

Cymru Fydd should have occasioned, at very least, an upsurge of nationalist sentiment in Wales, but it was undermined by the old Welsh divisions. The South Wales Liberal Federation flatly refused to amalgamate with the north. When Lloyd George, a northerner, campaigned in Newport, Monmouthshire, in 1896, he was heckled by an Alderman Bird, who declared, 'There are from Swansea to Newport thousands upon thousands of Englishmen, as true Liberals as yourselves, who will never submit to the domination of Welsh ideas.' Lloyd George was furious, storming from Newport in disgust and devoting the rest of his career to national politics in London. Cymru Fydd collapsed within a decade.

The reality was that the left of the political spectrum, from which nationalist opinion had drawn most of its oxygen, was seeing the emergence of a new and different struggle. The conflict was between a declining Gladstonian Liberalism and forces arising from an expanded franchise and an increasingly well-organised trade union movement. Scotland's Labour Party was founded by R. B. Cunninghame Graham and Keir Hardie in 1888, with a strong independence stance. But within seven years it had merged with the pan-British Independent Labour Party. Class identity trumped national identity.

Wales was a special case. It had in the 1880s and 90s seen the growth of the Glamorgan coalfields at a rate that bore comparison with America's Klondike gold rush. The county became for a while the richest industrial centre in Britain, if not in Europe. Cardiff was the world's greatest port by tonnage. Cardiff Coal Exchange, built in 1883, reputedly played host to more millionaires than anywhere in the world. Cardiff's civic buildings erected at this time were, and still are, the finest in any British city.

The result was that Wales in the early 1900s was reputedly second only to America for net immigration. That is why Lloyd George's heckler and his 'thousands of English' did not seem out of place. Such industrialisation and prosperity did not sit comfortably with the quainter rituals of traditional Welsh identity. To the historian Kenneth Morgan, this was 'Wales's Augustan age', but nationalism 'seemed to be as dead as the druids'.

What was not dead was Welsh industrial politics. Any downturn in coal prices or other disruption to trade instigated serious labour unrest, as was seen in the mines in 1898 and 1910. There were also prolonged strikes in the slate quarries of north Wales, notably at Penrhyn in 1900. Wales thus offered an early welcome to the emergent Labour Party. Hardie, MacDonald and Arthur Henderson all deserted Scottish politics to find safe parliamentary seats in south Wales. When elected for Merthyr Tydfil in 1900, Hardie declared himself for 'the Red Dragon and the Red Flag'. It is a measure of the shift in Glamorgan's demography that he distributed his election literature in English.

What these newcomers did not do was identify as specifically Welsh. They had no trouble adapting to the Welsh passion for music, Nonconformity and the Labour Party, but they felt no obligation to learn the Welsh language, nor were they infused with any desire for Welsh independence. Labour did later flirt with home rule in its 1918 election manifesto, when Henderson as party general secretary wrote an article supporting 'home rule all round'. But political reality held that a divided Britain was not in the interest of working-class solidarity. John Davies noted that Labour's 'role was to consolidate the process of integrating the Welsh into the British system'. In this respect it was as unionist ideologically as were the Tories.

Home rule in abeyance

The lesson of 1918–21 in Ireland was not entirely ignored. In 1918 a group of pragmatic Tory MPs professed themselves 'deeply impressed by the need for a far-reaching system of federal devolution for the United Kingdom'. The declaration of Irish independence in 1921 raised the cause of Scottish home rule but from an insignificant base. A Scottish National League was founded by a romantic aristocrat with a love of Gaelic, Ruaraidh (Rory) Erskine of Marr (1869–1960). This mutated into the Scottish National Party in 1934, with its initial presidents the Duke of Montrose and Cunninghame Graham. The cause was chiefly ensconced in the minds of romantics such as the Lallans poet Hugh MacDiarmid. He wrote grandly that 'He canna Scotland see wha yet/ canna see the Infinite,/ And Scotland in true scale to it'. The novelist MP John Buchan told the Commons in 1932 that 'every Scotsman should be a nationalist', but he acknowledged that this amounted to 'a desire that Scotland shall not lose her historic personality'. As for Wales, an attempt in 1922 to hold a conference on Welsh devolution – in Shrewsbury – failed utterly. Glamorgan refused to send even one delegate.

Welsh and Scottish radicalism now went in one direction, into the rise of Labour. Here the dominant issue of the day was the industrial struggle of miners, railwaymen and dockers, drawing its strength from collectivity, from acting together across national boundaries. After initial ideological conflicts, discipline in the Labour Party was strong. Just as trade union power depended on unity, so did that of the party. It had little time for borders or the inherent divisiveness of nationalists.

On entering Downing Street as prime minister, first in 1924 and again in 1929, Ramsay MacDonald made no move to honour his earlier enthusiasm for Scottish home rule. Lloyd George's successor as hero of Welsh politics, Aneurin Bevan, was equally emphatic. According to his biographer 'any form of devolution would draw Wales away from the mainstream of British politics . . . and be a blow to the unity of the British working class'.

Trade union solidarity led to widespread industrial turbulence culminating in the General Strike of 1926, for which support was particularly solid in South Wales. World coal prices collapsed and mining unemployment went from 1.8 per cent in 1924 to 28 per cent a year after the strike. The subsequent Great Depression (1929–32) hit Glamorgan hardest, as it was by then almost wholly dependent on coal, new reserves of which were opening up across Europe and America. Even with economic recovery, the Welsh jobless rate rose to a devastating 43 per cent. In the 1920s and 1930s, for the first time Wales's population fell as some 400,000 people emigrated. The Klondike days were over.

The emotional impact of the Depression on Wales was intense, etched deeper into the recollections of my Welsh grandparents than its impact on industrial Yorkshire or Lancashire. One preacher described Wales as covered by 'the ashes of Vesuvius'. In addition, Wales found someone to blame, the ancient foe, the English and English capitalism. This in turn drove local politicians to the demolition of Europe's most dramatic industrial architecture, that of the Merthyr valley. Yet even this did not stir the flames of nationalism. They rather stoked an adamant anti-Toryism. Labour's sixteen Glamorgan valley seats were to remain its most solid anywhere in Britain.

What sort of nationalisation?

The first majority Labour government that took office in 1945 was unlikely to champion devolution of any sort. Its vision of welfare socialism was that of a centralised state administering services through public corporations without local variation. The concept of what would today be called a postcode lottery was to be the scourge of British localism down to the present day. Measures not just for welfare but for all forms of public service had to be uniform across the union. The language was not that of socialisation but of 'nationalisation', and the nation was one Britain.

The 1945 government was the most emphatically unionist ever seen. Edward I would have been proud to see the English empire reborn. Labour's manifesto had deplored any concession to 'sectional interest'. The historian David Edgerton describes a regime enveloping every public service and institution – the 'commanding heights of the economy' – in a state ownership that would eventually embrace mines, railways, docks, hospitals, airlines, shipbuilding, oil, cars and even computer manufacture. To Bevan in 1951 a one-nation Britain had assumed 'the moral leadership of the world', and as such was the 'only one hope for mankind'. When a suggestion was made for a minister for Welsh affairs, Bevan called it 'escapism' and Attlee's chancellor, Stafford Cripps, was adamant that, even if just from 'the point of view of efficiency . . . it would be wrong'. Churchill later agreed, putting Welsh affairs under the Home Office.

County and county borough councils were the only tier of democratic government allowed to the Welsh or Scots. Secretaries of state appointed for Scotland (in 1885) and Wales (in

1965) did offer a nod towards Edinburgh and Cardiff, but their offices were firmly in Whitehall under the eye of the Treasury. Nationalism was tossed the occasional sop, a Welsh television channel or sports grant. The chief burden on English ministers allotted to Wales was having to learn – and sing – the Welsh national anthem.

British politics focused on Westminster was everywhere based on centrally organised parties. Their members were subject to national party discipline and received party patronage accordingly. Tory, Liberal and Labour parties contested virtually all Welsh and Scottish constituencies. While the Conservative Party was explicitly 'unionist', Labour was effectively so, if only through deriving much of its parliamentary strength from its Scottish and Welsh MPs. Scots ministers were prominent in both Tory and Labour cabinets.

Only Northern Ireland remained unchanged – and strangely unmentioned in British constitutional discussions. Stormont was detached from Westminster and highly federal in its remit. Local politics remained entrenched in the old religious divides. Attempts to form a Northern Irish Labour Party were abandoned in 1987. Domestic affairs were for Belfast to decide. No one thought it odd that Scotland and Wales were not entitled to follow suit. Nor was there any sign of a bond between the Scots and Welsh with Northern Ireland on the possible fashioning of a federal agenda.

Language was the one political issue grasped, at least by Welsh nationalists, as the most obvious token of identity in the absence of political devolution. Across Europe rural depopulation was driving minority languages to extinction, with Sami, Frisian, Tatar and Ruthenian among others confined to ever more isolated communities. Of British languages, Irish had by the 1950s dwindled to the Aran Islands and a few western villages heavily subsidised by the government. Scots Gaelic survived among similar groups of islanders in the Hebrides.

Cornish was long gone, while the last Manx speaker died in 1974. Only in Wales did the flame of language still flicker as a political issue.

As we have seen, it had survived principally on the prosperity and continuity of Welsh rural communities. By 1926 the proportion of the population claiming to be Welsh-speaking had fallen to a third, increasingly confined to the west and north. But this decline had stirred a minor nationalist revival in 1925. The initiators were a minister and language activist, Lewis Valentine, and a Liverpool-born writer, Saunders Lewis, who together founded a new party called Plaid Cymru.

The Welsh title was intended to focus on the Welsh language not just for its own sake but as a weapon against English 'dominion'. This was a risk. Lewis declared that language was 'the only political question deserving of a Welshman's attention' and was 'alone consistent with the aims and philosophy of Welsh nationalism'. This was greeted with hostility from non-Welsh speakers, who did not like the implication that they were not really Welsh, or that language was their only weapon against Englishness. This especially applied to the English-speakers of Glamorgan.

Valentine stood for Caernarvon at the 1929 election but failed to secure even 2 per cent of the vote. Saunders Lewis had little concern for politics, rather with 'taking away from the Welsh their sense of inferiority – to remove from our beloved country the mark and shame of conquest'. Lewis was not ideal for this task. A Catholic convert and early fan of Hitler, he spent much of his time demanding to be allowed to speak Welsh on the BBC.

As for enforcing Welsh in schools, Lewis confronted the same problem as had O'Connell in nineteenth-century Ireland. Among rural working-class communities, not to speak English was a barrier to advancement. By imitating the Irish Gaelic League and making language – a difficult language – an obsessive symbol of identity, Plaid Cymru distracted attention from the issue of devolution generally. The party was regularly bought off with grants to Welsh-speaking projects, while the firm hand of Whitehall became ever more dominant in Welsh national government.

Even Wales's writers seemed unmoved. Its finest twentieth-century poets, Dylan Thomas and R. S. Thomas, were devoid of nationalist romanticism. Both wrote in English. Dylan Thomas's sympathetic account of *Under Milk Wood* was of a charming but trapped and introverted people. 'As for the land of my fathers,' he added, 'my fathers can keep it.' To R. S. Thomas, who served as a village vicar in north Wales, 'There is no present in Wales,/ And no future:/ Only the past,/ Brittle with relics . . . an impotent people,/ Sick with inbreeding,/ Worrying the carcase of an old song.' It was a savage image of an ailing nation.

20

A Celtia of Sorts

A modern state in embryo

To pan-Celticists the year 1922 should have been one of triumph. The ideal of 'autonomy for small nations' was cited by the American president Woodrow Wilson in his 1918 programme for a new League of Nations. Under the 1919 Treaty of Versailles, new and revived states were springing into life across Europe, from the Baltics and Poland to Czechoslovakia, Hungary and the Balkans. Boundary commissions were crawling across the landscape, seeking to determine the allegiance of villages and towns to new governments. Leaders born of war had to mutate into leaders for peace. Their domains might have been conceived in violence but they must set violence aside in the cause of unity.

Britain's reluctant contribution to this movement was Ireland, a gift bequeathed bruised, divided and desperately poor, still notionally a Commonwealth dominion of the crown. For two years on either side of independence, pro- and anti-treaty factions fought each other, both in Dublin politics and within IRA factions on the streets. When Collins was assassinated by anti-treaty rebels in August 1922, Ireland lost its ablest leader since Parnell. Desultory fighting continued, with atrocities exchanged between Catholics and Protestants in Belfast. By the time of ceasefire in 1923 some 2,000 Irish had died by Irish hands.

In 1926 de Valera made a critical stabilising move. He

severed himself from Sinn Féin and founded a new party, Fianna Fáil. This established a formal parliamentary opposition to the governing Fine Gael and was probably crucial in keeping Irish politics off the streets through the remaining interwar years. Whatever debate was to take place on Ireland's future, it should be by representatives of the Irish electorate in peaceful conclave. De Valera took power from Fine Gael in 1932. First as prime minister and then as president, he was for thirty years the dominant figure in consolidating the new state. In 1937 he changed Ireland's name to Éire. In 1948, to Britain's fury, it left the Commonwealth and became simply the Republic of Ireland.

At the time of independence the border with the six counties of Ulster saw customs huts erected and duties imposed on all goods except for farm produce along what was a 300-mile boundary. These remained in place until the UK and Ireland both joined the European Economic Community in 1973. Partition now saw a gradual separation of Catholics from Protestants within Northern Ireland, driving it towards a de facto apartheid state. This further fuelled communal tension. One Catholic family living in a prosperous suburb of Belfast kept a car ready and permanently packed in their garage, to leave for the south 'in the case the Prods come for us'.

Probably Britain's most valuable donation to Dublin was virtually unseen. It was the leaving in place of the old Irish civil service, especially those administering the nation's finances. Ireland began independence as one of the poorest countries of Europe. Its economy was mostly agricultural and its productivity low, estimated at half that of similarly sized Denmark. The island's only substantial industry, engineering and shipbuilding in Belfast, was now on 'foreign' territory. The economic outlook was bleak.

The cold wind of fiscal reality was greeted with fierce conservatism from the Dublin bureaucracy. In the final years of

British rule, the Irish had been benefiting from the state pensions and unemployment pay introduced by Lloyd George. Ireland on its own could not afford them and officials advised austerity. The pension was cut by a shilling a week and wages and unemployment pay were frozen. When strikes broke out in 1922, former IRA units were deployed by the new government to suppress them. Each austerity measure was introduced into the Dáil as 'paying the price of independence'.

With 1920s inflation rampant across Europe, Collins, briefly finance minister in 1921, had been desperate that his new state should win a reputation for sound money. Before independence, he had been working from a private house, even succeeding in raising an international loan backed by gold hidden under its floorboards, some of which was lent to Russian revolutionaries in return for Tsarist jewels. These in turn were hidden in a chimney. Collins's legacy lasted even after his death. Throughout the interwar years, the Irish state maintained a tight monetary policy with a sound international credit rating.

Where Ireland held up its head was overseas. It appointed ambassadors and was active in the League of Nations, de Valera even becoming the League's president and a champion of neutralism. He was assiduous in maintaining a public hostility to Britain, though he kept doors open for a de facto alliance. In particular he needed co-operation over residual Irish debts to Britain and over the future of British sovereign ports.

Push came to shove with the outbreak of the Second World War, a conflict known as 'the Emergency' in Ireland. It evoked every kind of Irish ambivalence. Dublin's self-described 'pro-British neutrality' located behind Britain's maritime front line was to London insecure. Northern Ireland was British territory, its coasts guarding the northern approaches. Dublin was thought to be teeming with German spies, despite some 42,000 Irish soldiers having departed to serve in the British army. When Belfast docks were bombed by the Germans during the

Blitz, the south sent fire engines to its aid – de Valera declaring, 'these are our people'. Conversely, his signing of the German embassy book of condolences on Hitler's death appalled British opinion.

The search for an Irish identity

If the Irish were Gaels, they were first and foremost Catholic Gaels. Though the church was not mentioned in the 1922 constitution, a draft had declared 'that the true religion is that established by Our Lord Jesus Christ' and that it was 'the Catholic Church'. This phraseology caused de Valera much trouble, not least when it was revealed that it had been vetted, if not actually written, by the Vatican. The phraseology was not just sectarian, it negated any hope of Irish reunification. The measure was amended in favour of the church having a 'special position', which the pope diplomatically 'did not approve and did not disapprove'.

At first the Catholic clergy enjoyed a virtual veto on social and educational policy. Divorce and abortion were banned, working mothers were discouraged and literary censorship introduced. The church retained control over state education 'in Catholic schools by Catholic teachers under Catholic control'. Teachers were mostly clergy. Monasteries and convents also supplied much of social welfare, often in institutions whose behaviour and conditions were to shock later generations. But while Catholics continued to suffer discrimination in the north, Protestants rarely did in the south. They remained prominent in Dublin's professional establishment, though numbers declined with continuing emigration. Just 7 per cent of the south was declared Protestant by 1930.

Ireland in 1945, after two decades of wrestling with independence, was still enduring severe economic hardship. It received £150 million in post-war Marshall Aid and its government benefited from assistance from London on trade alignment, loans and migration. But when London's Labour government blessed Belfast in the north with its 'cradle-to-grave' welfare state, Dublin could not possibly follow suit. Throughout the 1950s and 60s increasing divergence in living standards between the south and the north weakened the southern economy and led to continued migration to the north and to Britain. The old Irish curse still applied: the brightest and best left home. In 1961, four decades after independence, southern Ireland's population hit a new low of 2.8 million, having roughly halved over fifty years during which populations across Europe had been rising. The cause of independence was not prospering.

An economic corner began to be turned with the 1958 Whitaker Report advocating a shift to state interventionism. Its aim was forcefully to move the country from an agricultural economy to an industrial one. Crucial to this was assistance from the International Monetary Fund and, in 1973, Irish membership of the then European Economic Community. The EEC opened Ireland to foreign loans and freer trade with Europe. The Dublin government responded with exceptionally low levels of corporate and personal taxation. Gradually, the impact of these innovations took hold. By the mid-1970s some 350 foreign firms had set up shop in Ireland. Net emigration ceased and the population moved back above 3 million.

As part of this process of reinvention, Ireland sought to free itself of the grasp of the Catholic church, whose authority over education and social welfare still had widespread support. A 1962 poll showed 87 per cent of Irish citizens saying they would support the church in any clash with the state. The government now devoted an exceptional one-third of its EEC structural funds to state education, drawing secondary schools away from church control and expanding universities.

In the 1960s Irish student numbers doubled, and for once

Irish graduates did not automatically seek to leave Ireland. The Protestant Trinity College Dublin even became fashionable for students from England. At last Ireland began to emerge from the torpor so often associated with post-colonial status. Half a century of independence at last gave it the muscles of economic manoeuvre, the strength of true autonomy.

The reborn Ireland also had little time for the nuances of Gaelic identity and gradually came to feel it did not require them. It knew and needed to know only that it was not English. None the less, in intellectual quarters independence initially yielded a mild identity crisis. As if by instinct, the 1921 settlement and its surrounding conflict had recalled symbols of an old Ireland. The Dáil was filled with alumni of the 1890s Gaelic League and its leaders were quick to demand primacy for the national language. Even if few spoke Irish, an independent Ireland should surely assert itself by speaking 'its own native tongue'. This would wipe out Matthew Arnold's gibe that Irish was 'the badge of a defeated race'.

To demand that all Irish now learn what was virtually an alien tongue seemed absurdly exclusive, another burden to add to that of economic self-sufficiency. It demonstrated the gulf that had arisen between the Gaelic-speaking leaders of the revolution and the mass of Irish people. In the 1911 census 17 per cent of the population claimed to speak Irish, but this was almost entirely on the isolated west coast.

None the less, lessons in Irish were made compulsory in schools and every child was expected to pass an exam in the language, notably if they wanted government employment. Educational documents sought 'to revive the ancient life of Ireland as a Gaelic state, Gaelic in language and Gaelic and Christian in its ideals'. The Gaeltacht – the Gaelic-speaking areas of the west – were designated a linguistic reservation and showered with money. The word was always Gaelic, never Celtic.

The project was severely hampered by a lack of Irish-language teachers. The Catholic church had long been English-speaking, but its eagerness to retain a dominant role in education made it supportive of the language project. Parents and pupils alike, the true victims of the policy, were almost totally opposed. Teaching was further complicated by Irish's impenetrable spelling, invented by academic orthographers but incomprehensible to non-speakers. I came across one spelling of the Irish word for 'bear' as *beirbhiughadh* and 'lament' as *beochaoineadh*. The prime minister was pronounced 'teesoc' but spelled *taoiseach*. To conservatives, the spelling was the essence of Irish subtlety; to others, it was a further obstacle to learning an already difficult tongue. Some reform did take place – 'bear' became *beiriú* – but nothing better illustrated elitist Gaelic obscurantism than the refusal of its champions to reform its spelling. Romantics might see the Irish tongue as a token of rebellion, the one-time voice of a 'not-English' peasant class. But England had gone and an Irish-speaking peasantry with it. The point had been made. Irish was becoming the private language of a Dublin mandarinate.

In 1988 a Dublin Education Board report admitted defeat. It stated that, given 'changes in Irish society . . . the previous mobilising rhetorics do not operate in the same way or as effectively as in the past'. The reality was that 'the symbolic significance attached to Irish as an official emblem' was not reflected by the 'vernacular in everyday life'. Compulsory Irish was also a deterrent to what was now being accepted as an absolute economic necessity – immigration. Compulsion should therefore end and learning Irish should be a matter of personal choice, in effect a hobby. It was an intriguing lesson in nationalist psychology. When its objectives had been achieved, its authoritarian disciplines could relax.

By the 1926 census just 18 per cent of the population claimed, dubiously, to have some Irish – a tiny increase on the

1911 figure. A later generation of compulsorily educated meant that by the 2016 census 40 per cent of respondents claimed an 'ability' in Irish, but just 1.7 per cent used the language on a daily basis. Activists scored occasional victories, such as reserving new housing in Connemara for Irish speakers.

Irish as a language remained a political issue where 'mobilising rhetorics' still applied, most significantly in the north. Here Sinn Féin encouraged adherents to learn Irish as a mark of loyalty. Later, during the troubles, inmates of Northern Ireland's Maze prison took Irish lessons and the prison came to be dubbed the 'jailtacht'. Belfast's Catholic Falls Road neighbourhood was even bizarrely designated a Gaeltacht area in 2018. Today, Irish-medium schools exist in both Belfast and Londonderry, against fierce Protestant resistance.

In the same way that Irish was coming to seem a relic of past conflicts, so too was Ireland's national anthem, 'Amhrán na bhFiann', 'The Soldier's Song'. It was a battle cry of Irish rebellion associated with Sinn Féin's early campaigns. It told the 'Sons of the Gael! Men of the Pale! . . . See in the east a silvery glow/ Out yonder waits the Saxon foe/ So chant a soldier's song'. The anthem had long been controversial for its outdated belligerence, a problem eased by many trying to sing it in phonetic Irish translation. Since 1995 it has often been replaced by an anodyne song 'Ireland's Call', particularly in such all-Ireland games as rugby.

The Tiger roars

The innovations made to Ireland's economic policy in the 1970s and 80s were startlingly successful. The term 'Celtic Tiger' was coined by Kevin Gardiner in a Morgan Stanley market report in 1994, suggesting that Ireland was mimicking the 'Asian Tiger' economies of Singapore, Hong Kong, South Korea and Taiwan. Why it was called Celtic is a mystery. It did not refer to any country other than Ireland, while the Irish did not refer to themselves as Celts.

Dublin was now aggressively marketing itself as a hub of the new and bracing international capitalism. It offered a base for business with minimal corporate and personal taxes, attracting European headquarters for such mammoths of the digital age as Microsoft, Apple, Amazon and Dell. By the 1990s Ireland was registering the fastest growth rates in the EU. Unemployment fell from 18 per cent in 1990 to 4.5 per cent in 2007. Immigration turned into a rush, and Dublin property prices soared.

Largely through the residency of big American corporations, Ireland now contrived to appear on lists of the 'world's richest countries' as measured in gross domestic product per head. The international cyber-economy was swirling through the ether, touching down wherever a quick-witted finance minister might give it floor space or a nameplate. Immigration was such that, soon, 10 per cent of Ireland's residents were born outside its shores. The economy matured from tax haven to serious manufacturing base for electronics, pharmaceuticals and processed foods, even if 70 per cent of new plant was American owned. By the end of the 1990s Ireland was producing 50 per cent of Europe's packaged digital products.

The Celtic Tiger was the subject of much controversy. To some it was mere froth, robbing its EU neighbours of tax revenue to garner a thin layer of speculative cash. To others it was laying aside the British incubus, allowing Irish self-rule to give full rein to home-grown enterprise and initiative. What was incontrovertible to those who had known Ireland in the 1970s was that it had become unrecognisable. In 2004 a much-trumpeted accolade from *The Economist* proclaimed Ireland to have 'the best quality of life in the world'. This was ahead of Norway and Switzerland, with Britain down at twenty-ninth. The Irish novelist Colm Tóibín remarked that 'the Word was no longer made flesh, it was made a set of astonishing statistics'.

In 1990 the election as Irish president of the civil rights activist Mary Robinson gave the Tiger a human face, and a secular one. The Catholic church was already losing its authority as well as its political status. Attendance at Mass fell from 85 per cent of adults in 1990 to under 60 per cent within a decade. Reforms came, albeit slowly, to contraception, divorce and homosexuality. Over it all hung the emerging shame of what the church's historian Derek Scally called its 'catastrophic failures of sexual and institutional abuse', which left Ireland's welfare services sorely in need of what he suggested should be 'a truth and reconciliation commission'.

The new state still had problems aplenty. Breakneck expansion slowed. In 2001 the governor of the Bank of Ireland, Maurice O'Connell, announced that 'the Celtic Tiger is over', while pockets of both urban and rural poverty remained. OECD figures showed the Gini coefficient, the gap between the richest citizens and the poorest, was well above the European average. The impact of EU grants was also mixed, blighting the Irish countryside with squalid half-built developments in the manner of Sicily. Dublin saw swathes of Georgian and Victorian buildings smashed to the ground. A Dublin planner told me that Georgian buildings were 'just the last relics of England' and had no place in a new Ireland. The truth was quick profit and an Irish blindness to townscape beauty.

Ireland was badly hit by the economic recession of 2008–9, when unemployment surged to 14 per cent. A financial crisis led to an IMF rescue of €85 billion and resulting austerity, with the nation's quality-of-life index diving from fifth to forty-first place. In the event the recession proved a blip and the economy recovered after 2010, though net disposable income in 2019 remained below the OECD average. The Tiger lived, but on a reduced diet.

Whatever the statistics foretold, what was undeniable was that southern Ireland had been transformed within two decades from being a minority contributor to its island's economy compared with the north to contributing ten times more in industrial output and fifteen times more in export value. Dublin's population had risen from 526,000 in 1980 to approaching a million four decades later. Net emigration from the south – endemic for two centuries – all but ceased. Ireland was now able to keep its talent.

A survey prepared for InterTradeIreland in 2013 looked back over a quarter-century and compared 'current industrial structures' north and south of the border. It found the south showing 'dynamism, export openness, attraction of foreign direct investment, intensity of R&D, patenting and SME innovation'. The north, on the other hand, suffered from 'industrial restructuring and social unrest . . . its economy is relatively more dependent on the public sector'.

Irish independence had come at the price of half a century of hard times, but its essence, self-government, had been vindicated. No Irish person of my acquaintance hankers after reunion with England. The tiger metaphor might be glib, but it rebutted the caricature of a 'Celtic' people genetically workshy, immersed in nostalgia and unsuited to self-government. At an end were Trevelyan's useless Celts compared with the 'orderly, moral, industrious and frugal' Anglo-Saxons, a caricature finally drowned in the mud of a Fermanagh bog.

The dreary steeples of the north

The 2015 DNA survey of the People of the British Isles identified ten Irish clusters. Seven in the south were overwhelmingly of 'Gaelic Irish ancestry'. The northern counties were quite different. One-third of their population was like the south – broadly identified with the Catholic population – while two-thirds fell into two groups. One shared links with those living across the Irish Sea in western Scotland, echoing the ancient Dalriadan diaspora. The others were descendants of the plantation from the Scottish Lowlands and England. Elsewhere in the British Isles such genetic differences might have vanished into the warp and weft of migration, intermarriage and political accommodation. This had not happened in Northern Ireland.

Whether the 1922 partition could have been avoided is now academic. Collins had known that the north would have been an intolerable challenge to his new state. De Valera had disagreed. To him, Ulster was 'an accident arising out of the British connection and which will disappear with it'. He even boasted of the Gaelic ancestry of many Protestant leaders. At the fiftieth anniversary of the Easter Rising in 1966, he declared Ulster to be 'the land of the O'Neills, the Ó'Cathains, the Mac-Donells, the Maguires, and the MacGuinnesses'. Surely they could be one happy family again?

In practice, it was not to be. Churchill after the First World War had remarked that, even 'as the whole map of Europe has been changed . . . as the waters fall short, we see the dreary steeples of Fermanagh and Tyrone emerging once again. The integrity of their quarrel is one of the few institutions unaltered in the catachysm which has swept the world.' This graphic depiction remained as true after the Second World War as after the first. England might feel it had washed its hands of Ireland. A 'home ruled' north could bury its own dead. But Churchill's quarrel was still England's legacy and England's responsibility. It remained the unfinished business of English imperialism. The Ulster poet Seamus Heaney portrayed the north as the bastard child of an English rape, a 'boom burst from within [that] sprouted an obstinate fifth column/ Whose stance is growing unilateral.' That fifth column was Catholic militancy.

By the 1960s the province was one of the most divided communities in Europe. It was supposedly a prize exhibit of home rule. London showered it with privileges previously denied to Catholic Ireland as a whole. The north had its own parliament, yet with equal representation in Westminster, a status denied to the Scots and the Welsh. It received a lavish annual 'subvention' and a commitment from London not to interfere in its internal policies, however archaic and divisive. It taught creationism in its schools and banned abortion. It perpetuated Protestant discrimination against the Catholic minority, making no moves to bring the communities together. Religion continued to determine admission to public housing, education and public-sector jobs.

Money did not buy harmony. While southern Ireland enjoyed an economic dawn, Northern Ireland slid into greater dependency on London. The province's core shipbuilding and linen industries went into decline. Since jobs in the former were largely confined to Protestants, this led to a build-up of resentment when any concessions were made to Catholics. Parts of Belfast and Londonderry where communities had previously been mixed now divided into separate zones, often with violent overnight evictions.

In the 1960s the IRA, now 'provisional' in the north, re-emerged as putative defenders of the Catholic interest. Over against it was a revived Protestant Ulster Volunteer Force. In the winter of 1968/9 tension exploded in battles between Catholics and the police in Londonderry, spreading to Belfast. In 1971 a Protestant preacher and demagogue, Ian Paisley, founded a new Democratic Unionist Party. In speeches of rabble-rousing power – I heard him mesmerise a freezing crowd in the rain on a Stormont hillside – he fashioned himself as a defender 'to the death' of Protestant majority rule. He was to be its unofficial champion for forty years.

These warning signs should have led to instant action from London. As it was, the British government did little to defuse the growing confrontation. All it did was form a reservist

Ulster Defence Regiment to aid the police, fuelling the flames. Street hostilities continued for four years into 1972, with civilian murders, kneecapping and retaliation. Gradually, the local constabulary lost control and the British army was drawn into policing the conflict, almost always a prelude to disaster. In January 1972 disaster occurred with the so-called Bloody Sunday massacre by British paratroops of fourteen unarmed Catholics. It was a sickening rerun of past Anglo-Irish wars, with IRA retaliation carried over into 'mainland Britain'. The IRA declared quaintly that they would not commit terrorist incidents in Wales or Scotland, as they 'stood with their Celtic brothers'.

Northern Ireland's devolved government, in being since 1921, now collapsed and Belfast fell under 'direct rule' from London. This led in turn to the Sunningdale Agreement of 1973, whereby the cabinet of Edward Heath agreed with Dublin a power-sharing executive in the north and a 'consultative' council of all Ireland. This structure failed largely through militant unionist opposition whipped up by Paisley. The moderate unionist first minister Brian Faulkner stood down and provincial politics fled to the extremes.

Northern Ireland now stumbled through a quarter-century of failed devolution, ruled sometimes from Stormont and sometimes by a London secretary of state resident in Hillsborough Castle. Hapless British ministers traipsed to Belfast like imperial apprentices with retinues in tow, all painfully inexperienced and at a loss as to what to do. Every dispute was soothed with money. Two-thirds of the Northern Irish population was working for the government or under its patronage. One home secretary, Reginald Maudling, returned from a visit and remarked to an aide, 'Get me a large Scotch. What a bloody awful country.' He seemed unaware it was his responsibility.

Direct rule was rolling chaos. Northern Ireland's democratic institutions, relieved of any job to do, became a display of polarised intransigence. Money seemed to subsidise division. Millions of pounds in grants were wasted on a dodgy American carmaker named DeLorean. Housing was ever more segregated, as were schools. Back in the 1960s a third of housing estates were mixed Protestant/Catholic. By the 1980s direct rule had reduced that proportion below 10 per cent. Britain was the only country in Europe where a government practised and financed religious apartheid, even as it lectured the rest of the world on such evils.

Emblems of division

In the 1980s, at conferences of the British-Irish Association and the Freiburg Institute for Advanced Studies, I would listen to Northern Ireland being grouped with South Africa and Israel/Palestine as implacably divided societies. Across Europe, the conflicts within the Christian faith that historically split nations apart might have left symbolic relics and fine buildings, but few left raw political wounds. Europe's Catholics and Protestants, torn asunder by the Reformation, had shown they could live together and govern together. They moved on. Only in Northern Ireland does such religious antipathy have a lasting reality. Foreign participants at these conferences were baffled that, in liberal Britain, Catholics should be unable to live alongside Protestants.

To visit the north during what came to be called 'the troubles' was to sense a people imprisoned by history, yet unsure of their jailers. The most public witness to this imprisonment was the erection of cynically entitled 'peace walls' between Catholic and Protestant neighbourhoods. These involved the emptying of whole streets and turning parts of inner Belfast and other towns into war zones. At the height of the troubles there were thirty-seven such walls in the province, a figure that by the 1990s had risen to eighty. These remain. In the Short Strand area of Belfast, Catholics put up Palestinian flags to vie with Israeli ones put up by Protestants. Local police stations and army barracks became fortresses of steel and barbed wire.

Cities everywhere have their divided communities, their outbreaks of gang violence and signs of communal collapse. But rarely on this scale and with this depth of hatred. When I walk the two-storey walls that divides the Catholic Falls and Protestant Shankill districts of Belfast, I see them festooned with the tribal symbols of an antique conflict. Round them lies a rubble of stones, weeds and barbed wire, an obscenity now witnessed by silent coachloads of grim-faced tourists and watchful minders. Is it possible to call this a United Kingdom?

Part Four

Rebirth of the Nations

21

A Tale of Four Parliaments

Identity gods and centralist demons

Most of the world's armed conflicts at the end of the twentieth century were internal to states, generated by the same issues of centralised authority, subnational identity and devolution that I have discussed in this book. Boundaries fixed since the Second World War had begun to fray. The collapse of the Soviet Union in 1989 saw old borders re-emerge and new nationalisms take shape. Within Europe, the EU's march towards 'ever closer union' lost its magnetism. The splintering of Yugoslavia in the 1990s and the partition of Czechoslovakia in 1993 echoed the historian Norman Davies's recall of Europe's *Vanished Kingdoms*, of Aragon, Burgundy, Etruria and Celtic-speaking Galicia and Strathclyde.

New regional parties sprang to life in Spain, Italy, France and Germany, adept at exploiting identities and grievances long thought dead. Separatist voices were heard from Basques, Catalans, Corsicans, Montenegrins and Kosovans. Many sought to follow in the steps of Luxembourg, Andorra and Monaco into micro-statehood. To the EU's twenty-four official languages – including Irish – another sixty minority tongues stepped forward to demand recognition. France alone registered twenty-five languages and Poland eight.

Amid this swirl of identities, 'Celt' nowhere featured. Terms such as 'Celtic fringe' and 'Celtic politics' did occur as a shorthand for what was still a declining 13 per cent of the United

Kingdom's population. In the conservative realm of soccer, Scotland, Wales and Northern Ireland retained 'national' status denied to Basques or Bavarians, but no one thought of forming a Celtic team. This did not prevent argument over whether a 'united' Olympics team should be called TeamGB or TeamUK. To its credit, Irish rugby football operated on an all-Ireland basis.

With the end of the twentieth century, the surviving nations of the United Kingdom lost some of their glue. The early signs were modest. In Wales, the creation of Plaid Cymru in the 1920s had been all but stillborn, the party surviving after the war as a small Welsh-speaking association. In 1966 its leader, Gwynfor Evans, won a by-election in Carmarthen, largely in reaction to the flooding of a Gwynedd village, Tryweryn, for a Liverpool reservoir. His party went on to win a scattering of local council seats and for a while gain control of Merthyr Tydfil. In Scotland, the SNP had won a by-election in 1945 but remained equally inconspicuous. In 1967 the maverick Winnie Ewing won a by-election in Hamilton on an independence platform. 'Stop the world,' she declared, 'Scotland wants to get on.'

These by-elections did produce a nervous twitch in the two main parties. At the 1970 general election, Labour went so far as to promise the Welsh and Scots their own devolved assemblies. The party lost the election but the victorious Tories took the message and set up a commission on the constitutional status of the two countries. The Kilbrandon Commission reported in 1973 with a mish-mash of options and minority reports, proposing referendums on the new assemblies.

The Kilbrandon Report was a damp squib, not helped by the prime minister and MP for Cardiff in 1976, Jim Callaghan, clearly opposing any devolution to Wales. He took what his biographer, Kenneth Morgan, called 'the traditional Labour view of endorsing a nationwide approach to social and economic planning and regarding devolution as a dangerous concession to parochial Celtic nationalism'. Callaghan was firmly in the twentieth-century tradition of left-wing political unionism.

Devolution was duly put to referendums in March 1979. Scotland voted in favour of a new assembly but failed to reach the requisite 40 per cent of the electorate, a requirement inserted at the last minute in the referendum bill by Labour unionists. The Welsh rejected an assembly outright, by a million votes to just a quarter of a million. Evans declared Wales to be 'degraded in the sight of the world and humiliated in the eyes of its own people'. The failure of the 1979 referendums was greeted at Westminster with a sigh of relief. The 1970s rank as a low point in Welsh and Scottish nationalist zeal.

Labour breaks with its past

One thing achieved by the debate over Kilbrandon was to dis-inter interest in home rule as such. In Wales, Plaid Cymru's poll share rose from insignificant to between 5 and 10 per cent in the 1980s, while in Scotland the SNP rose to over 20 per cent. Both movements were fuelled by a burst of bureaucratic centralisation by Conservative governments under Margaret Thatcher and John Major, in power from 1979 to 1997. Local government boundaries were redrawn and renamed for admin-istrative convenience. Local tax-raising powers were curbed and budgets capped. Schools, housing policy and planning were brought under Whitehall control. Decentralised democ-racy was demoted, dismissed as a back door for socialism if not anarchy. Britain was rated among the most centralised states in Europe.

There were occasional concessions to Welsh and Scottish sensibilities. When in 1982 Gwynfor Evans threatened a hunger strike if Thatcher did not fund a Welsh language television channel, she capitulated. The resulting S4C achieved barely

2 per cent of the Welsh audience. A south Welsh MP told me its replacement of the English-speaking Channel 4 evoked more local anger even than Thatcher's closure of the coal mines.

In Scotland in 1989 a convention of fifty-eight of Scotland's seventy-two MPs met and reasserted the ancient Arbroath declaration on Scottish autonomy. They affirmed 'the sovereign right of the Scottish people to determine a form of government best suited to their needs'. Thatcher's response came to be seen as her moment of madness. Against the pleadings of her colleagues she decided to replace Britain's progressive property tax with a flat-rate poll tax, deciding to 'pilot' it first in Scotland.

The impact of the poll tax on Tory support in Scotland and Wales was devastating. In Scotland the party slumped from twenty-two MPs in 1979 to none by 1997, at which election Wales also failed to return a single Tory MP. The Conservatives entered the twenty-first century as emphatically the party of England. Meanwhile, Major desperately tried to recover, abolishing the poll tax in 1992 and offering the Welsh language official status in 1993. A Scottish white paper declared that 'no nation could be held irrevocably in a union against its will'. But Major's government continued with the direct rule of both Scotland and Wales, largely through politically appointed boards and corporations devoid of local accountability. They came to be known as the 'quangocracy'.

Tory suppression of localism was a gift to Labour and its new leader in 1994, Tony Blair. He pledged that 'a sovereign Westminster Parliament will devolve power to Scotland and Wales', such that 'the union will be strengthened and the threat of separatism removed'. Scotland would get a parliament with law-making powers, but with limited scope to vary taxes. A less powerful Welsh assembly would provide a forum of democratic accountability for existing Welsh Office functions. Both institutions would be led by a first minister.

That Blair had seen fit even to breathe the word separatism was remarkable. Interviewing him at the time, I sensed that he saw devolution – including to elected city mayors – largely as a means of eroding the power of local Labour oligarchies, opponents of his New Labour project. But he and the British Parliament were taking a risk. They were proposing a new tier of democratic institutions within a British state that had not seen them for two centuries. John Major at the 1997 election strongly opposed the idea. He declared that devolution would be 'the end of the union . . . Wake up, my fellow countrymen, before it is too late!'

Referendums on the new devolved assemblies were held soon after Labour came to power, undoubtedly benefiting from Blair's current electoral popularity. Scotland's new parliament, the first since the Stuarts, was approved overwhelmingly. Wales's proposed Senedd Cymru, passed only by a whisker – 50.3 to 49.7 per cent – with serious opposition from counties along the border with England. But 50 per cent support was a huge advance on the 20 per cent of 1979. It was Wales's first ever assembly, at least since Glyndwr. The Welsh writer Jan Morris reflected that Wales had come within a percentage point of being virtually abolished. Had it voted against devolution, 'no passion of patriots, no ecstasy of linguists, no reasoning of history or ideology would persuade the English state that Wales was really a nation at all'. But a majority was a majority.

Two years later, the Queen opened new assemblies in Edinburgh and Cardiff amid much rejoicing. On 12 May 1999, Winnie Ewing marked the former with the words, 'The Scottish Parliament, prorogued on the twenty-fifth day of March 1707, is hereby reconvened.' For the first time in Great Britain, Westminster had diluted its democratic monopoly. In the words of a Welsh Tory devolutionist, David Melding, devolution was 'a common characteristic of modern European government' and one that had at last made Wales 'a political nation . . . Never again would the Conservative Party win in Wales and Scotland only by winning in England.'

The remits of the new assemblies expanded over time. They came to include health, education, housing, transport, farming, industry, employment and culture. The Scottish Parliament also had responsibility for justice. The assemblies could not, at least initially, raise their own taxes or exceed Treasury guidelines on borrowing or spending. Though some fiscal discretion was later granted, all three assemblies ran large budget deficits and had to rely on what were called Barnett subventions from London, determined by a formula of needs and resources. But the devolution in the case of Scotland was extensive, and in the case of Wales at least substantial.

Devolution bears fruit

The immediate effect of these innovations was to confirm Major's warning. It gave nationalist politics a legitimacy and status from which it swiftly drew strength. For two decades Scotland and Wales had been ruled from afar by Conservative politicians, for almost none of whom the Scottish or Welsh peoples had voted. What was intriguing was that Blair's Labour Party attracted no gratitude for the reform. Labour's traditional base in the working-class Scottish Lowlands and the Welsh valleys steadily diminished in favour of nationalist parties.

British subnationalism, unlike that in many parts of Europe, was predominantly left wing. The SNP under its charismatic leader Alex Salmond carefully positioned itself to the left of Labour. In the first election to the Scottish Parliament in 1999, Labour won fifty-six seats and the SNP thirty-five, Labour forming Scotland's first ruling executive, but by 2007 the nationalists had supplanted Labour as Scotland's largest party and formed its minority government. The SNP has retained power in Edinburgh ever since. The party also held an overwhelming majority of the fifty-nine Scottish seats at Westminster. In 2007 Labour was reduced to barely 20 per cent of the Scottish electorate, its worst performance since 1910.

Despite the SNP's electoral supremacy it remained strangely unable to convince a majority of Scottish electors to support its central goal, independence. When put to a referendum in 2014, independence was rejected by 53 per cent to 44 per cent, its cause eroded by a slew of new devolved powers offered to the Scots by the then prime minister, David Cameron. Salmond had played into Cameron's hands by rejecting his offer of a 'second question', on enhanced home rule known as 'devomax'. This might have given the Scots almost full control of their economy and taxation and was widely supported in opinion polls. Salmond preferred to pitch for total independence or nothing. He got nothing.

In Wales, as in Scotland, Labour won the first 1999 assembly election, by twenty-eight seats, and took power in coalition with the Liberal Democrats. But there was a surge in Plaid Cymru support, the party coming second with fourteen seats and making deep inroads into the Welsh Labour vote, notably in its south Welsh valley homeland. Plaid's chief handicap was its continued, divisive obsession with the Welsh language. The party's leader in 2012, Leanne Wood (described as 'Welsh-learning' not Welsh-speaking), was spotted wearing translation headphones at her own party conference. By 2011 Welsh devolution had become sufficiently accepted for a further referendum, on giving the Senedd law-making powers in twenty areas of government, to pass with 64 per cent support.

A Welsh 'non-party' lobby group for independence, YesCymru, emerged in 2014 at a time when support for independence hovered around 10–15 per cent. Five polls between 2019 and 2021 now showed support rising to between 27 and an impressive 35 per cent. Though this may have reflected younger Welsh voters described as 'indy-curious', or, to some cynics, 'vanity secessionists', the Welsh trajectory was similar to that of the SNP a decade earlier. Welsh independence, whatever it might mean, was no long unmentionable or unthinkable.

Even in long-dormant Cornwall the ghosts of home rule asserted themselves. The Liberal Democrats pledged a Cornish assembly, while Labour now offered support for regional governments across England. A small Cornish independence movement, Mebyon Kernow, demanded the customary status symbols of nationalism: Cornish road signs, Cornish teaching in school and, in 2001, 'Cornish' as a declared nationality on the census form. While these were not all granted, the party won five local council seats and a mayoralty, that of Camborne. Its support within the county as a whole never rose above 5 per cent of the poll.

Devolution coloured orange

The one place where devolution had never died, though it often needed life-support, was Northern Ireland. The 1980s saw no diminution in the IRA's campaign of violence, including on the British mainland. An attempt was made on the life of the prime minister Margaret Thatcher in a bomb attack on a Brighton hotel in 1984. Another bomb in 1992 caused immense damage to the City of London. The British government was no longer indolent. Thatcher had built a working relationship with the liberal Irish prime minister Garret FitzGerald, despite having declared Northern Ireland 'as British as Finchley'. A hesitant Anglo-Irish 'agreement' was reached in 1985 between London and Dublin and continued under John Major, designed to calm relations between Ireland's north and south.

Then came a breakthrough, the so-called Good Friday Agreement reached in Belfast in 1998 under the government of

Tony Blair. This achieved two goals. It acknowledged that self-determination by the people of the north should be the sole basis for any Irish reunion and it established a new devolved executive with power shared by both Protestant and Catholic communities. This approach won their joint agreement and ceasefires were declared by their militant wings. Inter-communal violence abated and a rough-and-ready acceptance of Protestant majority rule was ameliorated by a Catholic cabinet veto. When a year later a dissident-IRA bomb at Omagh killed twenty-nine people, it was condemned outright by the Sinn Féin leadership.

The 'official' unionist, David Trimble of the Ulster Unionist Party, became first minister, with the nationalist Social Democratic and Labour Party's Seamus Mallon as his deputy. But hovering over the shoulders of both were the DUP's Paisley, who rejected the agreement, and Sinn Féin's Gerry Adams. It was a nervous start to a new sort of home rule. An ominous sign was Blair's banality that 'the hand of history is upon our shoulders'. People asked which history and how firm was its grip.

The Good Friday Agreement undoubtedly laid the precondition for a more robust form of power-sharing. Protestants and Catholics were sitting round the same cabinet table and talking, not shouting at each other. Yet division was ingrained. The new assembly found itself suspended four times over the next decade as local politics reverted to the extremes. By 2007 the DUP and Sinn Féin had usurped the moderate 'official' unionists and the SDLP. The only refreshing note was that Paisley and Sinn Féin's Martin McGuinness shook hands and served together as first minister and deputy respectively.

This coming together of opposites was the north's one opportunity. In the south after 1922, independence had forced enemies to come together and rule by compromise. In the north, British direct rule had relieved them of any such need. Responsibility for tough decisions could always be shuffled onto a London minister. For a while the coming together worked, lubricated with London money. But Paisley retired in 2008 and McGuinness in 2017, and a new generation of leaders untutored in compromise took over.

Power-sharing degenerated into sleaze. A vast sum of £490 million was lost on what appeared to be a corrupt renewable energy project under the aegis of the DUP enterprise minister and party leader from 2015 to 2021, Arlene Foster. Periodic breakdowns in power-sharing resumed, with London always ready expensively to pick up the pieces. One in 2017 concerned a Sinn Féin demand that Irish be recognised as an official language in the north, to which the Unionists demanded equality for their dialect of Scots-Irish, Ullans. Foster resigned in 2021 to be replaced by two successors in a matter of weeks. Northern Ireland was looking like a banana republic.

Enter Brexit

Two events now occurred that were to traumatise relations between London and the devolved assemblies in Edinburgh, Cardiff and Belfast. The first was the decision in 2015 of David Cameron's Tory government in London to hold a referendum the following year on the UK's membership of the EU. Wales conformed to the English balance of opinion in favour of Brexit, both voting 53 per cent to 47 per cent to leave the EU. But Scotland and Northern Ireland voted 62 and 56 per cent respectively to remain. The union was divided.

The Brexit victory saw a variety of interpretations. It was a vote of provincial Britain against the metropolitan establishment in London. It was a reassertion of neglected English regions facing the persistent drift of jobs, wealth and talent to the south-east. It was also a vote against excessive immigration. The leave vote was heavily biased towards non-graduates, over-forty-fives, the rural population and the poor. Scotland's strong wish to remain in the EU further distanced its voters from English opinion, tilting Scotland further in the direction of independence.

In Northern Ireland opinion was more complex. London's drastic post-referendum decision not just to leave the EU but also to withdraw from the European single market transformed a political move into a severe impediment to the all-Ireland trading economy and to low-wage employment. Those affected included farming, fishing, tourism, care homes, and industries with complex continental supply lines. It also raised doubts about Northern Ireland's border with the south, a border which now divided Britain from the entirety of the European economy. This divide clearly broke the terms of the Good Friday Agreement stipulating an economic union across the whole island of Ireland. The only solution was a protocol whereby the province remained inside the EU single market while a new barrier was declared 'down the Irish Sea' between the north and Britain. This entailed customs checks on goods moving through Belfast port checks that were both disruptive and politically toxic to northern unionists. In 2019 the British prime minister Boris Johnson told those unionists that any such barrier would be 'over my dead body', then promptly agreed it.

This was precisely the crisis unionists most feared at the time of partition. They called it 'British treachery'. Easily resolved short-term conflicts yield knotty long-term problems. Irish nationalists were exultant that the logic of history was undermining partition. Protestant rioters took to the streets of Belfast in 2021, shortly before the first minister Arlene Foster's resignation. Northern Ireland's capacity to destabilise the union was undimmed.

A Pandemic devolved

Even as the trauma of Brexit was being absorbed, the British Isles, along with the rest of the world, was hit by the Covid-19 pandemic. As various lockdowns were introduced during 2020, London decided that what might be drastic curbs on personal freedom would be more acceptable locally if administered by the devolved executives. It was a stark acknowledgement of the virtue of localism when obedience to authority was critical. It seemed odd that 'the science' might be read differently in Bristol than in Cardiff, or in Newcastle than in Glasgow, but so-called 'national' first ministers were vested with unprecedented powers and used them eagerly. Every week there would be news of pandemic regulations varying between 'the four nations', of border checks, families migrating, newly prominent health officials declaring policy changes of considerable economic significance. Differences between the nations were on display every evening on the television news.

The result was that the three first ministers were often taking stances on lockdown divergent from those of the Johnson government in London, giving each newfound exposure. The nations were seen to have definable leaders making decisions on their peoples' behalf rather than taking orders from London. The result was undeniable. The 2021 'vaccine' elections to the devolved assemblies saw Wales's first minister, Mark Drakeford, score highly even against the run of his own Labour Party. As one Welsh interviewee in Merthyr told the BBC, 'I don't mind being told what I can and cannot do, so long as I am told it in Wales.' Such attitudes undoubtedly fed traditional anti-English hostilities. There were roadblocks on routes into and out of Wales and reports of local Welsh police waking up holidaymakers at night and ordering them 'back to England'.

In Scotland, Nicola Sturgeon likewise scored a steady 75 per cent approval rating against Johnson's 20 per cent. At the 2021 poll she was re-elected as first minister. Though she did not recover the SNP's overall majority, her coalition with the Green Party ensured a majority for another independence referendum.

While there was some evidence that Brexit and Covid had solidified the independence cause, Scotland did clearly remain in two minds. Though one 2020 poll at the height of lockdown showed support for independence peaking at 58 per cent, most polls hovered in the region of 50:50. Scottish voters under thirty-five were two-thirds in favour and only over-fifty-fives were for continued union, so it could therefore be said that independence was only a matter of time. But that time was not yet. The SNP's electoral dominance was not on the scale of Sinn Féin's in 1918 Ireland, when independence support reached 70 per cent.

Blair's 1999 devolutions had undoubtedly met the desire of the Scots and Welsh for more control over their domestic affairs. This desire for greater autonomy was shared by parts of England, such as the mayoralties of London and Manchester and the county of Yorkshire, where a One Yorkshire 'nationalist' movement emerged. Devolution, Brexit and lockdown were in their different ways all manifestations of a popular upsurge against over-centralised government.

An eerie sign of constitutional strain did appear just before Brexit when the so-called 'West Lothian question' raised its head. This concerned the anomaly – bluntly the unfairness – that English MPs under devolution had no say in the domestic affairs of Wales, Scotland and Northern Ireland, while MPs from those nations could debate and vote on the domestic affairs of the English. Why should forty-five SNP MPs have a vote on a road programme in Kent when Kent MPs had no say over one in Strathclyde?

In 2015 the Cameron government sought to resolve this asymmetry with a Commons protocol whereby only English MPs would vote on bills on English matters. This was known as English votes for English laws or EVEL. This ostensibly fair arrangement succeeded in enraging Scottish MPs by suggesting that they were less than full members of the Westminster Parliament. In the event, the protocol proved complex to apply to 'hybrid' bills and was almost never used. EVEL was abolished in 2021 and the West Lothian question remained unresolved.

British politics passed through a period of near unprecedented turbulence in the six years following the Brexit decision in 2016, years that saw the Conservative Party enjoy three leaders in succession, Labour two and the Liberal Democrats four. One outcome of that turbulence was that the issue of devolution, supposedly settled in 1999, was still very much alive. Forces at play across Europe were generating pressures of group identity and populist leadership that called for possibly radical constitutional reform. Of all the countries of Europe, the one that should have needed least warning of this was the United Kingdom. It has already lost Ireland and now faced a crisis in that country's relationship with its northern neighbour. And it had Scotland clearly on the brink of possible departure from the union. As for a solution, champions of that union had none.

22

The Great Identity Hunt

English or British?

In the 1930s the writer V. S. Pritchett toured Britain for a travelogue on the state of the nation. He found a people pulling itself together out of Depression. Yet he also detected not one people but many, and they were not wholly at peace. He pondered on the 'devilish inspiration of historical fate' that had for so long kept 'these four ill-assorted, quarrelsome peoples stuck on a couple of small islands off the wet and foggy Atlantic coast of Europe'. There they had been 'forced to live in one another's pockets for nearly 2,000 years'.

Pritchett did not ask who 'forced' them or what made them so quarrelsome. It certainly did not occur to him to draw a distinction between those whom some called Celts and others Anglo-Saxons, while a discussion of British versus English would also have seemed arcane. The United Kingdom was assumed united, and its components haphazard in their dissatisfactions. That said, Pritchett did not bother to embrace Wales or Scotland in his peregrination.

Since the rise of immigration as a political issue in the 1960s and the later rise of 'national' sensitivities, numerous attempts have been made to pin down who the British people think they are and whether it matters. In France and America, nationality is regarded as a civic definition of citizenship. To Germans it is ethnic. To some Britons, national identity is a civic concept; to others, it is genetic. To many, it is a mix of both.

The British Social Attitudes Survey, conducted annually since 1983, concludes merely that Britishness is a 'fuzzy' concept. It is an umbrella embracing ancestry, language, birthplace and longevity of residence. The surveys do show, however, that over three decades there has been a decline in 'pride in being British', in all but the over-sixty-fives. Those feeling 'very proud' had dropped from 43 per cent to 35 per cent. Indeed, Britishness is most marked in recent immigrant communities.

A 2018 poll by YouGov was intriguing in a different direction. Older people were more likely to identify as being 'English' as well as British than were younger people, by as much as 72 per cent to 45 per cent. The old are clinging to their English identity within Britain but the young are fleeing it. However, turn to Wales and Scotland and this phenomenon is reversed. It was the young who feel more Welsh or more Scottish than their elders.

What is certainly the case is that the number of people living in Britain and claiming to be Irish, Welsh or Scottish far exceeds the population of those three countries. When, as a boy and having lived all my life in England, I was asked my identity, I would always say Welsh, or possibly half-Welsh, in honour of my father's place of birth. But if I was within earshot of my mother she would forcefully correct me. 'You should say you are half-English.' I would do so to humour her, but think it unnecessary and not very exciting.

The desire of the young is clearly for a more 'interesting' background than the vague categorisation of Englishness. A Briton who identifies as anything-but-English appears to be more specific, more historic, almost more ready for an argument about it. It was as if, by instinct, we knew which side we were on (with King Arthur) at the Battle of Mons Badonicus. When asked, half my friends manage to cite elements of Welsh, Scottish or Irish in their pedigree.

England searches for itself

Englishness is now a subject of intense debate. Where bookshops would once be lined with works on Scottishness, Irishness and Welshness, it is the vexed identity of the English that now claims pride of place. To boast of being English was long thought of as being rather trite or pompous, like waving a Union Jack as Americans do the Stars and Stripes. There was an archaism to such phrases as 'English and proud of it', as there once was to 'God is an Englishmen' and 'mad dogs and Englishmen'. These phrases were used by G. K. Chesterton's 'secret people', who murmured, 'Smile at us, pay us, pass us; but do not quite forget;/ For we are the people of England, that never have spoken yet.'

English nationalism has often been regarded with some suspicion. The philosopher Roger Scruton called it 'the forbidden identity', variously associated with football misbehaviour, right-wing agitation and anti-immigrant marches. Other than on churches on St George's Day, the patron saint's red cross was a badge of working-class identity. But Englishness was thrust into a new prominence by the Brexit referendum, seen as expunging inhibitions over English identity, as 'taking back control' from anyone not English. The Brexit Party leader, Nigel Farage, openly called Brexit 'our very own English rebellion'.

The Brexit Party's roots were in the Referendum Party, founded in 1994 by James Goldsmith, which gave way to the UK Independence Party (UKIP), both coded euphemisms for English nationalist, although both fought elections beyond England's borders. David Cameron unwisely dismissed UKIP in 2006 as 'a bunch of fruitcakes, loonies and closet racists, mostly'. Yet in 2014 it achieved the highest popular vote of any party in the UK European elections. Two years later it could claim to be architect of the Brexit 'leave' vote. The trouble, as the historian Jeremy Black said at the time, was that 'English nationalism is too important to be left to the extremists'.

A study published in 2021 by Ailsa Henderson and Richard

Wyn Jones analysed the new Englishness as 'a political force transforming Britain'. But it was not doing so in the direction of the union. To them, the issue of who gained or lost most from union did not matter, rather the fact that the argument was reawakening, the wound reopening. For the time being, the antagonism of the Scots and Welsh to what they saw as England's ongoing hegemony merely had the effect of boosting the 'Englishness' of the English.

A serious rebuff to unionism came in 2020 with a YouGov poll that found under half the English, a mere 40 per cent, cared if Scotland went independent, the remainder regarding it as a matter for the Scots. Nor did two-thirds really care if Northern Ireland rejoined the south. It too was all Ireland's business. Even among expatriates, for whom unionist affection reflects a sort of ethnic guilt, there seemed a detachment from the old debate. The Irish writer Fintan O'Toole concluded in his sardonic epitaph on Brexit, *Heroic Failure*, that England was now engaged in 'a form of silent secession' from the United Kingdom. The unthinkable was happening. It was not the neighbours – dare I say the Celts – who were declaring independence from the United Kingdom, it was the English.

The very concept of a UK unionism seemed to be dissolving into little more than the patriotic mantra of London's political class. It was absurd for the Conservative Party to call itself (sometimes) the Conservative and Unionist Party when it had so few adherents and almost no MPs from Wales or Scotland. After Brexit, the Tories had no need of Scotland and Wales any more than they had 'needed' Ireland before 1922. They had Commons majorities without them. These places were as relics from a forgotten empire, tossed into the attic of the British Isles. O'Toole was right. If there was a political crisis looming in Britain it was one of British nationalism.

A vignette well illustrated this confusion. In the summer of 2021, a brush at the G7 summit in Cornwall had the French president Emmanuel Macron teasing Britain's Johnson for trying to rule four nations as one. Johnson was furious. His was one nation, he said, and no different from France. A French spokesman afterwards pointed out that he was policing the pandemic as four 'nations', playing soccer as four nations, rugby as three and the Olympics as just one, Team GB. Could Johnson not make up his mind? As if to press home the tease, the EU suddenly demanded that British cars on the continent carry UK stickers, not GB ones.

New landscapes of identity

Demography now added its contribution. Rural Wales, Scotland and Northern Ireland had long shared with much of England the fate of population depletion. This was a shift from the countryside towards the cities and suburbs – ongoing since the eighteenth century – and from the north to the south. For decades, indeed for centuries, rural communities had seen their populations decline and their young leave home. To sustain their prosperity and public services, such regions need sources of new blood, which means policies actively attracting new migrants. One-third of modern Londoners were born overseas. So too were half a million new (southern) Irish – a tenth of the population – overwhelmingly under the age of thirty-five. On them rests its future.

Since the turn of the twenty-first century, Scotland, Wales and Northern Ireland have seen modest rises in population compared with a surge into England's south-east. Now it appears that the severe population losses of the second half of the twentieth century have ended. While exhausted industrial communities are still declining, many rural areas have begun to hold their own. This has largely been through attracting those actively seeking new places to live, whether in retirement, for leisure or through a change in the nature of their work. Wales and western Scotland have seen inflows on a similar scale to the West Country and the Lake District, largely of holiday-makers and the retired, often on a drastic scale.

The political scientist David Goodhart defined these demographic changes as a divide between 'somewheres' and 'anywheres'. The somewheres are static, remaining in or near their place of birth, while the anywheres leave home and are on the move. The latter's geographical loyalty is more tenuous. This obviously has a close relationship to career choice among the young. A friend educated in Liverpool told me that every boy in his class saw success in terms of leaving Liverpool, the dream being a job in London.

This emigration is as old as the fact of industrialisation. But it is peculiarly sensitive in the case of Scotland and Wales, where feelings of national loyal naturally run high. When I asked a Welsh grandmother how many of her offspring still lived in her village, she beamed with pride: 'None, they've all done very well.' North Welsh dialect has a word for a sheep considered not worth taking to market and left on the hillside, a *cwlun*. It was sometimes used derogatively of Welsh local politicians who never made it to Cardiff or London.

The impact of this decline in 'somewheres' can be drastic. The English-identifying population of Wales is something approaching 30 per cent. These are mostly people living within half an hour of the English border, for whom Wales is in commuting distance of the Midlands or Bristol. Meanwhile, the coastal resorts of western Britain have seen an exodus of established residents in favour of retirement and holiday lets. Second-home owners are a particular bone of contention. Stories are now common of 70–80 per cent of some seaside villages, from Cornwall to Pembroke, from Gwynedd to the Lake District and from Argyll to Oban lying empty for much of the year, rendering many local shops and services impossible to sustain, to the detriment of the year-round population.

The impact of these changes to Scotland can be as devastating as the Highland clearances. Whether the Covid-fuelled move to working from home can recover some of that lost vitality remains to be seen. In many areas the brightest and most enterprising 'somewheres' left behind are the farmers and those who live off the land, their families and their businesses geographically rooted. Frequently there can be a sense of two communities, the farmers with their own pubs and shops, and the 'anywhere' newcomers.

The fragmentation of identity

These changes in the demography of rural Scotland, Wales and Northern Ireland are too recent to assess. Parts of Wales known to me have undergone a population turnover of 20–30 per cent in a matter of a decade, and anecdotal evidence is that the same applies to much of Scotland. This has altered everything from the balance of ages in the population to the proportion of residents with local 'links' and the nature of local leadership and institutions. Pubs, schools and churches find their regulars have gone. Art, music and drama groups have new members. A community's cohesion decays and resentments arise. Where this has special impact is on those communities professing a specific, indeed a national, identity. The concept of 'local' in a Welsh or Scottish village or town is different from the Cotswolds or East Anglia, or even the Yorkshire dales. The question then arises as to what is the status of that identity and what legal or other steps are appropriate to defending it.

At the same time, newcomers can bring new blood, new young people and, above all, new money, especially useful in communities in decline. If there is any lesson to be drawn from Ireland in the 1990s, it was that new blood is a communal elixir. As one local councillor told me, 'I prefer to have people at my meetings who have chosen to live in my village to people who want to keep them out, or whose children can't wait to leave.'

Governments, local and national, must wrestle with how far the civil rights of British citizens, such as those of freedom of movement and settlement, can be limited for the sake of trying to preserve historic communities. They intervene to protect the physical heritage. Should they do so to protect social heritage? Should immigration into a neighbourhood be restricted, as into an Irish Gaeltacht? Should property rights to buy and sell be circumscribed – denying local people the value of their houses? Can internal migration be rationed by ethnic identity, nationality or language ability? Strict controls already operate on council tenancies. Councils in Cornwall tend to reject planning applications from outsider house-buyers. Severe tax surcharges are levied on second homes in Wales.

Most of these measures merely nudge at the edge of what are seismic upheavals. The most serious and controversial have been those concerning the blatant badge of identity, language. Not just language courses but Irish-medium schools have started appearing in Belfast and Londonderry. A Gaelic-medium school has opened in the Hebrides. The most serious steps at language entrenchment have been in Wales, where it has become the emblematic policy of an otherwise empty Plaid Cymru manifesto.

Overtly championed by Saunders Lewis as the key to Welshness – and to the anger of the non-Welsh speaking Welsh – compulsory Welsh has since the 1980s been what the Irish would call Plaid's 'mobilising rhetoric'. Councils across Wales have found themselves vulnerable to concerted lobbying for ever more Welsh-medium schools, irrespective of whether local parents (or children) want them. By 2020 some 450 such schools, mostly primary, had been set up, with a quarter of Welsh children reportedly being taught in the language. Often the school is the only Welsh-speaking presence in a town or village, while parents who want their children taught in English must send them away from friends and neighbours to the nearest English-medium facility.

There is no doubt knowledge of Welsh has increased as a result, though a gulf still exists between such knowledge and 'Welsh-speaking' at home or work. Meanwhile, the language has become a nationalised industry, with local officials, teachers, care workers, broadcasters and actors being expected to acquire it to get a job, even though it is claimed to be used regularly by just 17 per cent of the population. A commissioner was appointed to hunt for 'anti-Welsh' discrimination, with the power of a £5,000 fine. In English-speaking Cardiff, Welsh-speaking has become the badge of the 'taffia', or ruling establishment, compared by some to a freemasonry. Universities are increasingly dividing into Welsh- and English-speaking. Aberystwyth even has a Welsh hall of residence.

Where this authoritarian approach leads is the subject of intense controversy. Young people are forced to learn in a language they are most unlikely to use at home, work or play. For whatever reason, Wales has gone to the bottom of the results league in Britain, in PISA ratings, GCSE passes and access to higher education. One observer commented that it was like Latin in medieval France – great for a job in the monastery, but that was all. Wherever I have seen such communally separate schooling, in South Africa, Northern Ireland and elsewhere, it has eroded social cohesion and deterred immigration. In my experience, middle-class families seem better able to handle it than working-class ones. It is highly divisive.

As De Barra found in Ireland, such policies are largely the product of identity politics. They have little impact 'in changing the primary language through which most students live and work once they leave school'. It is significant that when the Dublin government abandoned language compulsion in the

1980s, it was seen as a gesture of political maturity and confidence. It was no longer 'needed'.

What was intriguing in Ireland's case was that the end of compulsion brought, if anything, a surge in voluntary enthusiasm for learning Irish. It became a matter of cultural pride rather than revolutionary discipline. During lockdown Welsh experienced a particularly steep rise. The website Duolingo – where a language is learned for 'fun not function' – registered Welsh as its ninth most popular language among learners in the UK, beating French. During 2020 it was also the fastest riser, with a 44 per cent increase in the year. More people were claimed to be learning Welsh voluntarily, 1.5 million, than were doing so compulsorily in Welsh schools. Either way, I would rather learn Welsh as a matter of pride than of political obedience.

23

Independence Versus Federalism

The seduction of independence

The diverse cultures of the British Isles are both a glory and a symptom of the failure of the English state to assimilate them into one harmonious whole. They thus left open the question, for a minority of Britons, would they feel or do better casting off altogether the shackles of British rule? A hundred years ago the answer given by two-thirds of the Irish was yes. What now of some 9 million Northern Irish, Welsh and Scots, with the example of Ireland before their eyes?

There is no inherent problem in small-state independence. The world is awash with countries of 5 to 10 million people, which is why every report on Scottish independence cites variously Denmark, Finland, Iceland, Slovenia or New Zealand. Scotland's population of 5.5 million is larger than eight existing members of the EU. In 2018 Scotland's sustainable growth commission argued that the benign 'big-country model of economic growth' was simply untrue. The reason was that big countries 'always tend to hold back their smaller regions'. To the economist John Kay, 'there are few economies of scale in statehood . . . Size is as much a disadvantage as an advantage when carrying on the principal functions of government.' As for spreading public contentment, no big country has ever appeared in lists of the top ten happiest states. The median size for the ten happiest is 5 million.

A new Ireland

The least controversial and most straightforward candidate for independence from the UK is Northern Ireland, the objective being to proceed to reunion with the south. The island's 1921 partition of one-third of its population was intended to be temporary. As we have seen, the parties to the 1998 Good Friday Agreement on Northern Ireland's constitution accepted that the south had no claim to the north beyond the terms of northern consent. The possibility of that consent remains on the table. The province today is certainly more peaceful than during the troubles. Extremist sentiment is in decline and street violence has largely abated. But this has not ended underlying tensions.

One outcome of Brexit, which the Northern Irish voted against, was not predicted. A series of polls indicated a firm shift in opinion on reunion. Those in favour surged from 22 per cent pre-Brexit to 47 per cent in 2021. Irrespective of this balance, a full half of those questioned also anticipated reunion within ten years. A new factor was also present. Census returns showed the Catholic population was now approaching a majority over the Protestants. The province's child population was 51 per cent Catholic with only 33 per cent registered as Protestant. The student population was already evenly divided. The historic Protestant fears were being realised.

In 2020 the Sinn Féin leader in the north, Mary Lou McDonald, declared herself delighted that Brexit, 'the lowest common denominator of English nationalism', appeared to have evaporated the north's unionist majority. The issue was not Brexit as such but Johnson's insistence on a 'hard Brexit', withdrawing the north from a commercial union with the south, palpably against the interests of either. Public opinion, said MacDonald, would soon trigger a positive referendum.

An additional factor in a change of attitude among northern Protestants was the progress made to modernise the south, including a diminution of the Catholic character of its state. By 2016 only three-quarters of the south's population identified as Catholic. In matters of social policy, such as marriage, abortion and sexual relations, the south has become if anything more liberal than the north. It is hard to imagine the north electing a gay prime minister of Indian descent, as the south did in Leo Varadkar in 2017.

The fusing of the crippled Northern Irish economy with that of the south under reunion would undoubtedly be painful. There would need to be a settlement with Britain to cover the transition, notably over pensions and health care. Another issue would be how fast the economic environment of the south could be extended northwards. Whether a new united Ireland might form closer ties with Britain, perhaps under some refashioning of Britain's relationship with the EU, is as yet an unanswered question.

A federalist dawn

If Northern Irish independence poses problems, they are at least soluble. In the case of the rest of the United Kingdom, the concept of independence is different. When devolution was introduced in 1999 Blair stated that it was a necessary alternative to separatism. As we have since seen, there are many shades to devolution. English governments throughout history have had recourse to devolved institutions to appease or ward off Welsh, Scottish and Irish rebellions. A federal Wales was proposed under the Treaty of Montgomery (1267) and a federal Ireland under the Treaty of Limerick (1691). Scottish and Irish parliaments with varying degrees of autonomy existed down to the Acts of Union of 1707 and 1801. Even Joseph Chamberlain, in opposing Gladstone's home rule for Ireland, toyed with the modest federalism of an ill-defined 'home rule all round'. Northern Ireland has had a federal assembly since 1921.

British governments have long been averse to the word 'federal', as if it implied some loss of virility to the central state. Federalism is strictly the subdivision of authority within a sovereign state, especially a state composed of regions, provinces or nations with strong and articulate identities. It brought together the once diverse states of the USA and has bonded them in one union ever since. It enabled bilingual Canada and Belgium to remain as sovereign unions. It was introduced as a bulwark against the re-emergence of a powerful state in post-war Germany. It holds Spain in delicate thrall.

Federalism is the pressure valve of union. It allows tension to escape when unification has failed, when subnational sentiments boil to the surface. Nationalism itself, as Neal Ascherson writes in his *Stone Voices*, is strictly 'inaccessible to politics . . . Love of one's country has been held to be a private and intimate area rather than a public one.' Only when some superior power deeply offends that love – as was long the case in Ireland – does nationalism turn political. Then all hell can break loose.

In Britain's case federalism has bred hypocrisy. At the end of the twentieth century, the most ardent opponents of devolution within the UK were most strident in demanding it within the EU. When EU functions and powers were repatriated to London after Brexit, these same champions of subordinate control point-blank refused to devolve it downwards to the three other nations. EU regional grants had previously gone direct to the devolved governments. Under Brexit's Internal Market Act their UK Treasury replacements were kept firmly in the grip of Whitehall. Johnson even remarked that devolution had been 'a disaster'. All power does not necessarily corrupt, but it does necessarily centralise.

At the time of Britain's 1997 devolution debate, the Institute for Public Policy Research (IPPR) in London studied federalisms across Europe. The examples were diverse. In Spain and Italy different local histories gave rise to different patterns of devolution. Catalonia, Galicia and Euskadi (Basque) were 'high autonomy' regions, Castile, Aragon and Madrid 'low autonomy'. Italy likewise boasted 'special regions' for Sicily, Sardinia and Valle d'Aosta and 'ordinary' ones for Piedmont and Lombardy. France, long the most centralised of European states, became less so in 1982 under reforms initiated by interior minister Gaston Defferre, with the famed *préfets* stripped of authority and Corsica rendered virtually independent. Germany's post-war *Länder* were represented in a central upper house, a *Bundesrat*, with centre/local disputes decided not by central government but by a constitutional court.

Until 1999 Britain was the only member of the European Union without any internal devolution, other than to Northern Ireland. As the Conservative theorist Michael Oakeshott pointed out, all other European states 'began as mixed and miscellaneous collections of human beings precariously held together'. But they were 'disturbed by what they had swallowed' and found federalism an essential aid to digestion. It never occurred to the English that they too might be such a 'miscellaneous collection precariously held together'.

By the simple technique of writing histories of the British Isles in their own image, the English contrived to rest content in their unwritten constitution, in its morass of 'basic' statutes, precedents and common law. They assumed they need have no truck with federalism, except in the constitutional anomaly of Northern Ireland. Yet fifteen years after the 1999 assemblies were in place, a survey by Oxford's Nuffield College still indicated deeper dissatisfaction with devolution in Scotland and Wales than anywhere else in Europe. Catalonia and Brittany were in third and fourth place.

The devolved assemblies had undoubtedly been welcomed by Scotland and Wales, but now they wanted more. Within two decades further powers were being devolved even to once hesitant Wales. Following the 2008 Calman Commission on

Scottish Devolution, a Scotland Act was passed granting Edinburgh greater discretion over income tax and borrowing. By now these governments were responsible for health, education, housing, transport, planning, agriculture, industry, employment and culture. By far the biggest of these was health, consuming a half of all public spending. Scotland's Parliament also controlled policing and justice. Almost casually the United Kingdom had moved into the mainstream of European federalism.

The great fiscal stumbling block

At a certain point in every federalist debate talk turns to money. In none of Europe's federal systems studied by the IPPR was central control over national revenues, public spending and borrowing surrendered by the central authority. Also under central control were national borders, customs and tariffs, law and order, citizenship and migration. Even local budgets, where they were devolved, were often subject to equalisation formulas to prevent one region benefiting by impoverishing or unfairly competing with another.

In Britain the central government remains absolutely sovereign in the overall disbursement of revenues at its disposal. Funding from the British Treasury to the devolved governments is determined by the 'Barnett formula subvention', introduced in 1979 by the then Labour chief secretary to the Treasury, Joel Barnett, initially as a temporary solution. Throughout a quarter century of negotiations on devolution, the concept was unchallenged. Based as it essentially was on local 'need', these governments were found hopelessly in deficit, enjoying discretion only on switching resources between budgets. The Barnett subvention to Scotland currently covers 85 per cent of its annual budget.

As noted earlier, before Scotland's independence referendum

in 2014, Cameron had offered to the SNP's Salmond the option of a 'second question'. As described at the time, it was for so-called 'devo-max' or 'full fiscal autonomy' (FFA). According to the Nuffield team, it would have seen Scotland collecting all its taxes and determining all its spending, paying a percentage to London for such 'shared responsibilities' as defence, pensions and social welfare. This came close to the definitional limits of federalism. Polls at the time suggested that FFA, insofar as the Scots understood it, would have secured 53 per cent of the votes in favour. Salmond rejected it. A calculation by the Institute for Fiscal Studies indicated that it would have left Scotland's budget with a £7 billion gap, requiring huge increases in local taxation.

The 1999 devolution settlement drove public spending in Scotland and Wales – as already in Northern Ireland – ever deeper into dependency on London. By 2019 Scots were individually benefiting from the British Exchequer by £2,543 net of what they were paying in taxes, and the Welsh by £4,412. The equivalent figure for England was £91. These were massive cross-subsidies, the golden shackles of union with England. They suggested that, at best, devo-max was a vision well over the horizon. The path to small-country independence would be a long and hard one. But it would have to start somewhere. That somewhere would need to be to lower the deficit and increase Scottish and Welsh fiscal responsibility.

At present, independence declarations tend to read like student manifestos. They conclude their list of demands with an assumption that somehow 'big daddy will meet the bill', the daddy usually meaning some taxpayer over the horizon. Yet as a Scottish report in 2006 on devolution, the Steel Commission, put it bluntly: 'No self-respecting Parliament should exist permanently on a grant from another Parliament.' We might recall the American newspaper said to have carried the motto. 'As independent as resources permit'. This is why any plausible programme for pushing the devolved governments towards greater autonomy cannot dodge the fiscal question. It is central to any democratic economy.

A new Scotland

At first sight, the case for Scotland to follow Ireland into the promised land of full independence looks strong. Any Scots can look at the experience of Dublin from the 1920s to the 1990s and ask why should they not pursue the same narrative of the Brexiters to 'take back control'. A self-governing Scotland should eventually be in the same economic league as Ireland, Denmark and a dozen other states of 5 million or so people. The country has a strong labour base, outstanding universities and mature corporations in manufacturing and financial services. Its tourism assets are superb. It has lucrative if waning oil and gas resources. There are problems aplenty, not least Scotland's dire narcotics fatality rate and a penal system light years behind that of most European states. But as a self-governing state, Scotland should at least be better prepared than was Ireland in 1921.

Yet the challenge is awesome. Scottish nationalism has at its beck and call a veritable college of cardinals, from Tom Nairn and Tom Devine to Neal Ascherson, Ben Jackson, John Lloyd, Colin Kidd and many others. In most there is an eerie absence of economic realism, as there is in the speeches of Scotland's leaders, Salmond and now Sturgeon. Studies of the Scottish economy suggest it has the biggest budget deficit of any developed country in the western world, at 22 per cent of GDP. There is no way such an economy would be admitted to the EU, even with Sturgeon pleading with Brussels 'to leave a light on for Scotland'. One estimate holds that it would take ten to twenty years to bring Scotland's fiscal performance into the necessary balance. This is an economy that was once ahead of Denmark's, which in 2019 had a budget surplus of 4 per cent. That is the true measure of economic subordination to London.

This is one reason why half of all resident Scots are still hesitant about full independence. Scotland is not Ireland. The SNP officially wishes to retain the Queen as head of state. Most Scots seem comfortable with dual nationality and would, I am sure, regard themselves as part of Britain's cultural outreach abroad. The real issue is how to move from the present devolution to devo-max and the wilder shores of so-called 'indy-lite'. It is how to liberate a country from having its domestic policy and much of its national sovereignty at the mercy of distant politicians for whom its people have not voted in two decades. The issue is, in a nutshell, how to get Scottish rulers and voters ready to make the decisions necessary to achieve a balanced budget.

The lesson from Europe is that all forms of federalism are fluid. Few end in full independence. Examples of the full partition of established nations are rare. Only Czechoslovakia and Yugoslavia come to mind in modern Europe. But in an age of heightened local identity, constitutions should always be in flux – as indeed is that of the EU itself. For Edinburgh to be regularly renegotiating its relationship with London, as it is now, should be politically creative.

Only 'hard unionists' want to see Scotland forever bound to England's fiscal purse-strings. The answer has to be in further liberating Scotland to progress towards self-sufficiency. As we have seen, that can only be through reducing the scale of the Barnett formula and developing new sources of revenue for the Scottish Exchequer. As for the eventual destination – independence or not – that would remain, as it should, an open question. Paying for everything from pensions and debt to defence and foreign affairs would be for negotiation. A Scotland freed of budgetary subservience to England could have a relationship with London that acknowledged a shared historical frame-work, cultural, intellectual and commercial. The Scots and the English would remain in essence one people. There would be no need for full independence.

A new Wales

Full separation from England – borders, currency, citizenship and all – is not a sensible future for Wales. Most of the country's population is in regular and commutable contact with three of England's major conurbations, Merseyside, the Midlands and Bristol. It is geographically and historically tied to England and that bond has never in modern times constituted a serious problem. While I can understand the background in historical grievance, there is a tediousness to Wales's defensive rhetoric towards the English, evocative of R. S. Thomas's 'worrying the carcase of an old song'. I wonder whether any Welsh politician has ever thought to say thank you to England for the scale of the Barnett subsidy. Anyway, if Wales is ever to detach itself from economic reliance on England, it will need England's help. It should do everything to welcome its immigrants.

That said, there is no denying Wales's enthusiasm for further devolution. In 2011 a Welsh referendum agreed to the Senedd receiving new tax-raising powers, passed by a majority of 63 per cent to 37 per cent. This was despite the much-publicised poor performance of the devolved Cardiff administration compared with the rest of the United Kingdom, notably in the core services of health and schooling.

The referendum was followed by two reports in 2019–20 on Wales's economic state of health. One from Cardiff University, on 'Wales's Fiscal Future', pointed out that Wales was now the poorest region of Britain, with a public-sector deficit of 18 per cent of its domestic product. The population was ageing, youth and graduate emigration was persistent and the number of income-taxed workers was actually declining, especially in the more lucrative higher bands. A quarter of the Welsh economy was dependent on the public sector – including a third of the Glamorgan workforce – against 17 per cent in England. National statistics had Welsh in-work labour productivity at the lowest in Britain, at just 60 per cent of London's. The report concluded that there was therefore 'no expectation of delivering prosperity to the people of Wales' independent of the British Treasury. Simply, the Cardiff authors doubted whether 'a relative improvement in Wales's economic performance is possible let alone likely'.

A separate Independence Commission was set up in 2019 by Plaid Cymru under its new leader, Adam Price, an economist. It was remarkably frank and hardly more cheering. It boldly addressed the challenges that would face an independent Wales and admitted to 'chronic structural weaknesses'. It suggested that these were due to a British economy 'overwhelmingly shaped in the interests of the City of London'. As things stood, it had services the quality of those in Ireland but with revenues that would support only those of Portugal. Wales had for twenty years of devolution enjoyed unprecedented control over much of its economy, yet it 'had hardly made a good fist of it'.

The report indicated that the chief need of an independent economy would be to find new sources of innovation and enterprise and to show 'immigration friendliness', notably to potential high taxpayers. It must somehow keep its graduates and boost its skills. It also discussed possible new sources of revenue, including an ever elusive land-value tax, road tolls, tourist taxes and energy levies. A similar Holtham Commission in 2009 had gone so far as to suggest a separate Welsh level of corporation tax. (This would be anathema to London but was a key to southern Ireland's renaissance.)

Like similar reports on Scotland, the commission cited parallels with Ireland, Denmark and New Zealand. Like them it was at a loss as to how much 'cold turkey' it would take to get Wales off British subsidy, 'to do the trick' of converting Wales to the much-vaunted 'small country spiral'. The report bravely suggested at one point that it might benefit from a 'break-through' jolt with 'wide-ranging changes to both taxation and spending from day one'. Ultimately it could only pose the old question, 'If Ireland had not decided one hundred years ago to break with Britain, would it now be among the richest parts of these Isles, up there with London and the south-east?' Ireland was an intangible dream to independence enthusiasts – a Land of Oz but one whose yellow brick road was always paved with English gold.

The only constructive way for Wales to go down that road must be, as with Scotland, to win more fiscal discretion for the Welsh government, and to accompany that discretion with phased reductions in the Barnett subvention. This phasing lies at the heart of a tolerably constructive future relationship between Cardiff, Edinburgh and London. It should be termed the 'federal bargain'. There is simply no other roadmap to degrees of self-rule.

Fashioning a radical future

At no point in this debate did it seem to occur to the three devolved governments to work together on a joint federalist programme. During the pandemic, as during Brexit, outsiders might have expected the three to have liaised over relations with England. How might they handle any divergence in the scientific consensus? How might they learn from different forms of lockdown? I was told that Scotland's Sturgeon, Northern Ireland's Foster and Wales's Drakeford barely ever exchanged a word, let alone an attempt to co-ordinate policy.

The only movement of any sort down this road had previously come from Wales. In 2014 its then first minister, Carwyn

Jones, proposed a four-nation constitutional convention specifically to discuss federalism. This progressed nowhere. Scotland's government was interested only in independence, while Northern Ireland had its own problems. In 2021 Jones's successor, Mark Drakeford, repeated the call. He dismissed talk of independence as 'a slogan not a solution' and repeated Jones's argument that existing forms of devolution, however extensive, were not 'proper federalism'. To him the word implied 'a constitution in which power is not devolved to regions by a still all-powerful central legislature, but rather a system in which power is shared out by a constitution over which no single institution has unilateral control'. It should have been music to Scotland's ears. Still it did not progress.

Such a constitution – it has been termed 'radical federalism' – is admittedly hard to imagine in a British context, given the sovereignty embedded in Westminster's unwritten custom and practice. From Burke to Bagehot to Dicey, this sovereignty is rooted in longevity, as it is in the English public's contentment with it. For 85 per cent of British subjects, that constitution is unlikely to budge.

The only new element in the debate is that fact that British politics is passing through a period of uncertainty. The American Edelman Trust Barometer of OECD countries puts the British public's trust in its political institutions at a remarkable twenty-seventh out of twenty-eight, above only Putin's Russia. An extraordinary 90 per cent of British adults say they distrust politicians, an all-time low and clearly reflected in the Brexit vote. To this public opinion, the UK's 'soft' federalism appears to have no answer.

A movement in favour of radical federalism emerged within the Labour Party in the 2010s. It recognised Jones's argument that the periodical granting of powers by Westminster to devolved assemblies does not amount to constitutional partnership. The radicals stipulated one monarchy, one citizenship, one currency, one welfare regime, one defence force and hopefully joint membership of Europe's collective economic area. Apart from that, it proposed home rule for all. But the radicals still found it hard to decide how far to go, such as on the precise functions of the national assemblies and the fundamental question of the allocation of collective resources.

Devolution needs constant discussion. It requires the agency of a standing commission, gauging progress towards self-sufficiency and advising on appropriate tiers of accountability. At the very least there needs to be a decision on the composition and powers of a new 'English' House of Commons and of a new upper chamber, the latter perhaps the formal embodiment of the kingdom's unity. There is no way such basic constitutional issues can be dodged. Most other countries in Europe have been over this ground for decades, even centuries. There is no panacea. There are ongoing conflicts, of Catalonia with Spain and of Flanders with Brussels. Federalism is a process, seldom a destination. The tendency of every modern state is to centralise power. The purpose of federalism is to discipline that tendency, bluntly, to resist it.

All the models discussed above portray a British Isles that uncannily reflects the same division with which this book opened, between Britain's eastern half and its west. That division may or may not be embedded in the prehistoric origins of the British people. It has been the cause of many conflicts and much misery and it lives on in the parties to the federal debate, again mostly of the east and the west. But there is no reason why such a division should be seen as such. There is no reason why the Welsh and the Scots should view the English with such frequent disfavour. There is every reason for a so-called 'united' kingdom to be refashioned as a stable, contented and prosperous economy, one that can disperse its wealth more fairly round its shores than it has over the past half century.

I do not believe that the reunion of Ireland and the loss of

Scotland would be catastrophic to England. The reunion of Ireland would be a historic redemption. The loss of Wales is barely conceivable. The departure of Scotland would be desperately sad, if only because it would mean that London had failed to restore Scotland's former economic health sufficiently to make devo-max work. Besides, a new nation of 'England and Wales' would have a strange hollowness to it.

The brute reality is that these substantive European countries, long subordinate to England, have grown relatively and inexcusably poor. Their revived prosperity is crucial to their self-respect and to the wider economy of an England currently having to spend ever more on subsidising them. I believe the diverse peoples of the British Isles have no real wish to see their collective identity disintegrate, just as I believe they will one day wish to forge a new, closer relationship with the rest of Europe. But the solution lies with England. England, as always, holds the power and must take the initiative.

Epilogue

I started this book with a debunking of the idea of a Celtic people in any shape or form. There was no such tribe, country, culture or language. Not only that, but the peoples customarily identified as 'Celtic' have never behaved together so as to justify one name. They came in the eighteenth century to be classified as Celts because of their geographical proximity and because their ancestors spoke languages derived from one branch of Indo-European.

I believe these peoples should be regarded as they regard themselves, as Irish, Scottish or Welsh – or for that matter Manx, Cornish or Breton. Each has its own history, language and culture, deserving the dignity and status of uniqueness. In searching for authenticity in these peoples, I have tried at every turn not to lump them together, least of all as Celts.

Towards the end of her life I often discussed with the Welsh writer Jan Morris her aggressively romantic view of her compatriots. She placed great store behind the myths and legends of a glorious Welsh past. When I protested that myths cannot be treated as history she disagreed. Myths, she said, were facts, just as history was facts. I should never underrate the role of myths in a nation's identity. They could be among its most potent 'facts'.

I am afraid it is on such myths that the birth of the British people came to be built. One held that a people invaded and conquered the British Isles and eliminated the ancient Britons in or round about the Bronze Age. These were the so-called Celts. The other myth was that Saxons invaded and conquered these Celts, driving them westwards in the fifth and sixth centuries AD and bringing with them a new, increasingly all-pervasive language.

These myths have come to underpin the story of Britain. They posit the Celts as a humiliated people. They posit the Saxons as a horde of foreigners who replaced them as true 'Britons'. This fed a Victorian ideology of Saxon superiority, relegating the Irish, Scots and Welsh to the nuisance fringe of history. Celtic mythology became a loser's culture. It validated England's failure to understand and live at peace with the peoples of the west.

I remain astounded that the English people and their leaders have not been able to overcome these myths, indeed continue to hold to them. They have been unable to sustain a union with their neighbours in a prosperous modern federalism, as have most of the composite states of modern Europe. One of the world's richest and most liberal countries, that delights in lecturing every corner of the world on democracy and civil rights, still cannot fashion for its own people a constitutional equilibrium. It has been enriched over centuries by the mixing of its four component peoples, English, Irish, Scots and Welsh. This mixing is the true legacy of the domestic empire created over a thousand years by the rulers of the English people in London. That legacy is worth preserving. It must not fall victim to myth.

List of Illustrations

1. Wild west shores

Ireland: Early Celtic Christian ring fort cashel monastic settlement and fishermen's cottages, Innishmurray Island, County Sligo. Photo: David Lyons/Alamy

Scotland: Scara Brae neolithic village, Sandwick, Orkney. Photo: Stephen Coyne/Bridgeman Images

Wales: St Govan's hermitage, Pembroke. Photo: Martin Lawrence Photography

2. Edward's empire

Caernarvon Castle. Photo: Ken Walsh/Bridgeman Images

Edward I in Parliament, with the Archbishop of Canterbury, King Alexander III of Scotland, Welsh prince Llywelyn ap Gruffydd and the Archbishop of York. From the Wriothesley MS, 1523. Photo: World History Archive/Alamy

3. Resistance

Battle of Bannockburn: *Battle of Bannockburn, Day Two*, painting by Andrew Hillhouse

Ireland's Brian Boru: Sculpture head, Chapel Royal, Dublin Castle, Dublin. Photo: Gordon Hulmes Travel/Alamy

Owain Glyndwr: Bronze statue located in the Church of St Peter ad Vincula, Pennal, Gwynedd, Wales. Photo: The Photolibrary Wales/Alamy

4. English caricatures

Welsh harpist in despair: *The Bard* by John Martin (*c.* 1817). Oil on canvas. Photo: Bridgeman Images

262

List of Illustrations

Bonnie Scots piper. Photo: Bridgeman Images
Irish leprechaun. Photo: Bridgeman Images
John Bull. Photo: Bridgeman Images

5. The flight into exile
Ireland flees its famine: Thomas Nast, February 1880 cover of
   Harper's Weekly. Photo: IanDagnall Computing/Alamy
Highland clearances: Engraving, *c.* 1886. Photo: AKG-Images

6. Forms of revival
Perth station in high season: *Coming South*, by George Earl. Oil on
   canvas. Photo: Bridgeman Images
Klondike comes to Merthyr Vale: *Rolling Hills, Merthyr Tydfil*, by
   Thomas Horner. Photo: National Museum of Wales/AKG-Images
Rhondda ladies. Photo: William Clayton/Bridgeman Images

7. Faces of dissent
Henry Grattan. Engraving by J. Godby after a drawing by A. Pope.
   Photo: Kean Collection/Getty Images
Charles Parnell. Photo: Bridgeman Images
Keir Hardie, *c.* 1892. Photo: Hulton-Deutsch Collection/Corbis/
   Corbis via Getty Images
David Lloyd George, *c.* 1920. Photo: AKG-Images

8. Divided not ruled
Bloody Sunday graffiti in Belfast: *The Petrol Bomber* and *Bloody
   Sunday* murals, Bogside. Photo: George Sweeny/Alamy
A disuniting kingdom: Nicola Sturgeon and Alex Salmond launch
   the Scottish Government's White Paper outlining plans for
   independence, Tuesday 26 November 2013, Glasgow, Scotland.
   Photo: David Gordon/Alamy

While every effort has been made to contact copyright-holders of illustrations, the author and publishers would be grateful for information about any illustrations where they have been unable to trace them, and would be glad to make amendments in further editions.

Bibliography

Anthony, David, *The Horse, the Wheel and Language*, 2007

Ascherson, Neal, *Stone Voices: The Search for Scotland*, 2002

Black, Jeremy, *A New History of Wales*, 2000

Bogdanor, Vernon, *Devolution in the United Kingdom*, 1999

Chapman, Malcolm, *Celts: The Construction of a Myth*, 1992

Colley, Linda, *Britons: Forging the Nation 1707–1837*, 1992

—— *Acts of Union and Disunion*, 2014

Collis, John, *The Celts: Origins, Myths and Inventions*, 2003

Cunliffe, Barry, *The Ancient Celts*, 1997

—— *Facing the Ocean: The Atlantic and Its Peoples, 8000 BC to AD 1500*, 2001

—— *Britain Begins*, 2012

—— *Bretons and Britons: The Fight for Identity*, 2021

Cunliffe, Barry, and Koch, John, *Celtic from the West: Alternative Perspectives from Archaeology, Genetics, Language and Literature*, 2010

—— *Exploring Celtic Origins: New Ways Forward in Archaeology, Linguistics, and Genetics*, 2021

Darby, John (ed.), *Northern Ireland: Background to the Conflict*, 1983

Davies, John, *A History of Wales*, 1993

Davies, Norman, *The Isles: A History*, 1999

—— *Vanished Kingdoms: The History of Half-Forgotten Europe*, 2011

Davies, Rees R., *The First English Empire: Power and Identities in the British Isles 1093–1343*, 2000

De Barra, Caoimhín, *The Coming of the Celts, AD 1860: Celtic Nationalism in Ireland and Wales*, 2018

Bibliography

Devine, Tom, *The Scottish Clearances: A History of the Dispossessed, 1600–1900*, 2018
—— *The Scottish Nation, 1700–2000*, 1999
Duncan, Anthony, *The Elements of Celtic Christianity*, 1992
Esler, Gavin, *How Britain Ends: English Nationalism and the Rebirth of Four Nations*, 2021
Ferriter, Diarmaid, *The Border: The Legacy of a Century of Anglo-Irish Politics*, 2019
Foster, Roy, *Modern Ireland, 1600–1972*, 1988
—— *Paddy and Mr Punch: Connections in Irish and English History*, 1993
—— *Luck and the Irish: A Brief History of Change, 1970–2000*, 2007
Goodhart, David, *The Road to Somewhere: The Populist Revolt and the Future of Politics*, 2017
Gower, Jon, *The Story of Wales*, 2012
Haywood, John, *The Historical Atlas of the Celtic World*, 2001
Henderson, Ailsa and Wyn Jones, Richard, *Englishness: The Political Force Transforming Britain*, 2021
James, Simon, *The Atlantic Celts: Ancient People or Modern Invention?* 1999
Jenkins, Geraint, *The Foundations of Modern Wales: Wales, 1642–1780*, 1993
Johnes, Martin, *Wales Since 1939*, 2012
Jones, Edwin, *The English Nation: The Great Myth*, 1998
King, Richard, *Brittle with Relics: a History of Wales, 1962–97*, 2022
Koch, John, *An Atlas for Celtic Studies, Archaeology and Names in Ancient Europe and Early Medieval Ireland, Britain, and Brittany*, 2011
Koch, John, and Minard, Anton, *The Celts: History, Life and Culture*, 2012
Lloyd, Thomas, *Lost Houses of Wales: A Survey of Country Houses in Wales Demolished Since c.1900*, 1986
Maier, Bernard, *The Celts: A History from Earliest Times to the Present*, 2003
Manco, Jean, *The Blood of the Celts: The New Ancestral Story*, 2015

Marr, Andrew, *The Battle for Scotland*, 1992

Melding, David, *Will Britain Survive Beyond 2020?* 2009

Miles, David, *The Tribes of Britain*, 2005

Moffat, Alistair, *The Sea Kingdoms: The Story of Celtic Britain and Ireland*, 2001

Morgan, Kenneth, *Rebirth of a Nation: Wales, 1880–1922*, 1981

Morris, Marc, *The Anglo-Saxons: A History of the Beginnings of England*, 2021

Nairn, Tom, *After Britain: New Labour and the Return of Scotland*, 2000

—— *Old Nations, Auld Enemies, New Times: Selected Essays*, 2014

Oosthuizen, Susan, *The Emergence of the English*, 2019

Oppenheimer, Stephen, *The Origins of the British: A Genetic Detective Story*, 2006

O'Toole, Fintan, *Heroic Failure: Brexit and the Politics of Pain*, 2018

Paxman, Jeremy, *The English: A Portrait of a People*, 1998

Prebble, John, *The Highland Clearances*, 1963

Pritchett, V. S., *At Home and Abroad*, 1990

Pryor, Francis, *Home: A Time-Traveller's Tales from Britain's Prehistory*, 2014

Renfrew, Colin, *Archaeology and Language: The Puzzle of Indo-European Origins*, 1987

Roberts, Alice, *The Celts: Search for a Civilisation*, 2015

Scruton, Roger, *England: An Elegy*, 2001

Sims-Williams, Patrick, *The Celtic Inscriptions of Britain: Phonology and Chronology, c.400–1200*, 2003

Sykes, Bryan, *Saxons, Vikings and Celts: The Genetic Roots of Britain and Ireland*, 2006

—— *Blood of the Isles*, 2007

Tanner, Marcus, *The Last of the Celts*, 2004

Tindale, Stephen (ed.), *The State and the Nations: The Politics of Devolution*, 1996

Tombs, Robert, *The English and Their History*, 2014

Vaughan-Thomas, Wynford, *Wales: A History*, 1985

Williams, Gwyn Alf, *When Was Wales? A History of the Welsh*, 1985

Index

Index

Index

Index

Index

Index

Index

Index

Index

Index

Index